AIRSPEAK

FIONA A. ROBERTSON
Centre of Applied Linguistics, University of Franche Comté, France

Pearson Education Limited
Edinburgh Gate
Harlow
Essex
CM20 2JE

and Associated Companies throughout the world

www.pearsonlongman.com

First published in 1988 by Prentice Hall International (UK) Ltd as *Airspeak, Radiotelephony Communication for Pilots*

Updated 2008
Second impression 2009
ISBN: 978-1-4058-9757-0 (book)
ISBN: 978-1-4058-9985-7 (book for pack)

Set in 10/11.5pt Times by 35

Printed in Italy by G. Canale & C.S.p.a.

Acknowledgements

The author would like to thank Mr A. Fossard for his assistance with the technical aspects in the first draft, Mr Ewout Wothers for his support and technical assistance with the recent revision, and also Stephen Nicholl (Publishing Manager), Ben Greshon (Senior Editor) and Phil Lawrence (Sound Engineer) at Pearson Longman.

The publisher would like to thank the following for their kind permission to reproduce their photographs:

Cover images: Front: Photolibrary.com: Nancy Ney

Picture Research by: Sally Cole

Every effort has been made to trace the copyright holders and we apologise in advance for any unintentional omissions. We would be pleased to insert the appropriate acknowledgement in any subsequent edition of this publication.

CONTENTS

ABOUT THE AUTHOR

Fiona A. Robertson, who comes originally from Scotland, started her English language teaching career in Finland. She subsequently settled in France working for the Centre of Applied Linguistics in the University of Franche Comte, where she specialised in aviation English training for pilots. She has also contributed to the improvement of the quality of English in aviation worldwide by founding and helping to run the International Civil Aviation English Association.

INTRODUCTION

Purpose

This course contains a carefully sequenced selection of training materials, giving progressive, systematic practice in radiotelephony phraseology for pilots.

The exercises are designed primarily to teach operational fluency in the ROUTINE phraseology for IFR flights. Unlike routine phraseology, the language of NON-ROUTINE situations in PLAIN ENGLISH is not highly predictable. However, practice is also provided for a selection of non-routine situations, plus additional vocabulary work.

This course is suitable for pilots or pilot trainees who wish to learn, or revise, the language used for radiotelephony communications. It is particularly suitable for people working at home or in a learning resources centre. All the exercises are self-correcting.

Organisation

There are five parts to the course. Parts 1–4 trace the normal pattern of a flight as follows:

Part One	Pre-flight to line-up
Part Two	Take-off to top of climb
Part Three	Cruise to descent
Part Four	Approach to parking

Each Part is divided into Sections which follow the normal sequence of events for each stage of a flight. For example, Part One (Pre-flight to line-up) is divided as follows:

1. Departure information
2. Route clearances
3. Start-up
4. Push-back
5. Taxi

Each Section is divided into ROUTINE phraseology practice, and then NON-ROUTINE exercises in PLAIN ENGLISH. These events are then followed by a REVIEW, which serves to bring together the phrases learned in each Section. Each Review contains:

- Model Flight
- Live Traffic

All the exercises build up gradually to Part Five, which is the FINAL REVIEW. In this part there are two simulations of complete flights, one an imaginary model flight, the other based on live traffic.

Level of English

The minimum level of English required to start this course is what language teachers call 'lower intermediate', i.e. a knowledge of the basic verb tense structures, how to make questions and negative verb forms, an ability to make simple, correct statements and to understand fairly easy dialogue — in other words, the result of about three years of positive learning experience at school.

Additionally, the learner should know the international alphabet (Alpha, Bravo, Charlie, etc.) and the system of numbers used in aviation. The learner should also have a basic knowledge of flying procedures.

Recordings

Except for a few supplementary vocabulary exercises, ALL the exercises in this book are recorded. The recorded exercises are of the following types:

a. routine phraseology practice
b. non-routine situations
c. simulation of a flight with an imaginary scenario
d. simulation of a flight using live traffic
e. supplementary vocabulary practice

All the callsigns and place names used in this book are imaginary, except for those in the live recordings of ATIS, VOLMETS and METARS, and in the Dublin to Paris flight. The sound quality of the live recordings reflects the working environment.

It should be emphasised that the live recordings have been chosen, not as exemplary models, but as practice to help learners get to grips with reality.

Warning

This course is based on a considerable amount of authentic material, but it does not attempt to teach:

— flying procedures
— anything about aviation other than English words and phrases used in RT
— *all* the words that can be found in *any* situation during a flight

References

The ICAO radiotelephony phraseology is to be found in the following documents:

The International Civil Aviation Organisation, *Manual of Radiotelephony*, DOC 9432 AN/925

The International Civil Aviation Organisation, *Procedures for Air Navigation Services, Air Traffic Management, DOC 4444*

Individual member states may file differences with ICAO. These slight variations are published by the different civil aviation bodies concerned.

NOTES TO THE TEACHER

This material can be used in the classroom, with a computer or CD player, and it is ideal for self-study.

Suggestions for classroom work

Key words and phrases

Before looking at the list of key words and phrases, find out what students already know by 'brainstorming', as follows:

Write the section title on the board (e.g. Departure ATIS) and ask the class to write down all the words they know related to the subject, first individually, then in pairs. Finally put together the whole class's knowledge of the vocabulary connected with Departure ATIS, either by writing it up on the board or by pinning up pieces of paper used by the class to list their words. Check that all the words mentioned in the book have been covered. If not, teach those that remain.

Another approach to this list is to ask the students to organise it into categories. Each student may see a different way to organise the words, but this is not a problem — in fact, it can be enriching. Try to help the students to understand that there is no 'right answer' here. The exercise is aimed at helping students remember words by thinking about them, and coming to their own individual decisions about them. Different ways to categorise the Departure ATIS list could be: (i) units, weather words, navigation words; (ii) abbreviations, single syllable words, two syllable words, three syllable words, phrases. Once each student establishes different categories, they can be shown and explained to the rest of the group.

Check the pronunciation and accentuation of the words in the list.

Typical exchange

This presents an analysis of a typical exchange, and it shows the layout of the pilot-controller exchange which will be practised in the exercises.

A useful preparation for the listening and speaking exercises which follow is to elicit this kind of analysis from the class. If that seems too difficult, write up the dialogue layout with a few elements missing. Then ask the class to supply the missing items.

Routine phraseology

Routine phraseology has been divided into short model dialogues for each phase of flight; and for each phase, the recorded material is presented in the same sequence:

Listen
Listen and Repeat
Write
Check
Listen and Speak
Check

This sequence has been chosen so that the learner hears and says the phrases before seeing them in print. Since the 'answers' also appear in the book, the learner has to be dissuaded from reading the answers before doing the exercise. With adult learners it is fairly easy to show that the objective is to understand the spoken word without written support and hence to accept the discipline of listening and repeating before looking at the written text. However, it would be counter-productive to be too authoritarian in this matter. The learner should take responsibility for his or her own learning, and therefore has a choice whether to accept advice or not.

All the material presented here can be used for classroom work or self-study. Each section contains 10–20 minutes of recorded audio material on routine phraseology, the contents of which provide ample material for $1^1/_2$ hours of classwork, including 40–45 minutes of individual work or pairwork.

The initial **Listen and Repeat** practice can be usefully done in a group with the teacher correcting pronunciation. The written exercise is important so that the learner knows exactly the words which will be used in the **Listen and Speak** exercise. The written phrases must therefore be carefully checked. In the classroom, time must be given for the writing phase.

The **Listen and Speak** exercise can be practised in pairs with the use of the *Audioscript of Controller's Part* (pages 203–219). In pairs, students take turns as the controller and the pilot. With an odd number of students, the odd-one-out could check the 'pilot', using the CHECK pages. In classroom practice of this kind, insist on the use of 'say again' for any parts of messages which are not understood.

Non-routine exercises

These take the form of listening comprehension followed by 'auto-dictation' blank-fill. The listening comprehension can be done in the classroom, but the blank-fill is best done individually. However, it can be used as a recall exercise, rather than an 'auto-dictation'.

Preparation for these exercises can take the form of classroom discussion on possible non-routine situations that could occur at the particular phase of flight, with students recounting any personal experiences they may have had.

Supplementary vocabulary exercises

Although these are grouped at the end of each Part of the course, they should be used in small doses along with the sections on phraseology. You may want to enlarge these sections with other kinds of activities centred on learning vocabulary. Many of the word games used in general language courses can be adapted to suit specific areas. One could have activities such as: What's My Job in Aviation? (a yes/no guessing game); Describe and Arrange, with matching sets of pictures of different types of planes; aviation crosswords; number games.

Suggestions for other activities

Remember that for the learner, a little RT practice goes a long way. Never try to cover more than one Routine RT Section and one Non-routine RT Section in one lesson. Classroom time can be usefully spent reviewing basic English structures in an aviation context, for example:

— describe your last flight (past tense)
— what do you do before you board the plane (present simple tense)?
— what are the essential qualities for a pilot ('should')?
— how will civil aviation develop in the next 20 years (expressions of futurity)?

A collection of pictures of planes, airports, ground vehicles, etc. is very useful, as the learner can talk about the pictures within his or her own level of competence.

Accident and incident reports always arouse a spark of interest, although the formal language used in this type of text can be difficult.

Always encourage the learners to extend their knowledge of English in general. Routine RT phraseology is not enough to cope with non-routine situations when pilots have to draw on their own knowledge of plain English.

NOTES TO THE LEARNER – HOW TO USE THIS BOOK

You will need:

- the recordings
- pencil and paper for notes
- a CD player or computer
- an aviation dictionary

A typical Section of the book

Example: 1.1.1 Departure information (routine)

1 **Key Words and Phrases.** Check that you understand each word on the list.

2 **Typical Exchange.** This shows the kind of dialogue that will be practised in the following exercises. You can see on the PILOT side what you will have to say, and on the CONTROLLER side what you will have to understand.

3 **Listen.** Put on the CD and play track 1.1.1. Listen to the dialogue.

4 **Listen and Repeat.** Repeat the pilot's words. Practise until you can do it easily. *Do not look at the* **Listen and Write** *Section yet. You must learn to understand the controller's words without looking at the text.* Remember, there is no text of the controller's words when you are in the cockpit.

5 **Write.** Write the pilot's words in the boxes (the controller's words are given). Check with the recording if necessary.

6 **Check.** Check that your written words are *exactly* the same as the words in the CHECK section. If there is a mistake, correct it, and listen to the recording again.

7 **Listen and Speak.** This is a role-play exercise using the same phraseology as the first three exercises (**Listen, Listen and Repeat, Write**). The example is recorded again, and then you can play the pilot's role for each of the six different flights. The six callsigns are listed on page 4. If the pauses on the CD are not long enough for you to speak, you can make them longer by pausing the CD, speaking, then restarting the CD.

8 **Check.** A correct version of the pilot's words in the **Listen and Speak** exercise is given in the CHECK section. If the **Listen and Speak** exercise is difficult at first, you can read aloud from the CHECK section as you play the CD once through, then try again *without* looking at the CHECK section.

Exercises with non-routine situations

When you know the routine phraseology very well, you can turn to the non-routine section.

Example: 1.3.2 Start-up (non-routine) p. 180

1 **Listen and Write.** Play track 1.2.3. Read the question for the first dialogue. Listen to the first dialogue and the question at the end of it. Pause the CD. If you know the answer, write it down; if not, listen again. If the questions seem too difficult, come back to them after the second **Listen and Write** exercise.

Continue in the same way with dialogues 2 and 3.

2 **Check.** Check your answers to the questions in the CHECK section.

3 **Listen and Write.** Play the track again and use it for 'auto-dictation' to write in the words in the blank spaces.

4 **Check.** Check your answers by looking at the pilot's words in the CHECK section.

Review section

Near the end of each Part there is a review of the phraseology learned. The review is done in two simulations. The first is an imaginary scenario, the second is based on live traffic.

Example: 1.7.1 Flight from Rexbury to Winton (from ATIS to line-up) p. 48.

1 **Read.** Look at the information given to help prepare the flight.
2 **Listen and Read.** Listen to the CD and follow the information given in the book about the phase of the flight.
3 **Listen and Speak.** Think about the flight information (callsign, route, parking stand) and be ready to play the pilot's role. Have pencil and paper ready to take notes for clearances, etc. Play track 1.7.1 and reply to the controller and follow the instructions on the CD. If you find the pace too fast at first, practise by making the pauses longer — stop the CD, speak, then play the track again. But remember, try again without pausing the CD.
4 **Check.** Check your words with the model answers. If you want to read the controller's words, you can find them in the *Audioscript of Controller's Part*, pages 203–219.

Example: 1.7.2 Flight from Dublin to Paris (initial contact to line-up) p. 48.

1 This simulation uses live traffic. The procedure is the same as for the Rexbury–Winton simulation.

   NOTE: Real time has been compressed in these simulations, and there are no long pauses without RT. In a real flight there are often quite long periods without RT communciations.

Supplementary vocabulary

At the end of each Part there is practice with supplementary vocabulary. These exercises use various techniques to help you learn words related to the phases of flight practised in the RT sections. These words do not appear in routine phraseology, but they are useful for non-routine situations when you have to use plain English. The exercises are grouped at the end of each Part. You may prefer to do them bit by bit.

STANDARD WORDS AND PHRASES

(ICAO definitions)
The following words and phrases shall be used in radiotelephony communications as appropriate and shall have the meaning given below.

Word/Phrase	*Meaning*
Acknowledge	Let me know that you have received and understood this message.
Affirm	Yes.
Approved	Permission for proposed action granted.
Break	I hereby indicate the separation between portions of the message. (To be used where there is no clear distinction between the text and other portions of the message.)
Break Break	I hereby indicate the separation between messages transmitted to different aircraft in a very busy environment.
Cancel	Annul the previously transmitted clearance.
Check	Examine a system or procedure. (Not to be used in any other context. No answer is normally expected.)
Cleared	Authorised to proceed under the conditions specified.
Confirm	I request verification of: (clearance, instruction, action, information).
Contact	Establish radio contact with. . . .
Correct	True or accurate
Correction	An error has been made in this transmission (or message indicated). The correct version is. . . .
Disregard	Consider that transmission as not sent.
How do you read	What is the readability of my transmission?
I say again	I repeat for clarity or emphasis.
Maintain	Continue in accordance with condition(s) specified, or in its literal sense, e.g. 'Maintain 3500 ft'.
Monitor	Listen out on (frequency).
Negative	No *or* Permission not granted *or* That is not correct *or* Not capable.
Over	My transmission is ended and I expect a response from you. NOTE: *Not normally used in VHF communications.*
Out	This exchange of transmissions is ended and no response is expected. NOTE: *Normally used to indicate the end of an exchange of transmissions.*
Read back	Repeat all, or the specified part, of this message back to me exactly as received.
Recleared	A change has been made to your last clearance and this new clearance supersedes your previous clearance or part thereof.
Report	Pass me the following information.
Request	I should like to know . . . , or I wish to obtain. . . .
Roger	I have received all of your last transmission. NOTE: *Under no circumstances to be used in reply to a question requiring '**Read back**' or a direct answer in the affirmative (**Affirm**) or negative (**Negative**).*

Say again	Repeat all, or the following part, of your last transmission.
Speak slower	Reduce your rate of speech.
Standby	Wait and I will call you. NOTE: *No onward clearance to be assumed. The caller would normally re-establish contact if the delay is long. Standby is not an approval or denial.*
Unable	I cannot comply with your request, instruction or clearance. NOTE: *UNABLE is normally followed by a reason.*
Wilco	(Abbreviation for 'will comply'.) I understand your message and will comply with it.
Words twice	a) *As a request:* Communication is difficult. Please send every word or group of words twice. b) *As information:* Since communication is difficult, every word or group of words in this message will be sent twice.

Part One

Pre-flight to line-up

1.1 DEPARTURE INFORMATION

1.1.1 Departure information (routine)

Key words and phrases

Check that you understand all the words and phrases in this list. Look up any new words in an aviation dictionary.

ATIS (Automatic Terminal Information Service)
surface wind
temperature
dew point
runway
runway in use
gusting
visibility
no sig (no significant change)
kilometres (kms)
feet (ft)
degrees
knots
plus
minus
Celcius (previously centigrade)
mist
millibars (mb)
QNH
CAVOK (visibility: cloud and present weather better than presented values or conditions)
ILS (Instrument Landing System)
noise abatement procedure
transition level
cumulonimbus
wet
breaking action
trend
RVR (runway visual range)
threshold
taxiway
SID (standard instrument departure)
hecto*p*ascal (hpa)
flock of birds
sky clear; few; scattered; broken; overcast
swifts

Typical exchange

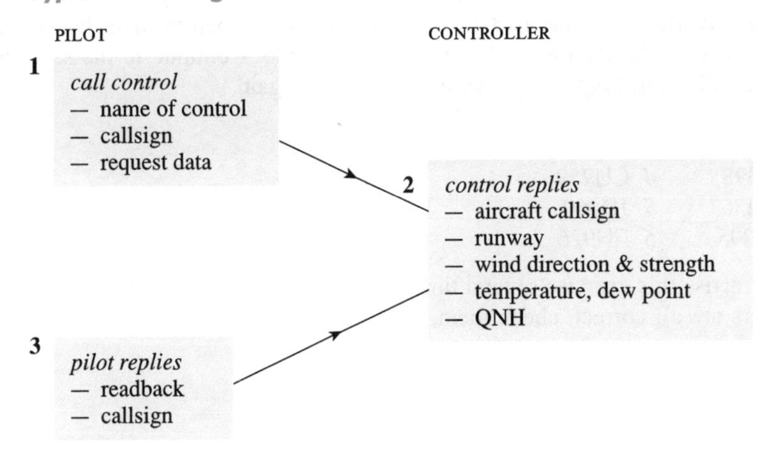

NOTES
- The controller usually gives the information in the following order: runway in use, wind direction and strength, visibility, temperature, dew point, QNH, other information.
- The pilot generally reads back the essential bits – wind data, QNH and runway number.

Phraseology practice

Listen If the airport has no ATIS (Automatic Terminal Information Service) recording, the pilot must ask for departure information. Listen to the recording.

Listen and Repeat Listen again and repeat the pilot's words.

Write Complete the text below by writing in the pilot's words. Check with the recording if necessary.

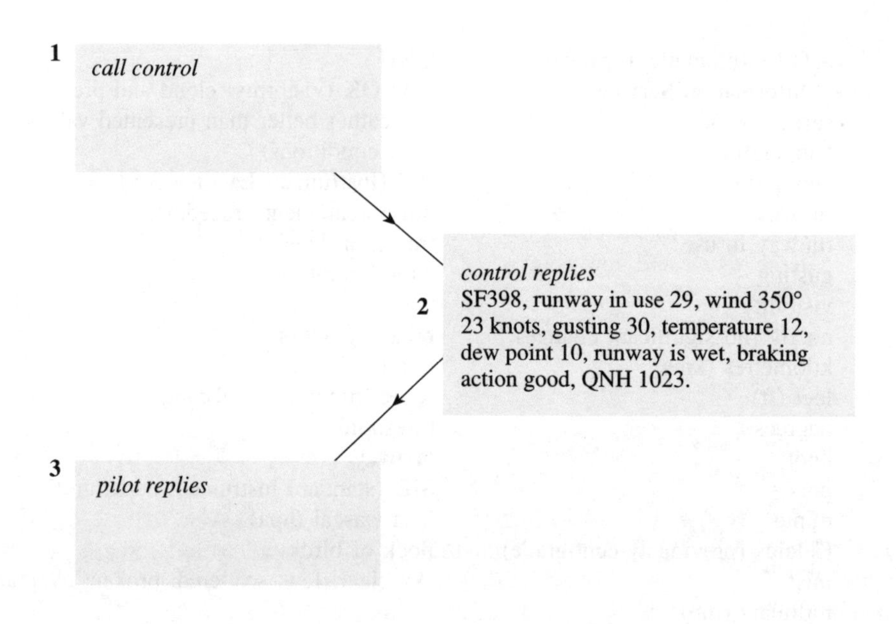

1
call control
2
control replies
SF398, runway in use 29, wind 350° 23 knots, gusting 30, temperature 12, dew point 10, runway is wet, braking action good, QNH 1023.
3
pilot replies

Check Check your answers, page 7.

Listen and Speak Take the part of the pilot, ask for departure data in the same way, and give the read-back. Listen to the example. Continue in the same way for the following flights. Start with the example again.

Callsigns

1 SF398	*4* CU759
2 KM563	*5* JD460
3 SV295	*6* EN926

Check Practise this exercise several times. When it seems easy, and you think your answers are all correct, check them, page 7.

1.1.2 Departure information (ATIS)

A typical ATIS recording

Some airports have separate departure and arrival ATIS, and others have one for both arrival and departure. The different items in the ATIS also vary according to the weather. A typical ATIS has the following items. Those in brackets ( ) depend on the weather and the type of information.

airport name
information code
time
runway(s) in use
(runway condition: wet, snow, slush, ice, braking action)
transition level
(operational information: expect ______ departure, flocks of birds, restricted areas, etc.)
wind direction (in degrees) and strength (in knots)
visibility in metres, kms up to 'ten kms or more'
(RVR)
(present weather: mist, fog, snow, drizzle, etc.)
(cloud cover: sky clear, few, scattered, broken, overcast; height of base of clouds in feet or metres)
(CAVOK, pronounced 'CAV-O-KAY')
temperature and dew point
QNH
(QFE)
trend ('no sig' *or* bcmg-becoming)
(extra information)

Listen and Read If the weather is good, the ATIS recording is short. Listen and follow the text.

> This is Heathrow departure information N, 1109 hours weather, 330°, 18 knots, temperature +2, dew point –3, QNH 1021 millibars*, departure runway 28R.

* CAA UK has kept 'millibars', others have changed to 'hectopascal' which is numerically the same.

If the weather is poor, the recording is longer. Listen to this example of an ATIS recording.

> This is Orly information H, recorded at 1300 Z time. ILS approach runway 07, take-off runway 08, expected 3V standard departure, transition level is 50. Wind 080° 12 knots, visibility 7 kms. Temperature –1, dew point –4, QNH 1008, QFE 997. Roissy is facing East*. At first contact advise you have received information H; and caution taxiway 2A, taxiway 21A and B area are closed.

* Roissy is facing East means that aircraft are taking off from Paris, Roissy Charles de Gaulle towards the East. There are two large international airports in the Paris region, Paris Orly and Paris Roissy Charles de Gaulle and the direction in which a/c take off at one airport affects which SID's (Standard Instrument Departure) may be used at the other.

Remember that you can listen several times to an ATIS recording.

Phraseology practice

Listen and Write Before start-up or before taxi, the pilot listens to the ATIS. If there is no ATIS, the controller gives the latest weather data.

Listen to the following ATIS recordings and make notes for each one in the tables below, as in the examples. *You will have to listen more than one time to each one to get all the details.*

1

A	wind 270° 19, temperature 6, DP3, QNH 1001, runway 29
B	wind ... , temperature..., DP..., QNH ...., runway ....
C	
D	
E	
F	
G	

Check When you think you have all the correct details, check your answers from the texts on page 8.

2

1 Heathrow	E, 200° 09, 21 09, 1017, 286
2 Heathrow	
3 Narita	
4 Malpensa	
5 le Bourget	
6 Kirkwall	
7 Athens	
8 Blagnac	

Check When you think you have all the correct details, check your answers from the texts on page 8. Remember that you will have to listen several times to each ATIS.

1.1 CHECK

1.1.1 **Write** (from page 4)

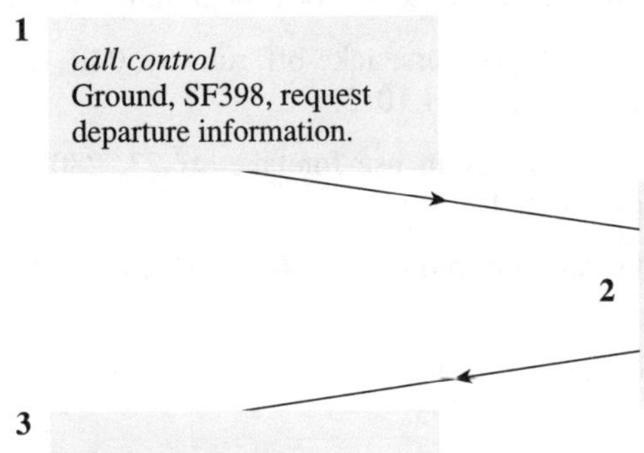
1
call control
Ground, SF398, request departure information.
2
control replies
SF398, runway in use 29, wind 350° 23 knots, gusting 30, temperature 12, dew point 10, runway is wet, braking action good, QNH 1023.
3
pilot replies
350° 23 knots, QNH 1023, runway 29, SF398.

1.1.1 **Listen and Speak** (from page 4)

The dotted lines (. . . . . .) show when the controller speaks.

1 PIL Ground, SF398, request departure information.
CTL . . . .
PIL 350° 23 knots, QNH 1023, Runway 29, SF398.

2 PIL Ground, KM 563, request departure information.
CTL . . . .
PIL 060° 18 knots, QNH 1008, runway 08, KM 563.

3 PIL Ground, SV 295, request departure information.
CTL . . . .
PIL 180° 9 knots, QNH 1014, runway 23, SV 295.

4 PIL Ground, CU 759, request departure information.
CTL . . . .
PIL Wind calm, QNH 1015, runway 33R, CU 759.

5 PIL Ground JD 460, request departure information.
CTL . . . .
PIL 260° 10 knots, gusting to 25, QNH 1005, runway 19L, JD 460.

6 PIL Ground, EN 926, request departure information.
CTL . . . .
PIL 320° 5 knots, QNH 1019, runway 21, EN 926.

1.1.2 **Listen and Write,** ***1*** (from page 6)

Departure information: texts of the ATIS recordings.

A This is Rexbury departure information Alpha, 00.05 hours weather, surface wind 270°, 19 knots, temperature 6, dew point 3, QNH 1001, departure runway 29.

B . . . departure information Bravo, 00.30 hours, take-off runway 04R, wind 050° 9 knots, temperature 25, dew point 18, QNH 1013.

C . . . departure information Charlie, runway in use for take-off 23, 280° 03 knots, QNH 1017, temperature 27, dew point 15.

D . . . departure information Delta, take-off runway 25, 030° 02 knots, QNH 1002, temperature 04, dew point 04.

E . . . departure information Echo, runway in use 36, wind 340° 10 knots gusting to 25, temperature 12, dew point 09, QNH 1005.

F . . . departure information Foxtrot, 02.30 hours weather, surface wind 250° 10 knots gusting to 20, temperature 8, dew point 6, QNH 1011 millibars, departure runway 33.

G . . . departure information Golf, take-off runway 28R, 330° 20 knots, visibility 10 kms or more, temperature +1, dew point –3, QNH 1022, no sig.

1.1.2 **Listen and Write,** ***2*** (from page 6)

Texts of ATIS recordings

1 This is Heathrow Departure information E, 18.15 hours weather, 200° 09 knots, temperature +21, dew point +09, QNH 1017 millibars, departure runway 28L.

2 This is Heathrow Departure information B, 15.45 hours weather, 200° 11 knots, temperature 24, dew point 12, QNH 1017 millibars, departure runway 28L.

3 Narita international airport information Oscar 0130, ILS runway 16R approach and ILS runway 16L approach, using runway 16R and 16L, parallel approach in progress, departure frequency 124.2, inform your assigned runway for Narita approach on initial contact. Wind 170° 8 knots, visibility 6 kms, light rain, mist, few 400 ft stratus, broken 600 ft stratus, temperature 23, dew point 21, QNH 1005 hectopascal, 2968 inches, advise you have information Oscar.

4 This is Malpensa Airport departure information India Alpha at 1327 runway in use 35L and 35R according destination, transition level 70, local report: wind 270° 3 knots, visibility 10 kms or more, cloud scattered 3500 ft broken 7000 ft, temperature 27, dew point 16, QNH 1013 hectopascal, and no significant change. You have received departure information India Alpha.

5 This is le Bourget info, information Hotel recorded at 1213 UTC. Expected approach ILS 27 landing runway 27 take-off runway 25, expected standard departure 1 Charlie, transition level 40. Caution: taxiways Charlie and Victor 1 closed. Caution: swifts reported on the field. Wind 240° 10 knots, visibility 10 kms clouds scattered 2800 ft, scattered 25000 ft, temperature +21°, dew point +13°, QNH 1016, QFE runway 27 1010, QFE runway 25 1009.
Inform on initial contact that you have received information Hotel.

6 Kirkwall information, acknowledge receipt of information Romeo, time 1250 runway in use 09, surface wind 130 14 knots, visibility 6 kms slight rain; scattered 500 ft, broken 900 ft, broken 1900 ft; temperature +13, dew point +11; QNH 1001; runway wet. Forecast period 13 to 20 hours, 140 15 gusting 25 knots 10 kms or more; few 800 ft, scattered 2500 ft, tempo period 13 to 20 hours, 8 kms, moderate showers of rain, prob 30, tempo period 13 to 15 hours, 4000 metres, moderate rain and drizzle, broken 400 ft, Kirkwall information.

7 This is Athens Airport information S. Weather report 09.00 hours: wind 280° 8 knots, CAVOK, temperature 27, QNH 1011 mb, 2985 inches, transition level 65. Runway in use 33R, taxiway Charlie between runway 33R and taxiway Bravo closed. It is reminded to follow strictly the noise abatement procedures.

8 This is Blagnac information L recorded at 1208R approach ILS 32R runway in use 32R, planned departure route 5 B, transition level 050, 32L closed NOTAM A2664, taxiway M2 S2 S3 S6 W50 W60 S60 W90 W100 S11 M10 P100 T101 closed NOTAM A2665, wind 330° 2 knots, CAVOK temperature +24, dew point +10, Quebec November Hotel 1018, QFE 1000. Inform Blagnac at first contact that you have received information Lima.

1.2 ROUTE CLEARANCES

Key words and phrases

Check that you understand all the words and phrases in this list.
Look up any new words in an aviation dictionary.

flight planned route	ATC (Air Traffic Control)
left/right turn out	clearance
climb	SID (standard instrument departure)
maintain	approach
*request	initially
level change	frequency
en route	heading
airborne	flight level (FL)
squawk	*contact
*cleared	

(* These words are explained in the section on Standard Words and Phrases, pages xvi–xviii.)

Typical exchange

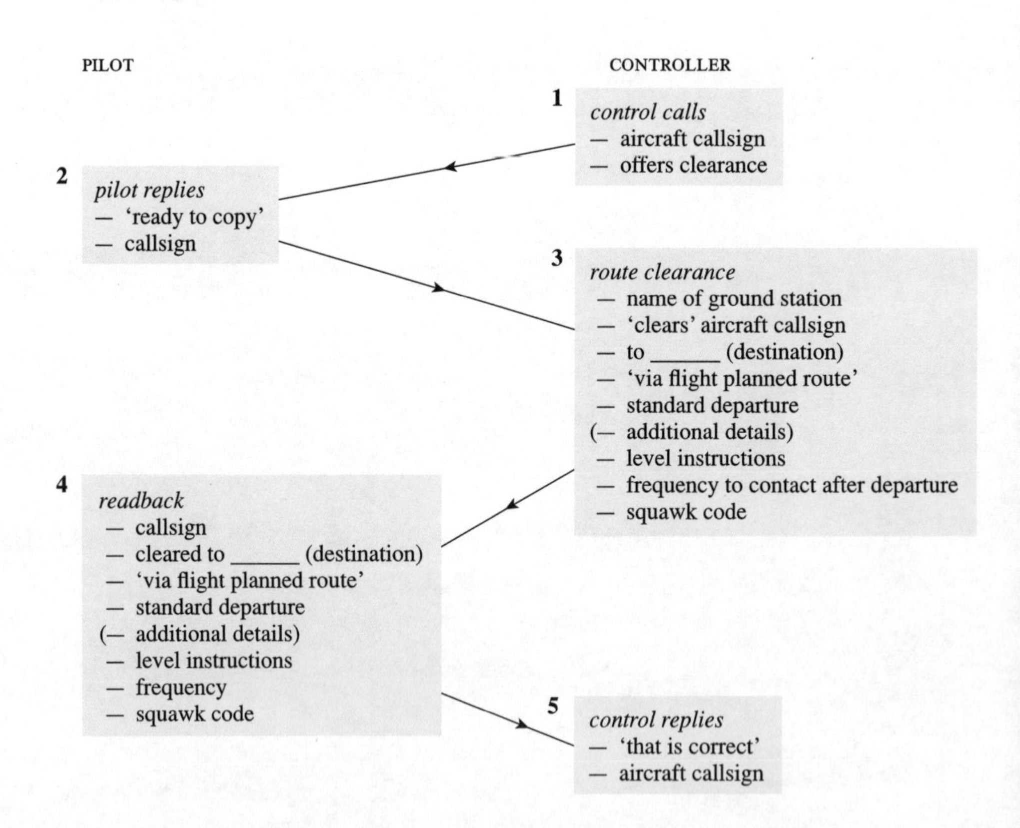

NOTES

– 'Additional details' added to a standard departure usually just repeat some essential points (e.g. left/right turn out after departure; climb on runway heading to . . .) or may contain a modification.
– Level instructions in route clearances often contain restrictions (e.g. 'FL190 initially, request level change en route').

Phraseology practice

Listen Route clearance is given before engine start-up or during taxiing. Listen to the recording.
Listen and Repeat Listen again, take notes, and repeat the pilot's words.
Write Complete the text below by writing in the missing words. Check with the recording if necessary.

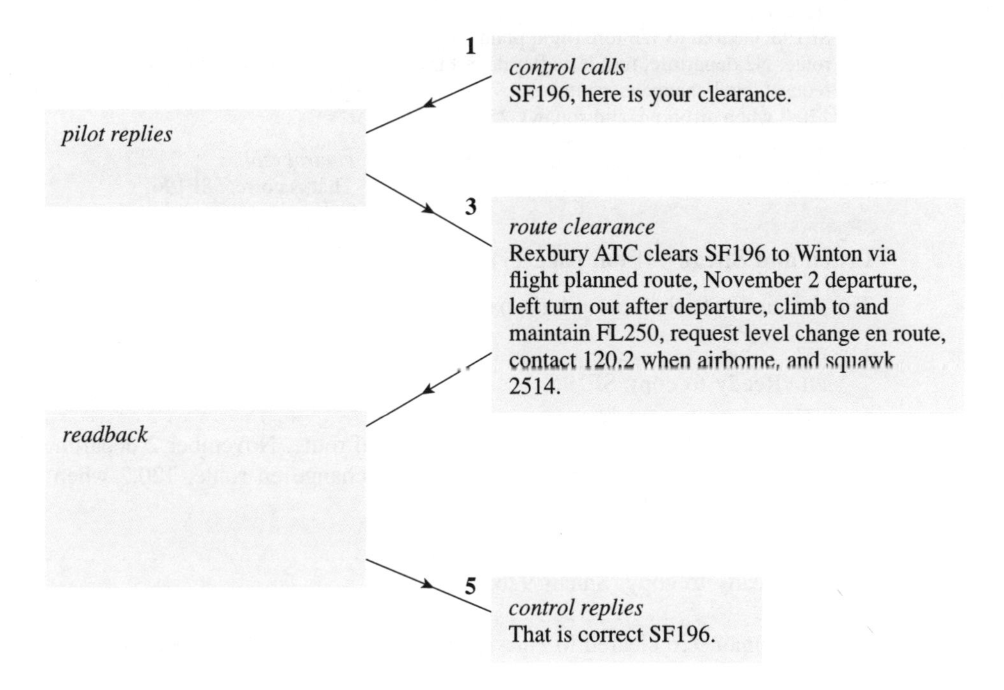

1
control calls
SF196, here is your clearance.
pilot replies
3
route clearance
Rexbury ATC clears SF196 to Winton via flight planned route, November 2 departure, left turn out after departure, climb to and maintain FL250, request level change en route, contact 120.2 when airborne, and squawk 2514.
readback
5
control replies
That is correct SF196.

Check Check your answers, page 12.
Listen and Speak Take the pilot's part and reply to the controller for the following flights:

1. SF196 to Winton
2. Sunair 926 to Paris Charles de Gaulle
3. Sunair 831 to Winton
4. Sunair 435 to Rexbury
5. Sunair 921 to Rexbury

Check Practise this exercise several times. When it seems easy, and you think your replies are correct, check your answers, page 12.

CHECK

1.2 **Write** (from page 11)

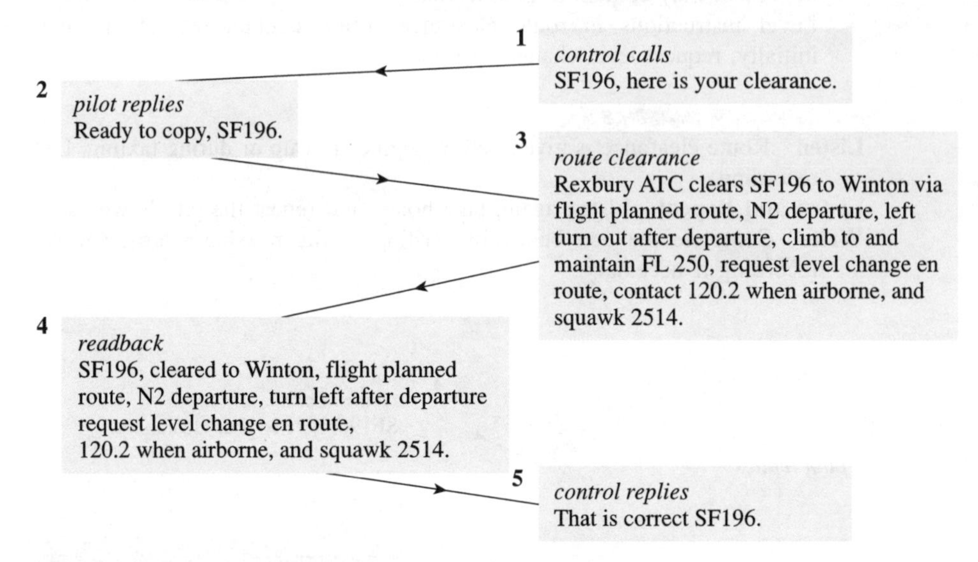
1
control calls
SF196, here is your clearance.
2
pilot replies
Ready to copy, SF196.
3
route clearance
Rexbury ATC clears SF196 to Winton via flight planned route, N2 departure, left turn out after departure, climb to and maintain FL 250, request level change en route, contact 120.2 when airborne, and squawk 2514.
4
readback
SF196, cleared to Winton, flight planned route, N2 departure, turn left after departure request level change en route, 120.2 when airborne, and squawk 2514.
5
control replies
That is correct SF196.

1.2 **Listen and Speak** (from page 11)

The dots indicate the controller's part.

1 CTL . . . .
PIL Ready to copy SF196.
CTL . . . .
PIL SF196 cleared to Winton, flight planned route, November 2 departure, FL250, turn left after departure, request level change en route, 120.2 when airborne, squawk 2514.

2 CTL . . . .
PIL Ready to copy, Sunair 926.
CTL . . . .
PIL Sunair 926 cleared to Paris Charles de Gaulle via Upper Red 10, Departure 31, FL290, 120.1 when airborne.

3 CTL . . . .
PIL Ready to copy, Sunair 831.
CTL . . . .
PIL Sunair 831 cleared to Winton, flight planned route, Romeo 1 departure, turn left after departure, FL210 initially, request level change en route, 120.2 when airborne.

4 CTL . . . .
PIL Ready to copy, Sunair 435.
CTL . . . .
PIL Sunair 435 cleared to Rexbury, Oscar 3 departure, to climb on runway heading to FL160, squawk 1537, 121.3 when airborne.

5 CTL . . . .

PIL Ready to copy, Sunair 921.

CTL . . . .

PIL Sunair 921 cleared to Rexbury, Whisky 1 departure, flight planned route, FL180 initially, request level change en route, squawk 1525, 121.3 when airborne.

1.3 START-UP

1.3.1 Start-up (routine)

Key words and phrases

Check that you understand all the words and phrases in this list. Look up any new words in an aviation dictionary.

*go ahead	stand number
stand	callsign
*approved	slot
*standby	slot time
gate	at your discretion
destination	expect
*say again	call you back

(* These words are explained in the section on Standard Words and Phrases, pages xiv–xv.)

Typical exchange

PILOT / CONTROLLER

1 (pilot)
call control
— name of ground station
— callsign
— greeting

2 (controller)
control replies
— 'go ahead'
— callsign

3 (pilot)
pilot replies
— callsign
— stand number
— ATIS information code
— request start-up
— name of destination

4a (controller)
control replies
— aircraft callsign
— 'start-up approved'

5a (pilot)
pilot replies
— 'starting up'
— callsign

3 or 4b (controller)
control replies
— aircraft callsign
— 'stand by for start'

5b (pilot)
pilot replies
— 'standing by'
— callsign

NOTE

— In *control reply* **2**, the controller may use: aircraft callsign, name of ground station, greeting; *or* name of ground station, greeting, aircraft callsign.

Phraseology practice

Listen Listen to the recorded dialogue.

Listen and Write Listen to the dialogues on the CD. Write down the callsign, stand (or gate), information code and destination in the table below.

No.	Callsign	Stand/Gate	ATIS Information	Destination
1				
2				
3				
4				
5				
6				

Check Check your answers from the texts on page 20.

Listen and Repeat Listen to the first two dialogues again, and repeat the pilot's words.

Write Complete the texts of the dialogues by writing in the pilot's words below. Listen to the recording again if necessary.

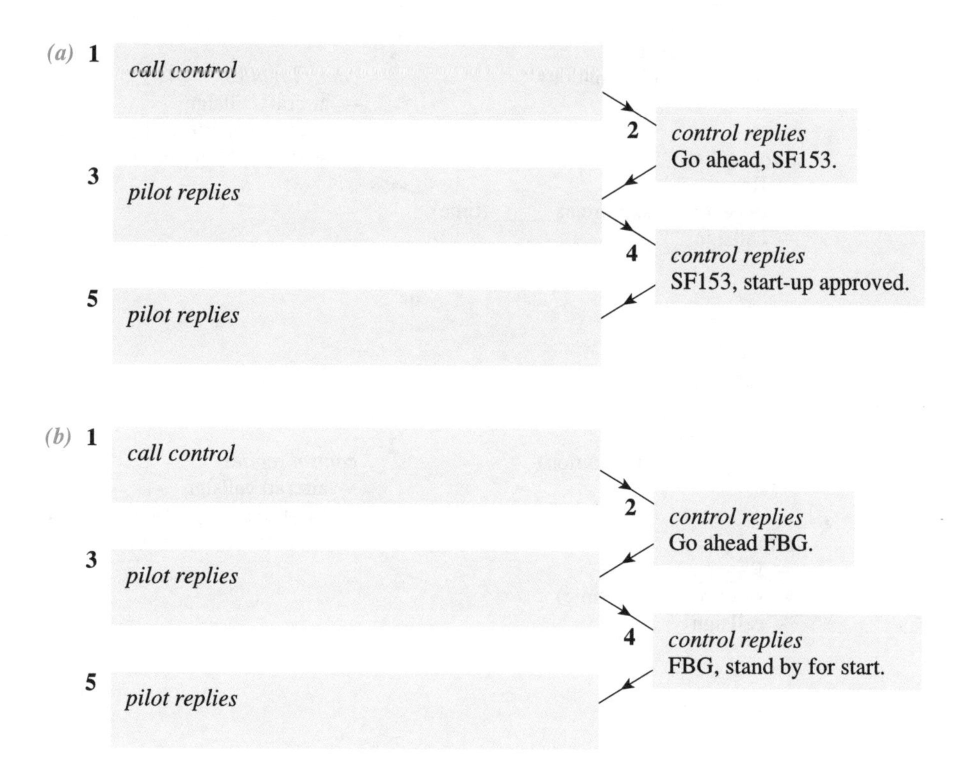

Check Check your answers, page 21.

Listen and Speak Now look again at the table you filled in on page 15. Using the recording, ask for start-up for each flight, and reply to the controller.

Listen to the example. Then continue in the same way, starting with the example again.

Check Check your answers, page 20.

Typical exchange

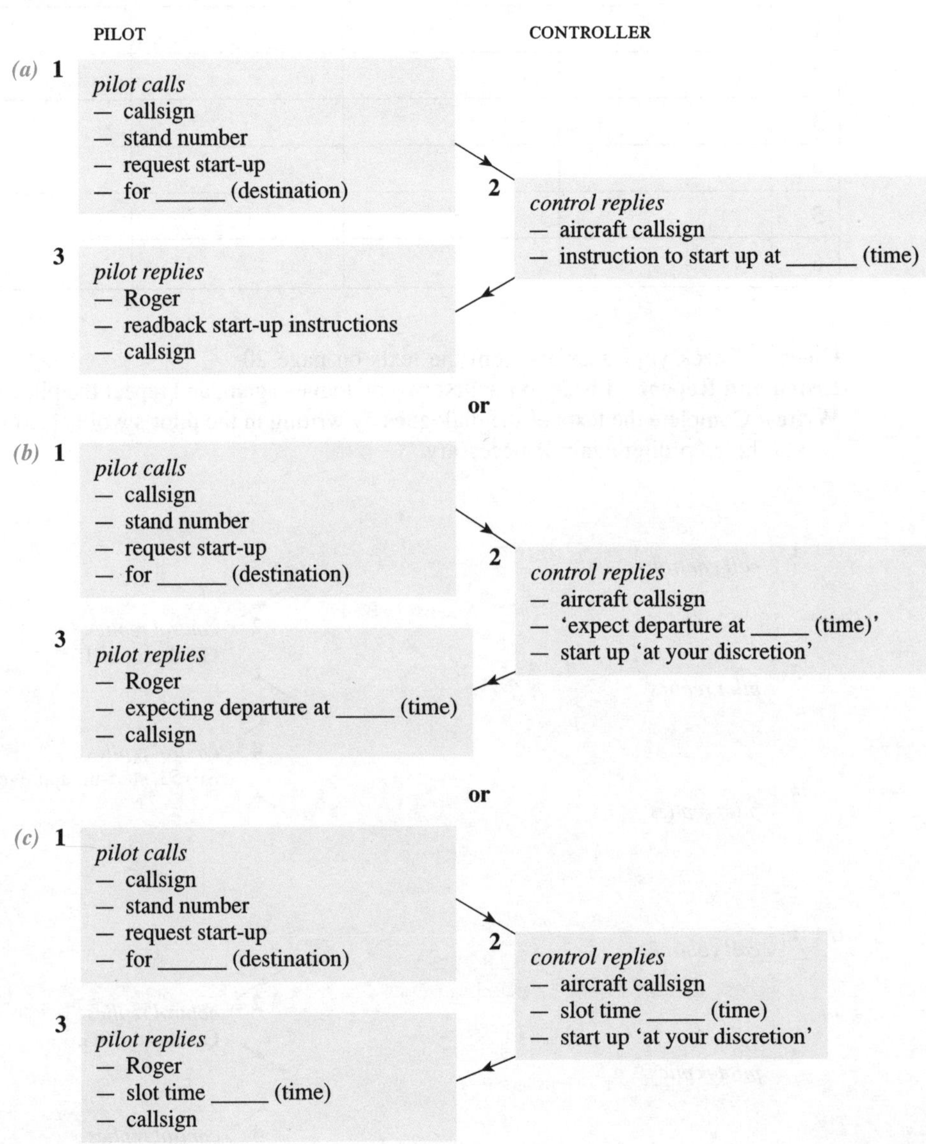

Phraseology practice

Listen At a busy airport, there is often a queue for departure, and the controller has a slot for each flight. Listen to the recording.

Listen and Repeat Listen again and repeat the pilot's words.

Write Complete the dialogues by writing in the pilot's words.

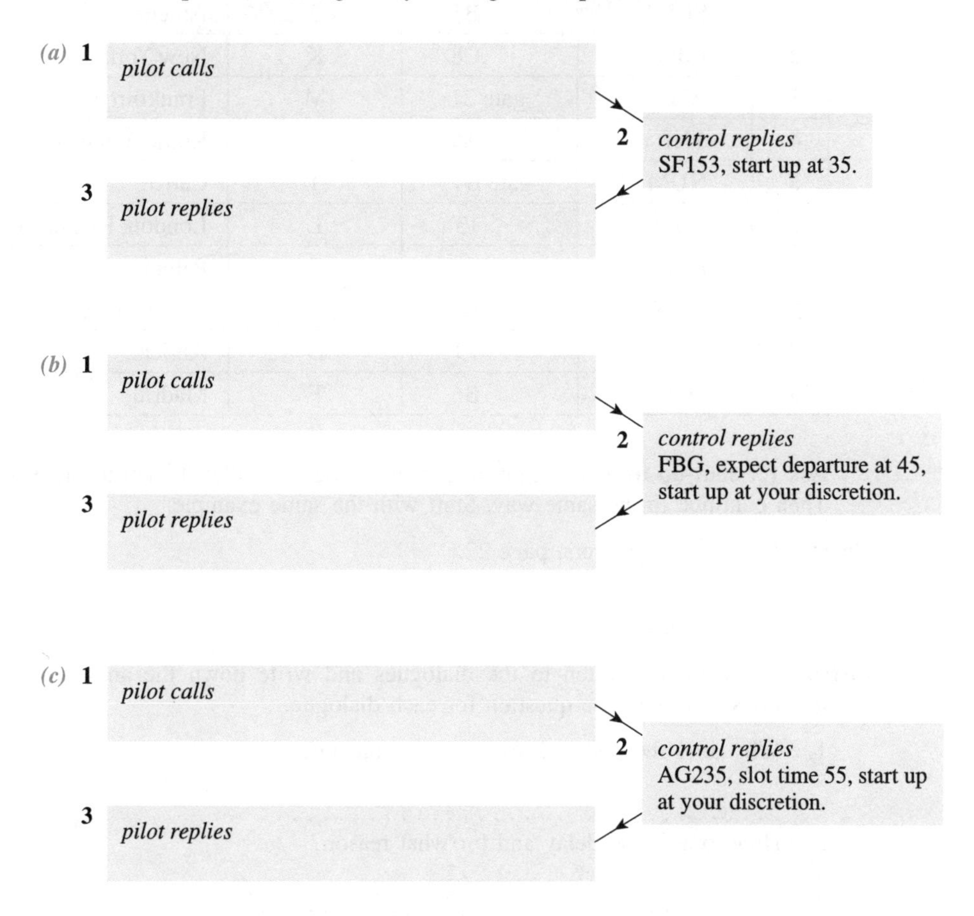

(a) 1 pilot calls
2 control replies
SF153, start up at 35.
3 pilot replies
(b) 1 pilot calls
2 control replies
FBG, expect departure at 45, start up at your discretion.
3 pilot replies
(c) 1 pilot calls
2 control replies
AG235, slot time 55, start up at your discretion.
3 pilot replies

Check Check your answers, page 21.

Listen and Speak Look at a longer version of the table you filled in on page 15. Data for 10 flights.

No.	Callsign	Stand/Gate	ATIS	Destination
1	SF153	B5	J	Athens
2	FBG	C8	K	New York
3	AG235	gate 21	M	Frankfurt
4	THI	A9	C	Rome, Fiumiccino
5	NUM	gate D7	I	Cairo
6	WJD	13	L	London, Heathrow
7	ESQ	5	P	Palma
8	KVX	A4	R	Copenhagen
9	YFL	19	D	Algiers
10	OPR	B6	F	Madrid

Ask for start-up for each flight, and reply to the controller. Listen to the example. Then continue in the same way. Start with the same example.

Check Check your answers, page 22.

1.3.2 Start-up (non-routine)

Listen and Answer Listen to the dialogues and write down the answers to these questions. There is one question for each dialogue.

1. Why does the pilot ask for an early start-up?

. . . .

2. How long is the delay and for what reason?

. . . .

3. Why does the pilot want to delay his departure?

. . . .

Check Check your answers, page 23.

Listen and Write Listen again to the same dialogues and complete the texts below:

1 PIL Rexbury Ground, Sunair ___________, good morning ___________ start-up.

CTL Sunair 670, ___________ departure 50, ___________ for start.

PIL ___________ start-up quickly please. We've got ___________ in the ___________.

CTL Stand by one.

CTL Sunair 670, start-up ___________.

PIL Starting up.

2 PIL Rexbury Ground, Sunair 539, good morning, ___________ to start.

CTL Good morning Sunair 539, there's a ___________ this morning due to a ___________, your ___________ is 09.45.

PIL 09.45, roger, Sunair 539.

3 PIL Rexbury Ground, Sunair 692, good morning ___________ start-up.

CTL Good morning Sunair 692, ___________, start-up ___________.

PIL (readback) ___________ ___________ ___________.

PIL (at 25) Sunair 692, we wish to delay our start-up due to ___________. We have one passenger ___________.

CTL Roger, Sunair 692.

Check Check your answers, page 23.

Your word list

Write down any words in the dialogues you do not understand, or are not sure about. Try to guess the meaning, in English or in your own language, and write it down. Then check with a dictionary.

Make your own vocabulary notebook, like this:

Words or expressions	Your idea about the meaning	Dictionary meaning

CHECK

SECTION 1.3

1.3.1 **Write** (from page 15); *also* **Listen and Speak** (page 16).

1 PIL Winton Ground, Sierra Foxtrot 153, good morning.
CTL . . . .
PIL Sierra Foxtrot 153, stand Bravo 5, information Juliet, request start-up for Athens.
CTL . . . .
PIL Starting up, Sierra Foxtrot 153.

2 PIL Winton Ground, Foxtrot Bravo Golf, good morning.
CTL . . . .
PIL Foxtrot Bravo Golf, stand Charlie 8, information Kilo, request start-up for New York.
CTL . . . .
PIL Standing by, Foxtrot Bravo Golf.

3 PIL Winton Ground, Alpha Golf 235, good morning.
CTL . . . .
PIL Alpha Golf, gate 21, information Mike, request start-up for Frankfurt.
CTL . . . .
PIL Gate 21, Alpha Golf.
CTL . . . .
PIL Starting up, Alpha Golf 235.

4 PIL Winton Ground, Tango Hotel India, good morning.
CTL . . . .
PIL Tango Hotel India.
CTL . . . .
PIL Tango Hotel India, stand Alpha 9, information Charlie, request start-up for Rome Fiumiccino.
CTL . . . .
PIL Standing by, Tango Hotel India.

5 PIL Winton Ground, November Uniform Mike, good morning.
CTL . . . .
PIL November Uniform Mike, gate Delta 7, information India, request start-up for Cairo.
CTL . . . .
PIL Gate Delta 7, November Uniform Mike.
CTL . . . .
PIL Standing by, November Uniform Mike.
CTL . . . .
PIL Starting up, November Uniform Mike.

6 PIL Winton Ground, Whisky Juliet Delta, good morning.
CTL . . . .
PIL Whisky Juliet Delta.
CTL . . . .

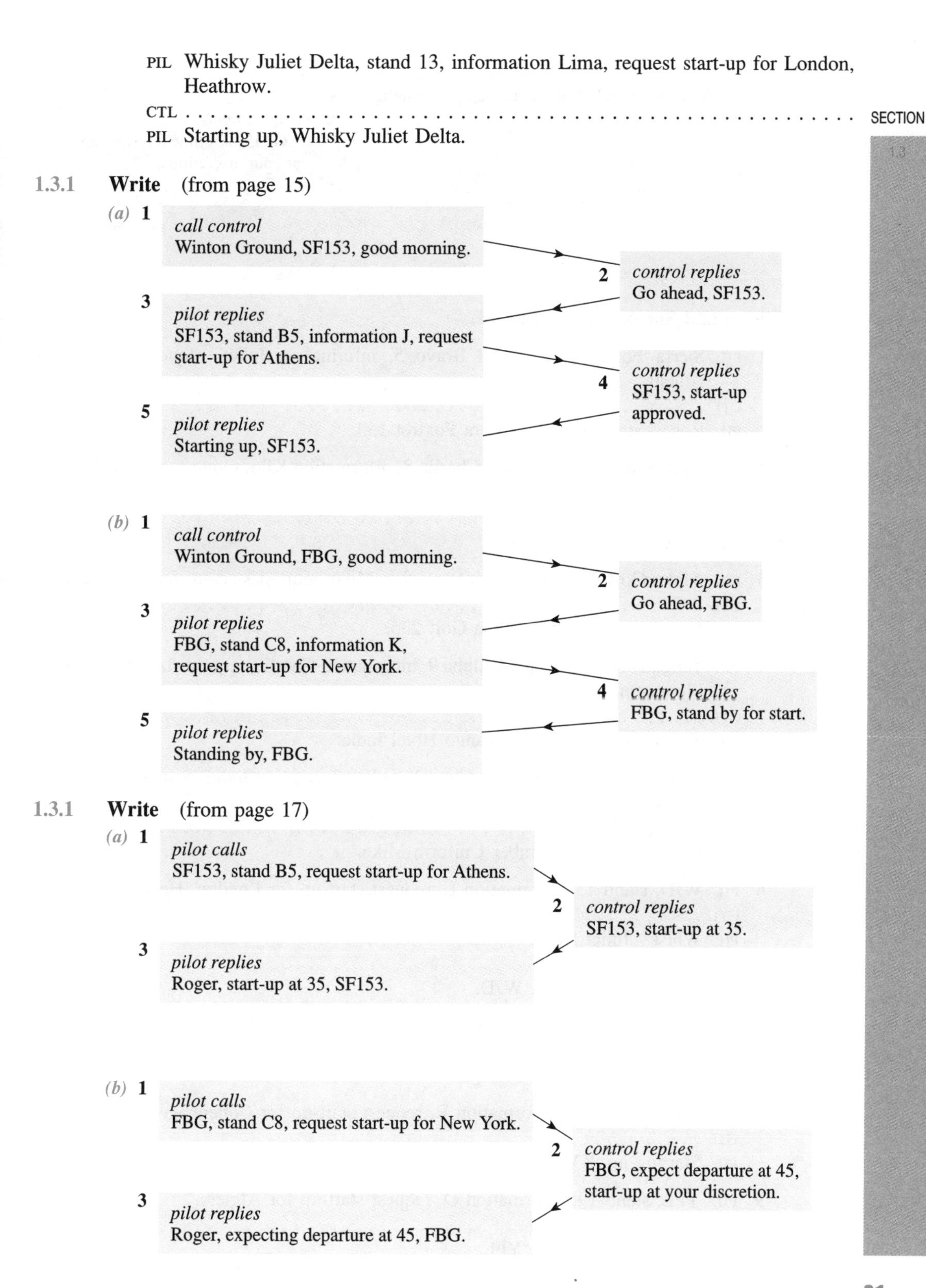

PIL Whisky Juliet Delta, stand 13, information Lima, request start-up for London, Heathrow.

CTL . . . .

PIL Starting up, Whisky Juliet Delta.

SECTION 1.3

1.3.1 Write (from page 15)

(a)

1 *call control*
Winton Ground, SF153, good morning.

2 *control replies*
Go ahead, SF153.

3 *pilot replies*
SF153, stand B5, information J, request start-up for Athens.

4 *control replies*
SF153, start-up approved.

5 *pilot replies*
Starting up, SF153.

(b)

1 *call control*
Winton Ground, FBG, good morning.

2 *control replies*
Go ahead, FBG.

3 *pilot replies*
FBG, stand C8, information K, request start-up for New York.

4 *control replies*
FBG, stand by for start.

5 *pilot replies*
Standing by, FBG.

1.3.1 Write (from page 17)

(a)

1 *pilot calls*
SF153, stand B5, request start-up for Athens.

2 *control replies*
SF153, start-up at 35.

3 *pilot replies*
Roger, start-up at 35, SF153.

(b)

1 *pilot calls*
FBG, stand C8, request start-up for New York.

2 *control replies*
FBG, expect departure at 45, start-up at your discretion.

3 *pilot replies*
Roger, expecting departure at 45, FBG.

(c) 1 *pilot calls*
AG235, gate 21, request start-up for Frankfurt.

2 *control replies*
AG235, slot time 55, start-up at your discretion.

3 *pilot replies*
Roger, slot time 55, AG235.

1.3.1 Listen and Speak (from page 18)

1 PIL Sierra Foxtrot 153, stand Bravo 5, information Juliet, request start-up for Athens.
CTL . . . .
PIL Roger, start-up at 35, Sierra Foxtrot 153.

2 PIL Foxtrot Bravo Golf, stand Charlie 8, information Kilo, request start-up for New York.
CTL . . . .
PIL Roger, departure at 45.

3 PIL Alpha Golf 235, gate 21, information Mike, request start-up for Frankfurt.
CTL . . . .
PIL Roger, slot time 55, Alpha Golf 235.

4 PIL Tango Hotel India, stand Alpha 9, information Charlie, request start-up for Rome Fiumiccino.
CTL . . . .
PIL Roger, departure at 05, Tango Hotel India.

5 PIL November Uniform Mike, Gate Delta 7, information India, request start-up for Cairo.
CTL . . . .
PIL Gate Delta 7, November Uniform Mike.

6 PIL WJD, stand 13, information L, request start-up for London, Heathrow.
CTL . . . .
PIL Whisky Juliet Delta.
CTL . . . .
PIL Roger, slot time 10, WJD.

7 PIL ESQ, stand 5, information P, request start-up for Palma.
CTL . . . .
PIL Roger, start-up at 50, ESQ.

8 PIL KVX, stand A4, information R, request start-up for Copenhagen.
CTL . . . .
PIL Starting up, KVX.

9 PIL YFL, stand 19, information D, request start-up for Algiers.
CTL . . . .
PIL Roger, slot time 15, YFL.

10 PIL OPR, stand B6, information F, request start-up for Madrid.
CTL . . . .
PIL Stand B6, OPR.
CTL . . . .
PIL Roger, departure at 25, OPR.

1.3.2 **Listen and Answer** (from page 18)

1. Why does the pilot ask for an early start-up?
   There is livestock on board.
2. How long is the delay and for what reason?
   A 55-minute delay due to a computer failure.
3. Why does the pilot want to delay his departure?
   Because of a baggage identification process due to a missing passenger.

1.3.2 **Listen and Write** (from page 19)

1 PIL Rexbury Ground, Sunair 670, good morning, request start-up.
CTL Sunair 670, expect departure 50, I'll call you back for start.
PIL Could we start-up quickly please. We've got livestock in the hold.
CTL Standby one.
CTL Sunair 670, start-up approved.
PIL Starting up.

2 PIL Rexbury Ground, Sunair 539, good morning, ready to start.
CTL Good morning Sunair 539, there's a 55-minute delay this morning due to a computer failure, your slot time is 09.45.
PIL 09.45, roger, Sunair 539.

3 PIL Rexbury Ground, Sunair 692, good morning, request start-up.
CTL Good morning Sunair 692, slot time 35, start-up 10 minutes before.
PIL Slot time 35, start-up 10 minutes before, Sunair 692.
PIL (at 25) Sunair 692, we wish to delay our start-up due to passenger baggage identification process. We have one passenger missing.
CTL Roger, Sunair 692.

1.4 PUSH-BACK

1.4.1 Push-back (routine)

Key words and phrases

Check that you understand the following words and phrases:

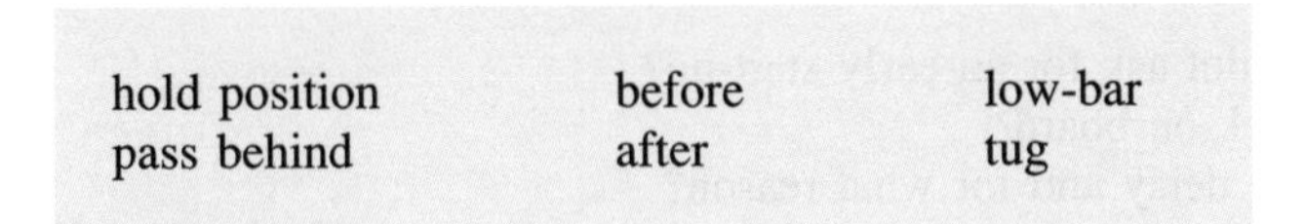

hold position
before
low-bar
pass behind
after
tug

Typical exchange

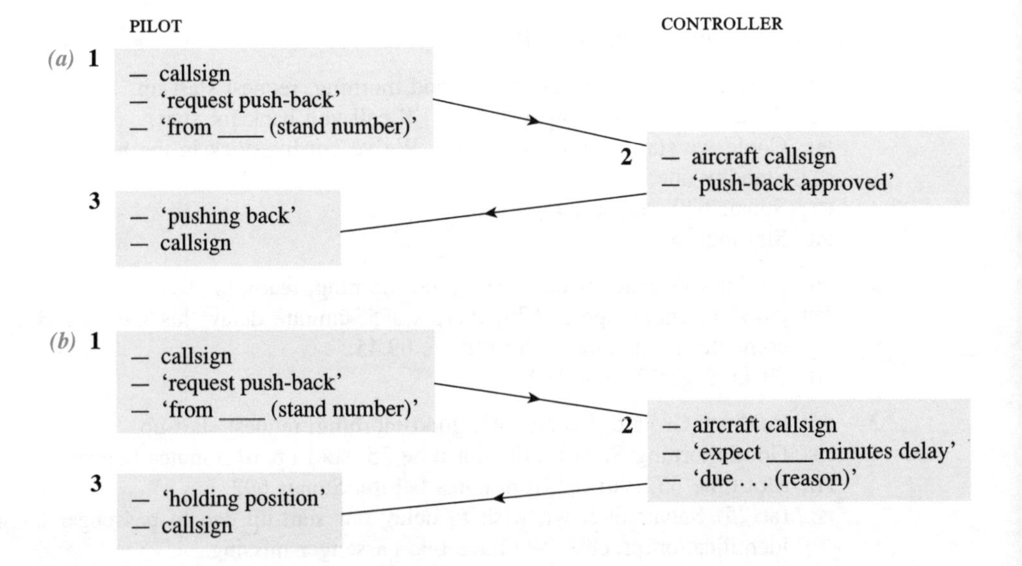

Phraseology practice

Listen Listen to the recorded dialogues.
Listen and Repeat Listen to the dialogues again and repeat the pilot's words.
Write Complete the texts of these dialogues by writing in the pilot's words.

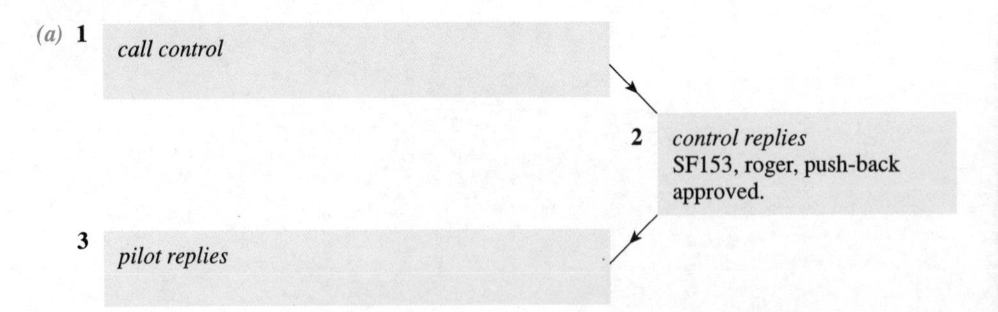

(*b*) **1** *call control*

2 *control replies*
FBG, expect 2 minutes delay, due 747 taxiing behind.

3 *pilot replies*

Check Check your answers, page 27.

Listen and Speak Ask for push-back for flights 1–6 below. Listen to the example, then continue in the same way, starting with the example again.

	Callsign	Parking stand
1	SF153	B5
2	FBG	C8
3	AG235	gate 21
4	THI	A9
5	NUM	gate D7
6	WJD	13

Check Practise this exercise several times. When it seems easy, and you think it is all correct, check your answers, page 27.

1.4.2 Push-back (non-routine)

Listen and Answer Listen to the dialogues and write down the answers to these questions. There is one question for each dialogue.

1. Where is the 747 going?

   . . . .

2. What is causing problems?

   . . . .

3. Why will there be a delay?

   . . . .

Check Check your answers, page 28.
Listen and Write Listen again and complete the texts below.

1 PIL Sunair 559, request push-back.

CTL Sunair 559, there's a 747 to ____________ and ____________, after him, ____________.

PIL After the 747, pushing back.

2 PIL Sunair 310, we're ___________ with the ___________. We're waiting for ___________.

CTL Roger Sunair 310, call me back when ___________.

3 PIL Sunair 892, we're going to be ___________. The ___________ seems to have ___________.

CTL Roger Sunair 892, call me back for taxi when you've got it ___________.

Check Check your answers, page 28.

Your word list

Write down any words in the dialogues you do not understand, or are not sure about. Try to guess the meaning, in English or in your own language and write it down. Then check with a dictionary.

CHECK

1.4.1 **Write** (from page 24)

(*a*)

1 *call control*
SF153, request push-back, stand B5.

2 *control replies*
SF153, roger, push-back approved.

3 *pilot replies*
Pushing back, SF153.

(*b*)

1 *call control*
FBG, request push-back, stand C8.

2 *control replies*
FBG, expect 2 minutes delay, due 747 taxiing behind.

3 *pilot replies*
Holding position, FBG.

1.4.1 **Listen and Speak** (from page 25)

1 PIL SF153, request push-back from stand B5.
CTL . . . .
PIL Pushing back, SF153.

2 PIL FBG, request push-back from stand C8.
CTL . . . .
PIL Holding position, FBG.
CTL . . . .
PIL Pushing back, FBG.

3 PIL AG235, request push-back from gate 21.
CTL . . . .
PIL Holding position, AG235.

4 PIL THI, request push-back from stand A9.
CTL . . . .
PIL Pushing back, THI.

5 PIL NUM, request push-back from gate D7.
CTL . . . .
PIL Holding position, NUM.
CTL . . . .
PIL Holding position, NUM.

6 PIL WJD, request push-back from stand 13.
CTL . . . .
PIL Holding position, WJD.
CTL . . . .
PIL Stand 13, WJD.
CTL . . . .
PIL Holding position, WJD.

1.4.2 **Listen and Answer** (from page 25)

1. Where is the 747 going?
   It is passing behind to park.
2. What is causing problems?
   The tow-bar.
3. Why will there be a delay?
   The tug has broken down.

1.4.2 **Listen and Write** (from page 25)

1 PIL Sunair 559, request push-back.
CTL Sunair 559, there's a 747 to pass behind and park behind, after him, push-back approved.
PIL After the 747, pushing back.

2 PIL Sunair 310, we're having problems with the tow-bar. We're waiting for another one.
CTL Roger Sunair 310, call me back when ready.

3 PIL Sunair 892, we're going to be delayed for a while. The tug seems to have broken down.
CTL Roger Sunair 892, call me back for taxi when you've got it sorted out.

1.5 TAXIING

1.5.1 Taxi (routine)

Key words and phrases

Check that you understand all the words and phrases in this list. Look up any new words in an aviation dictionary.

first	overtake
second	follow
third	straight ahead
turning	intersection
on your right/left	in front of you
give way	turn off

Phraseology practice

Look, Listen and Write Listen to the taxi instructions, look at the diagrams and identify which aircraft the instructions apply to. Write the correct aircraft in the table.

Example: 1. Take the second turning on the left.

This instruction applies to aircraft November, so write N beside Instruction 1 in the table.

Instruction number	Aircraft
1	
2	
3	
4	
5	
6	
7	
8	
9	

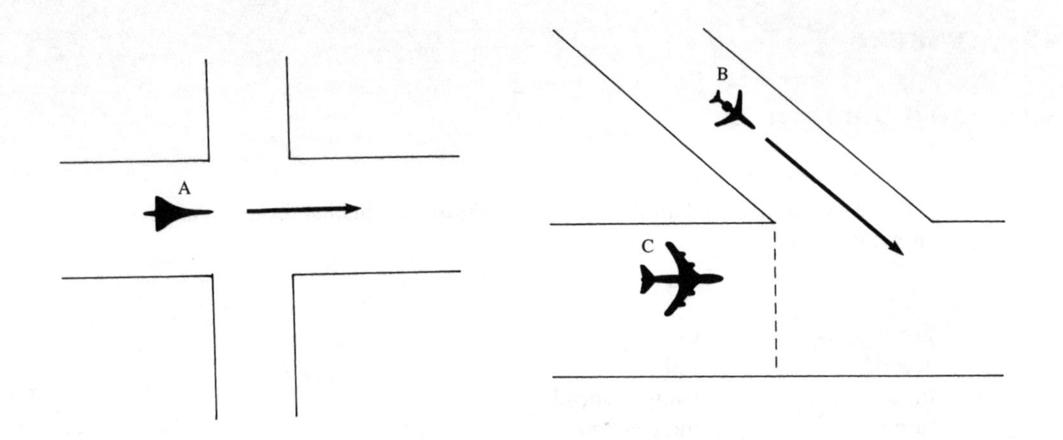
A
B
C

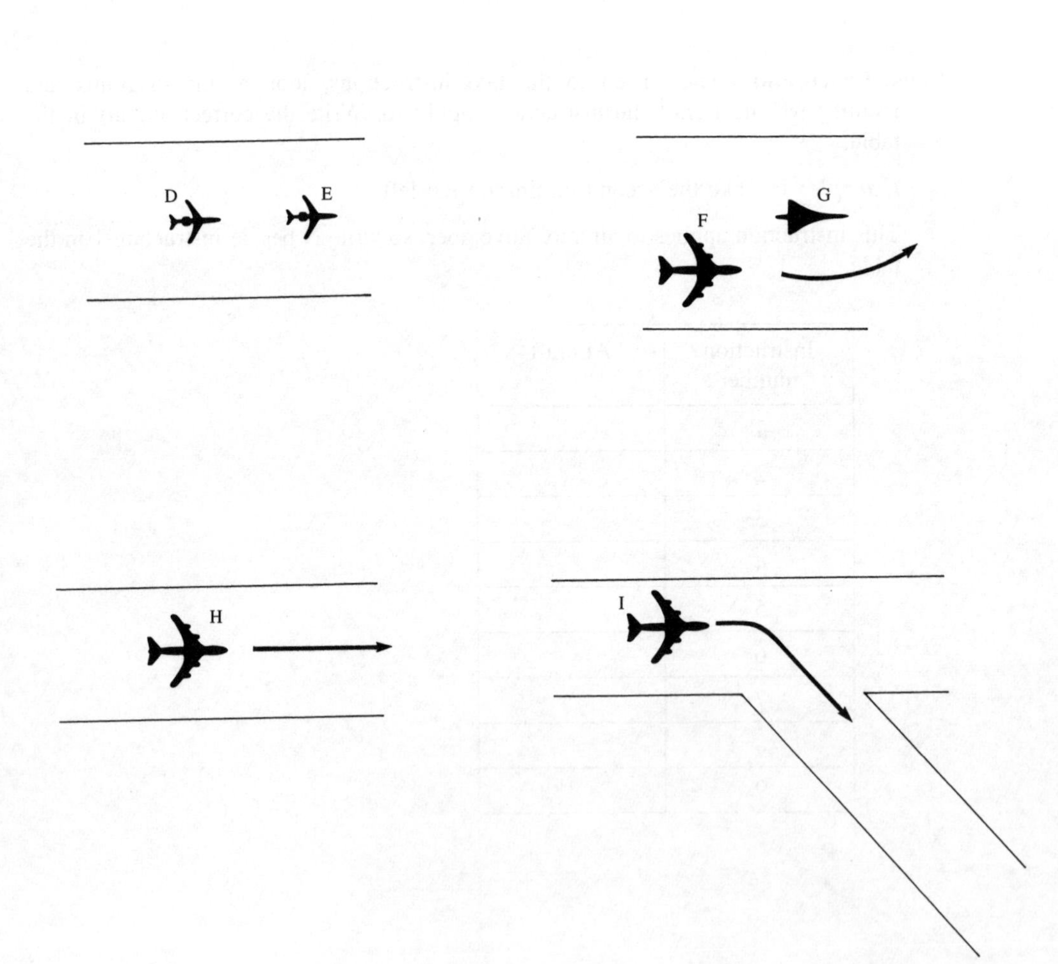
D
E
F
G
H
I

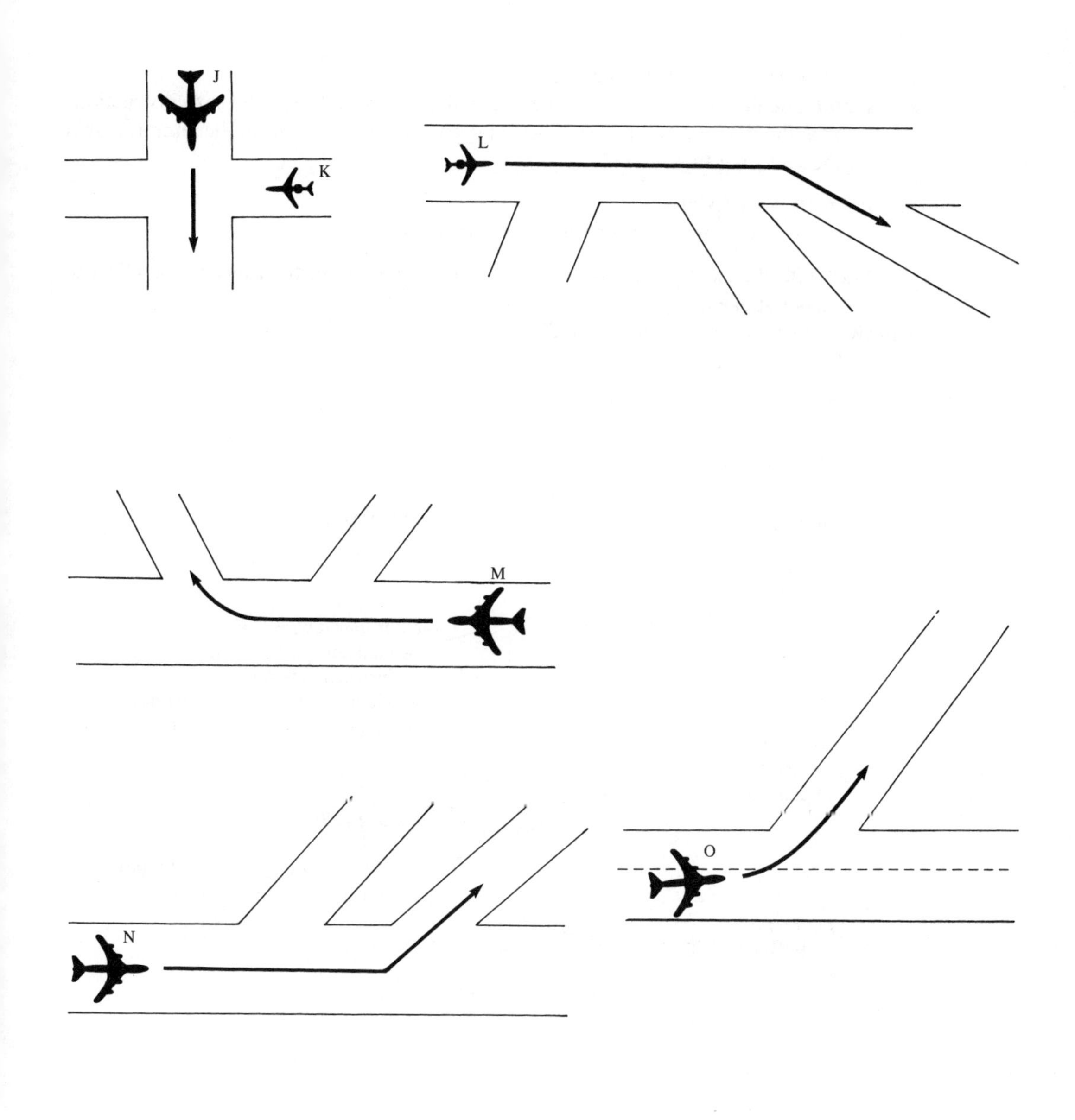
J
K
L
M
N
O

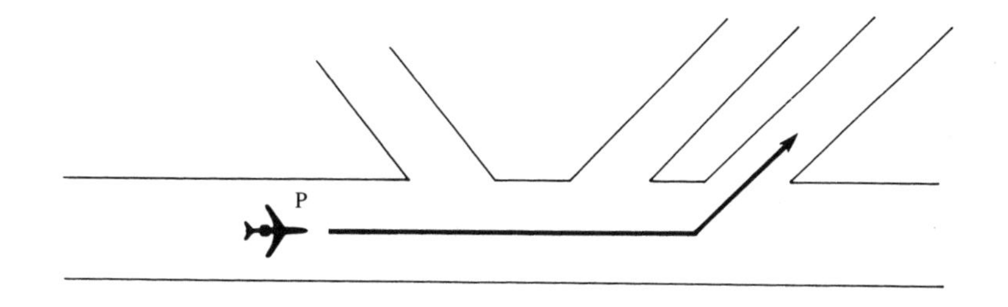
P

Check Check your answers, page 37.

Look and Speak This time, take the controller's part and give the taxi instructions. Look at the diagrams on pages 30–31 and give taxi instructions to the aircraft named on the CD, like this:

Example: A (Alpha)
Go straight ahead at the intersection.

Start with the example again. You will hear the correct instructions on the CD after you have spoken.

Check Check your answers, page 37.

1.5.2 Taxi (routine exchanges)

Typical exchanges

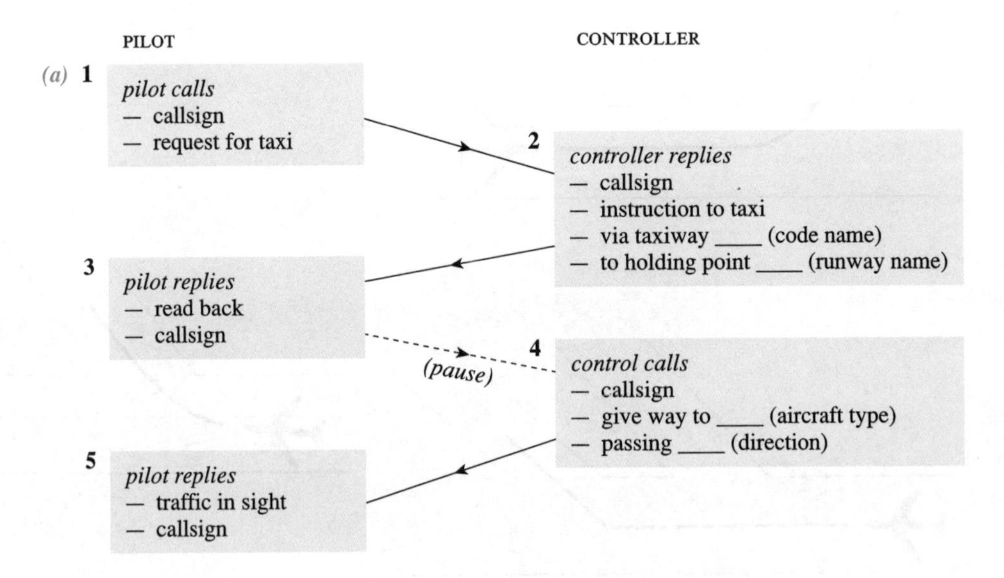

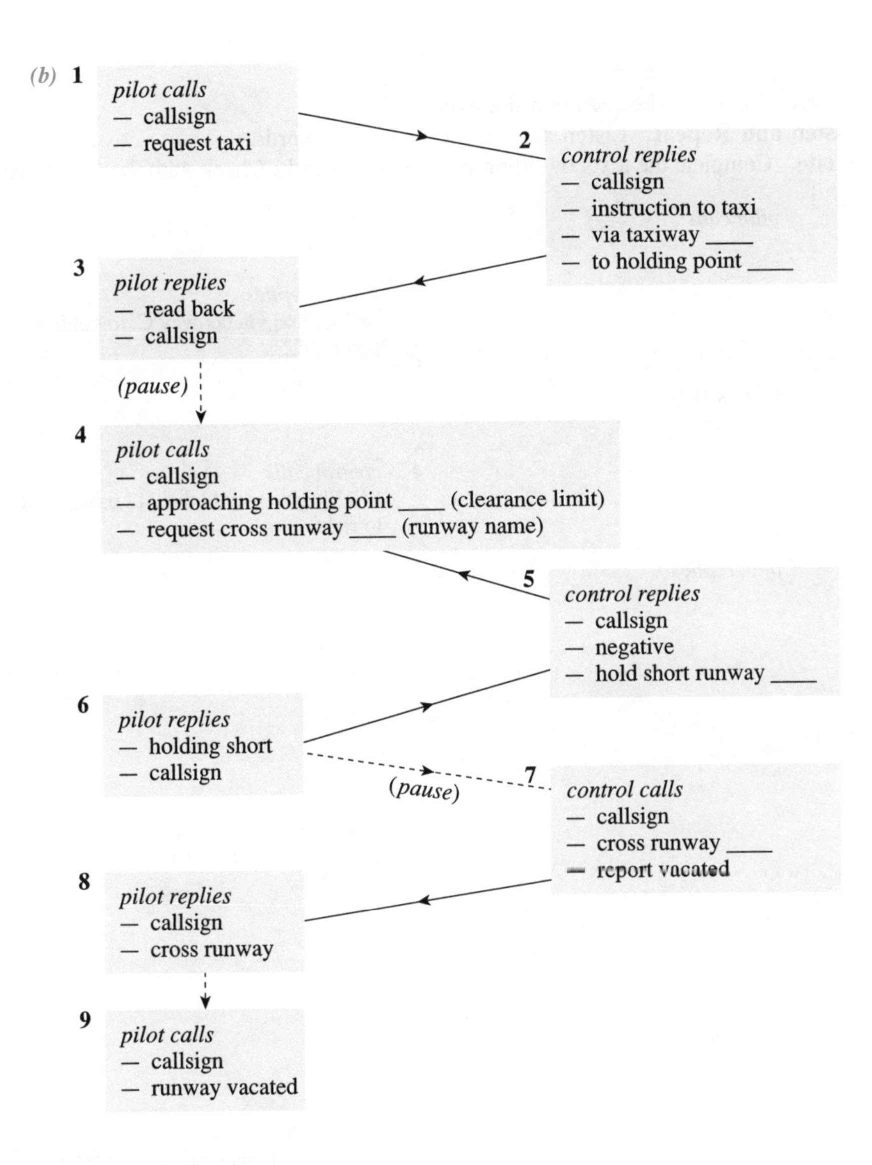

NOTES

- In practice, the language used for taxi instructions is affected by each particular airport layout.
- There is a time lapse and/or dialogue with other traffic between:

  pilot reply **3** and *control call* in ***(a)*** **4**
  pilot reply **3** and *pilot call* in ***(b)*** **4**
  pilot reply **6** and *control call* in ***(b)*** **7**
  pilot reply **8** and *pilot call* in ***(b)*** **9**

Phraseology practice

Listen Listen to the recorded dialogues.

Listen and Repeat Listen and repeat the pilot's words.

Write Complete the texts by filling in the pilot's words. Check with the CD if necessary.

(a)

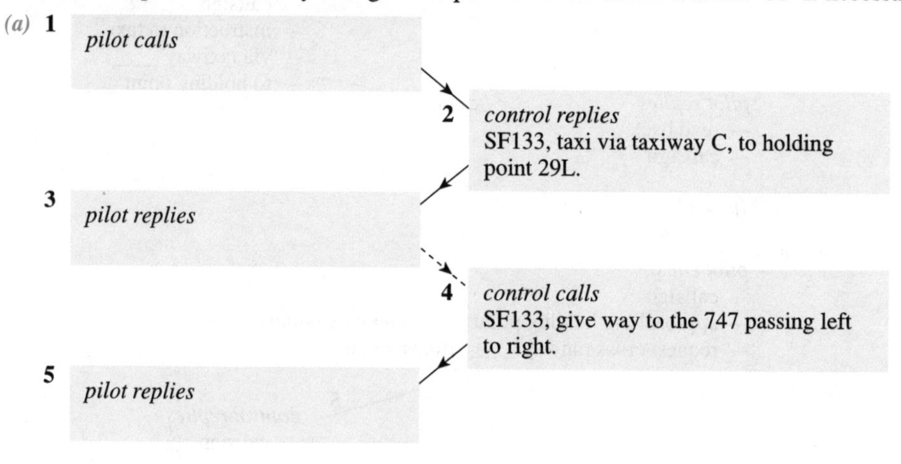

1 *pilot calls*
2 *control replies*
SF133, taxi via taxiway C, to holding point 29L.
3 *pilot replies*
4 *control calls*
SF133, give way to the 747 passing left to right.
5 *pilot replies*

(b)

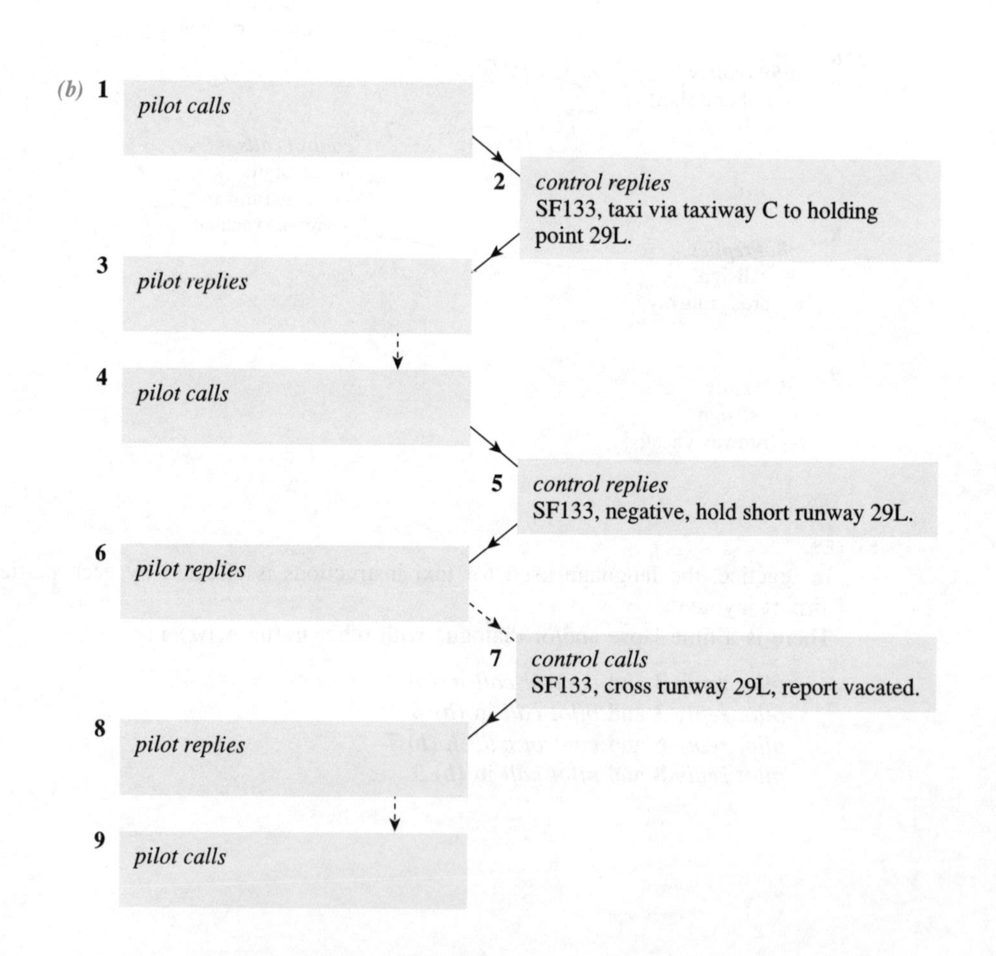

1 *pilot calls*
2 *control replies*
SF133, taxi via taxiway C to holding point 29L.
3 *pilot replies*
4 *pilot calls*
5 *control replies*
SF133, negative, hold short runway 29L.
6 *pilot replies*
7 *control calls*
SF133, cross runway 29L, report vacated.
8 *pilot replies*
9 *pilot calls*

Check Check your answers, page 38.

Listen and Speak Ask for taxi instructions and reply to the controller. Listen to the example and continue in the same way, starting with the example again. Your callsign is SF133.

Check Practise this exercise several times. When it seems easy, and you think it is all correct, check your answers, page 39.

1.5.3 Taxi (non-routine)

Listen and Answer Listen to the dialogues and answer these questions. There is one question for each dialogue.

1. Which runway must the pilot backtrack, and which runway must he cross?

   . . . .

2. What crossed in front of the plane and where was it going?

   . . . .

3. Why must the plane pull in?

   . . . .

4. Why does the aircraft have to wait for the 'follow me'?

   . . . .

Check Check your answers, page 40.

Listen and Write Listen again and complete the texts below:

1 PIL Sunair 978, request taxi.

CTL Sunair 978, ____________, ____________, ____________, call me back ____________.

PIL (readback) ____________ ____________ ____________ ____________ ____________ ____________ ____________.

PIL Sunair 978, reaching ____________ runway 32.

CTL Sunair 978 ____________ runway 32.

PIL ____________ runway 32.

2 PIL Sunair 978, a ____________ dog ____________ the taxiway ____________.

CTL Sunair 978, ____________ was it going?

PIL ____________ ____________.

CTL Thank you Sunair 978, we'll try to get someone ____________.

3 CTL Sunair 385, ____________, there's a 747 ____________, ____________.

PIL ____________, Sunair 385.

4 CTL Sunair 497, ____________, You ____________. Wait there ____________.

PIL Sunair 497, wilco.

Check Check your answers, page 40.

Your word list

Write down any words in the dialogues you do not understand, or are not sure about. Try to guess the meaning in English or in your own language, and write it down. Then check with a dictionary.

CHECK

1.5.1 **Listen and Write** (from page 29)

Instruction number	Aircraft
1	N
2	A or J
3	C
4	I
5	K
6	G
7	O
8	P
9	D

1.5.1 **Look and Speak** (from page 32)

A (Alpha) Go straight ahead at the intersection.
C (Charlie) Give way to the aircraft on your left.
D (Delta) Follow the aircraft in front of you
G (Golf) There's an aircraft overtaking you on your right.
H (Hotel) Taxi straight ahead.
I (India) Take the first turning on the right.
K (Kilo) Give way to the aircraft on your right.
L (Lima) Take the third turning on the right.
M (Mike) Take the second turning on the right.
N (November) Take the second turning on the left.
O (Oscar) Take the first left turn-off.
P (Papa) Take the third turning on the left.

1.5.2 **Write** (from page 35)

(a)

1 *pilot calls*
SF133, request taxi.

2 *control replies*
SF133, taxi via taxiway C to holding point 29L.

3 *pilot replies*
Taxiway C to holding point 29L, SF133.

4 *control calls*
SF133, give way to the 747 passing left to right.

5 *pilot replies*
Traffic in sight, SF133.

(b)

1 *pilot calls*
SF133, request taxi.

2 *control replies*
SF133, taxi via taxiway C, to holding point 29L.

3 *pilot replies*
Taxiway C to holding point 29L, SF133.

4 *pilot calls*
SF133, approaching holding point 29L, request cross runway 29L.

5 *control replies*
SF133, negative, hold short runway 29L.

6 *pilot replies*
Holding short, SF133.

7 *control calls*
SF133, cross runway 29L, report vacated.

8 *pilot replies*
SF133, cross runway 29L.

9 *pilot calls*
SF133, runway vacated.

1.5.2 **Listen and Speak** (from page 35)

1 PIL SF133, request taxi.
CTL . . . .
PIL Taxiway C to holding point 29L, SF133.
CTL . . . .
PIL Traffic in sight, SF133.

2 PIL SF133, request taxi.
CTL . . . .
PIL Taxiway C to holding point 29L.
PIL SF133, approaching holding point 29L, request cross runway 29L.
CTL . . . .
PIL Holding short, SF133.
CTL . . . .
PIL SF133, cross runway 29L.
PIL SF133, runway vacated.

3 PIL SF133, request taxi.
CTL . . . .
PIL Taxi to holding point runway 09, traffic in sight, SF133.
CTL . . . .
PIL Following the 767, SF133.

4 PIL SF133, request taxi.
CTL . . . .
PIL Taxiway E to holding point runway 18, SF133.
CTL . . . .
PIL Hold at next intersection, traffic in sight, SF133.
PIL SF133 approaching holding point runway 18, request cross runway 18.
CTL . . . .
PIL SF133, cross runway 18.
PIL SF133, runway vacated.

5 PIL SF133, request taxi.
CTL . . . .
PIL Taxiway I to holding point runway 31, traffic in sight, SF133.
CTL . . . .
PIL Expediting, SF133.
PIL SF133, approaching holding point runway 31, request cross runway 31.
CTL . . . .
PIL Holding short, SF133.
CTL . . . .
PIL SF133, cross runway 31.
PIL SF133, runway vacated.

6 PIL SF133, request taxi.
CTL . . . .
PIL Taxiway D to holding point runway 14, SF133.
CTL . . . .
PIL Hold at next intersection, traffic in sight, SF133.

1.5.3 Listen and Answer (from page 35)

1. Which runway must the pilot backtrack, and which runway must he cross?
   He must backtrack runway 11, and cross runway 32.
2. What crossed in front of the plane and where was it going?
   A large dog crossed in front going from right to left.
3. Why must the plane pull in?
   The plane must pull in to allow a 747 to overtake on the left.
4. Why does the aircraft have to wait for the 'follow me'?
   He missed the correct taxiway.

1.5.3 Write (from page 35)

1 PIL Sunair 978, request taxi.
CTL Sunair 978, taxiway D4, cross runway 32, backtrack to threshold runway 11, call me back reaching 32.
PIL Taxiway D4, backtrack 11, call you back reaching 32, Sunair 978.
PIL Sunair 978, reaching intersection with runway 32.
CTL Sunair 978, cross runway 32.
PIL Crossing runway 32.

2 PIL Sunair 978, a large dog has just crossed the taxiway ahead of us.
CTL Sunair 978, which direction was it going?
PIL It crossed from right to left.
CTL Thank you Sunair 978, we'll try to get someone to catch it.

3 CTL Sunair 385, pull in to the right, there's a 747 overtaking you, on your left.
PIL Pulling in, Sunair 385.

4 CTL Sunair 497, you've gone too far. You missed taxiway D4. Wait there for the 'follow me' car.
PIL Sunair 497, wilco.

1.6 LINE-UP

1.6.1 Line-up (routine)

Key words and phrases

Check that you understand the following words and phrases.
Look up any new words in an aviation dictionary.

holding point
wait
on final
in sight
landing
behind
hold short
number 2 for departure
negative departure

Typical Exchanges

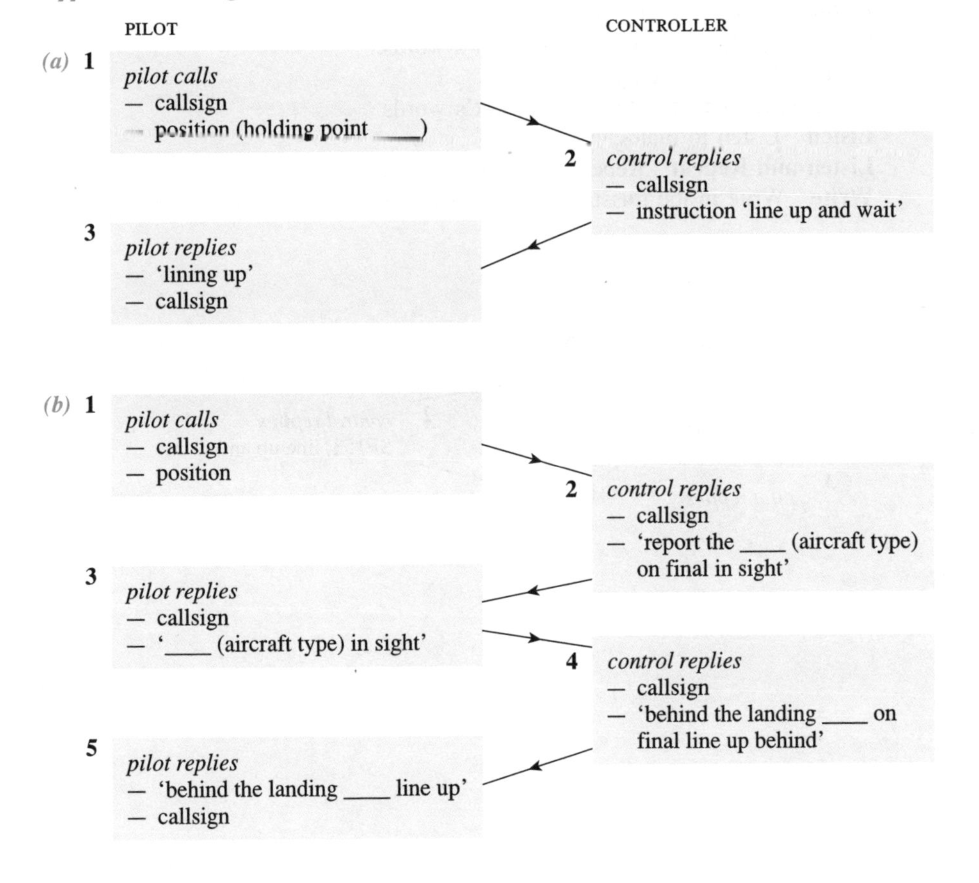

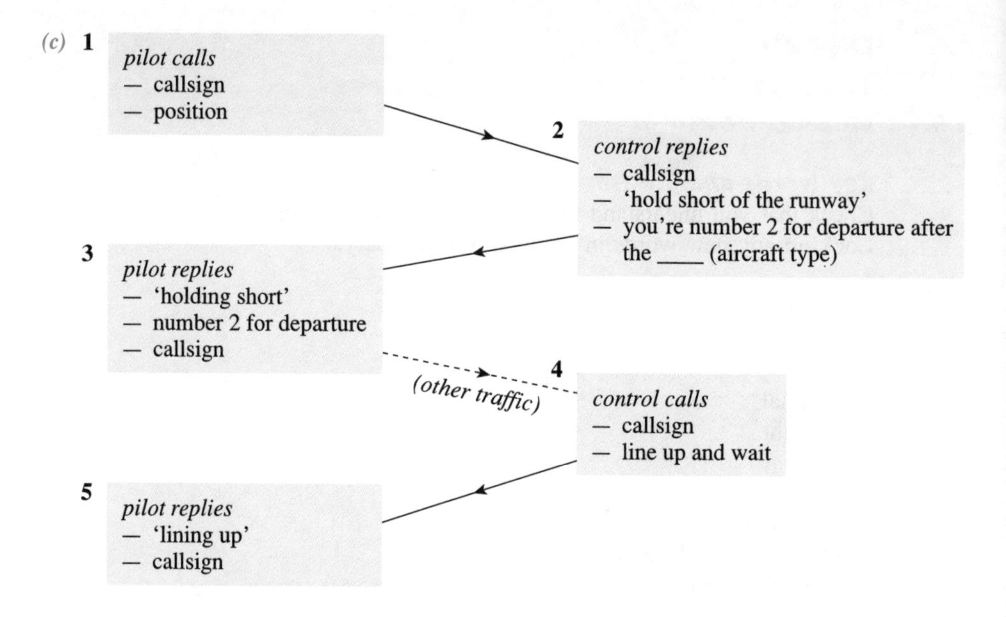

Phraseology practice

Listen Listen to dialogue (***a***).
Listen and Repeat Repeat the pilot's words.
Listen Listen to dialogue (***b***).
Listen and Repeat Repeat the pilot's words.
Listen Listen to dialogue (***c***).
Listen and Repeat Repeat the pilot's words.
Write Write in the missing words. Listen to the CD again if necessary.

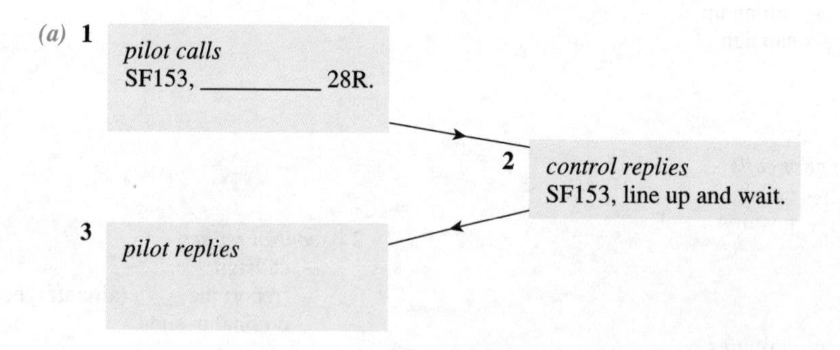

(a) 1
pilot calls
SF153, _________ 28R.
2
control replies
SF153, line up and wait.
3
pilot replies

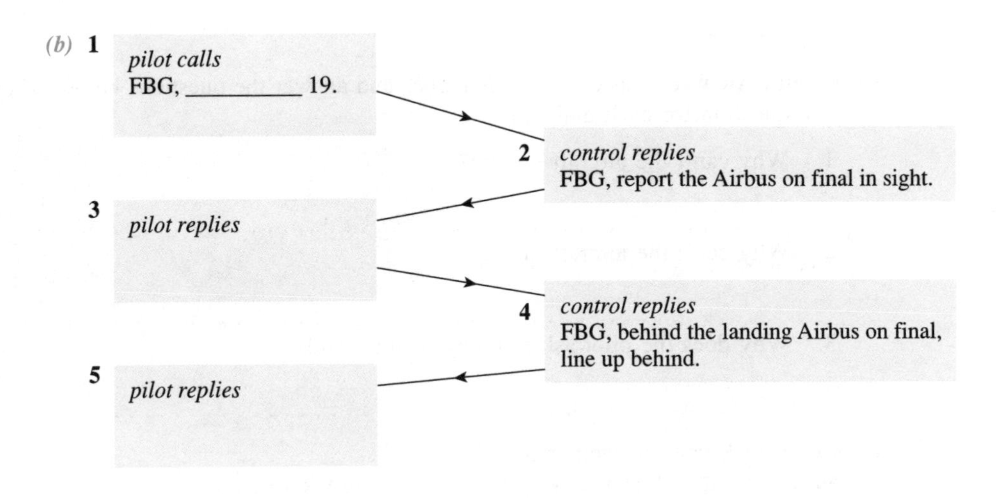

(b) 1
pilot calls
FBG, __________ 19.
2
control replies
FBG, report the Airbus on final in sight.
3
pilot replies
4
control replies
FBG, behind the landing Airbus on final, line up behind.
5
pilot replies

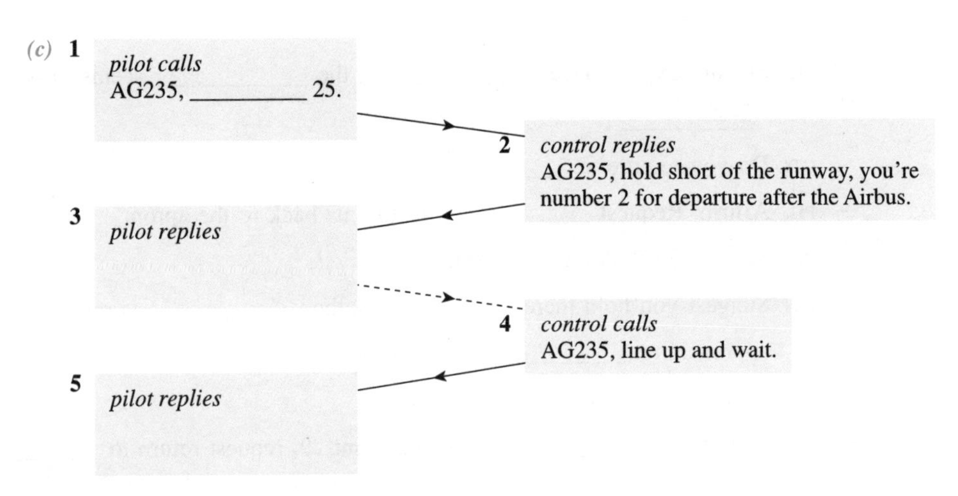

(c) 1
pilot calls
AG235, __________ 25.
2
control replies
AG235, hold short of the runway, you're number 2 for departure after the Airbus.
3
pilot replies
4
control calls
AG235, line up and wait.
5
pilot replies

Check Check your answers, page 45.

Listen and Speak Using the information below, call the Tower from the correct holding point and reply to the instructions, as in the recorded example.

No.	Callsign	Holding point
1	SF153	28R
2	FBG	19
3	AG235	25
4	ESQ	13L
5	KVX	05
6	YFL	33
7	OPR	18
8	ZE692	09

Check Practise this exercise several times. When it seems easy, and you think it is all correct, check your answers, page 46.

1.6.2 Line-up (non-routine)

Listen and Answer Listen to the dialogues and answer the questions below. There is one question for each dialogue.

1. Why can't the aircraft line up?

   ....

2. Why can't the aircraft line up?

   ....

3. Why does the pilot ask to return to the stand?

   ....

Check Check your answers, page 46.

Listen and Write Listen again and complete the texts below:

1 PIL Sunair 329, ____________ 32.

CTL Sunair 329, line up and ____________.

PIL Sunair 329, we have a ____________, the ____________ seems to be ____________.

CTL Do you require a ____________?

PIL Affirm. Request ____________ to tow us back to the apron.

2 PIL Sunair 473, holding point 18L.

CTL Suggest you hold there ____________, the ____________ is rapidly approaching ____________ of the runway.

PIL Wildo, Sunair 473.

3 PIL Sunair 968, ____________ holding point 29, request return to ____________, the ____________ are ____________.

CTL Roger, Sunair 968, turn in the ____________, take the first ____________, onto ____________ J.

PIL ____________ turn onto ____________ J.

Check Check your answers, page 47.

Your word list

Write down any words in the dialogues you do not understand, or are not sure about. Try to guess the meaning, in English or in your own language, and write it down. Then check with a dictionary.

CHECK

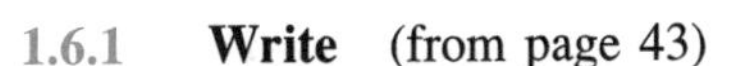

1.6.1 **Write** (from page 43)

(a)

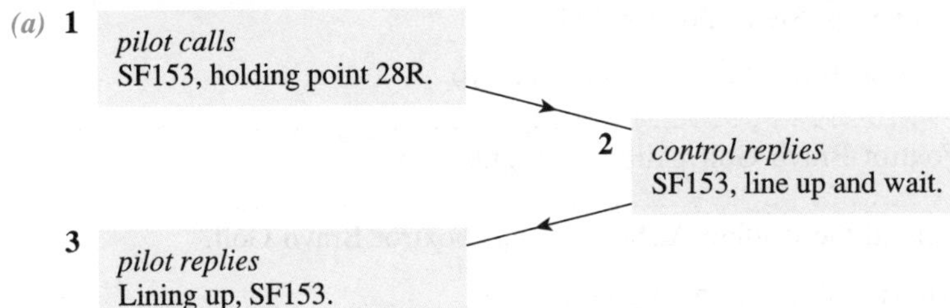

(b)

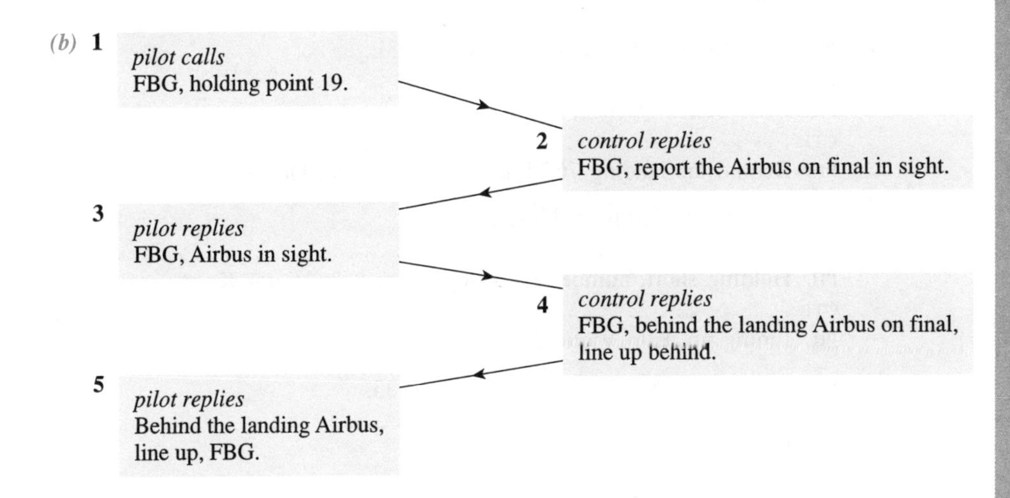

(c)

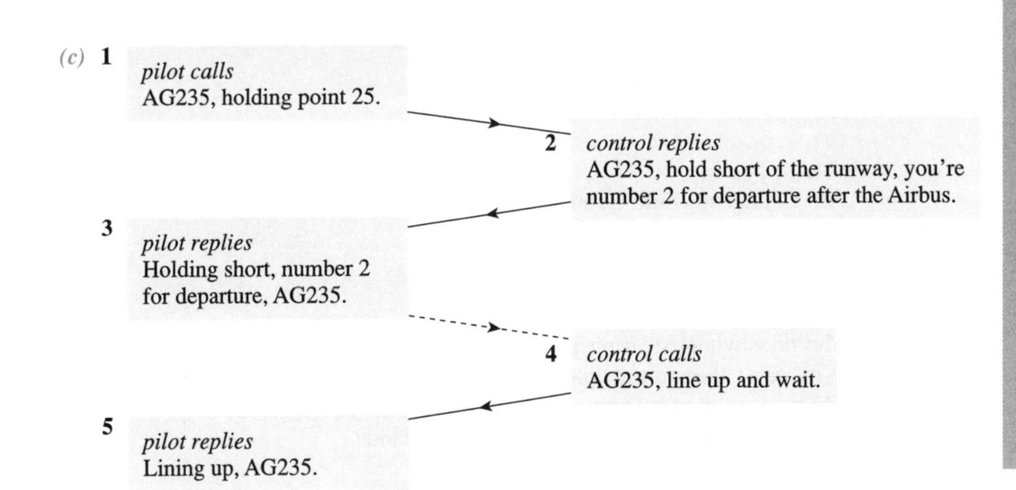

1
pilot calls
AG235, holding point 25.
2
control replies
AG235, hold short of the runway, you're number 2 for departure after the Airbus.
3
pilot replies
Holding short, number 2 for departure, AG235.
4
control calls
AG235, line up and wait.
5
pilot replies
Lining up, AG235.

1.6.1 Listen and Speak (from page 43)

1 PIL Sierra Foxtrot 153, holding point 28R.
CTL . . . .
PIL Lining up, Sierra Foxtrot 153.

2 PIL Foxtrot Bravo Golf, holding point 19.
CTL . . . .
PIL Foxtrot Bravo Golf, Airbus in sight.
CTL . . . .
PIL Behind the landing Airbus line up, Foxtrot Bravo Golf.

3 PIL Alpha Golf 235, holding point 25.
CTL . . . .
PIL Holding short, number 2 for departure, Alpha Golf 235.
CTL . . . .
PIL Lining up, Alpha Golf 235.

4 PIL Echo Sierra Quebec, holding point 13L.
CTL . . . .
PIL Echo Sierra Quebec, 767 in sight.
CTL . . . .
PIL Behind the landing 767 line up, Echo Sierra Quebec.

5 PIL Kilo Victor X-ray, holding point 05.
CTL . . . .
PIL Holding short, number 2 for departure, Kilo Victor X-ray.
CTL . . . .
PIL Lining up, Kilo Victor X-ray.

6 PIL Yankee Foxtrot Lima, holding point 33.
CTL . . . .
PIL Lining up, Yankee Foxtrot Lima,

7 PIL Oscar Papa Romeo, holding point 18.
CTL . . . .
PIL Holding position, number 2 for departure, Oscar Papa Romeo.
CTL . . . .
PIL Lining up, Oscar Papa Romeo.

8 PIL Zulu Echo 692, holding point 09.
CTL . . . .
CTL . . . .
PIL Lining up, Zulu Echo 692.

1.6.2 Listen and Answer (from page 44)

1. Why can't the aircraft line up?
   The nose wheel steering is jammed.
2. Why can't the aircraft line up?
   There is a thunderstorm approaching the far end of the runway.
3. Why does the pilot ask to return to the stand?
   The brakes are overheating.

1.6.2 Listen and Write (from page 44)

1 PIL Sunair 329, holding point 32.
CTL Sunair 329, line up and wait.
(*pause*)
PIL Sunair 329, we have a problem, the nose wheel steering seems to be jammed.
CTL Do you require a tug?
PIL Affirm. Request tug to tow us back to the apron.

2 PIL Sunair 473, holding point 18L.
CTL Suggest you hold there for a few minutes, the thunderstorm is rapidly approaching the far end of the runway.
PIL Wilco, Sunair 473.

3 PIL Sunair 968, reaching holding point 29, request return to stand, the brakes are overheating.
CTL Roger, Sunair 968, turn in the holding bay, take the first convenient left turn, onto taxiway Juliet.
PIL Left turn onto taxiway Juliet.

1.7 REVIEW OF PART ONE

1.7.1 Routine phraseology review

Start-up and push-back

Write The dialogue for start-up and push-back has been mixed up. Put it into the correct sequence:

(1) — Sunair 369, request push-back from C6.
(2) — Starting up, Sunair 369.
(3) — Sunair 369, stand C6, information Foxtrot, request start-up for Winton.
(4) — Sunair 369, push-back approved.
(5) — Sunair 369, start-up approved.
(6) — Sunair 369, hold position, I'll call you back.
(7) — Go ahead Sunair 369.
(8) — Rexbury Ground, Sunair 369, good morning.

Check Check your answers, page 52.

Taxi and line-up

Write Put the dialogue for taxi and line-up into the correct sequence.

(1) — Holding point 12, Sunair 369.
(2) — Sunair 369, line up and wait.
(3) — Winton Ground, Sunair 369 ready to taxi.
(4) — Lining up, Sunair 369.
(5) — Reaching holding point 12, Sunair 369.
(6) — Sunair 369, taxi to holding point 12.

Check Check your answers, page 52.

1.7.2 Flight from Rexbury to Winton (from departure ATIS to line-up)

Scenario

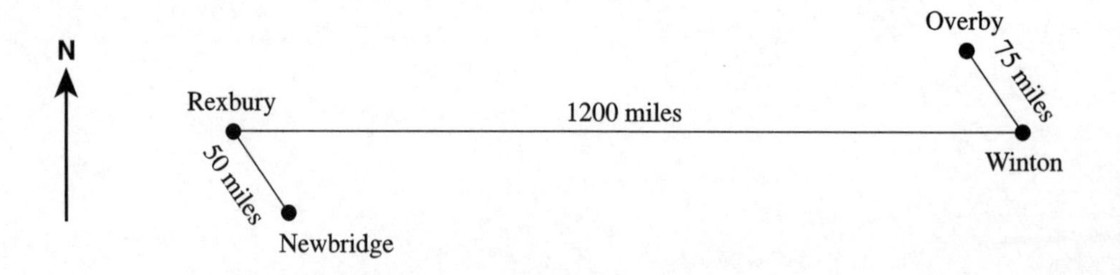

Winton is 1200 nautical miles East of Rexbury. The alternate for Winton is Overby, 75 nautical miles North West of Winton. Newbridge Airport is 50 miles South East of Rexbury.

Rexbury Airport
Runway: 29
Taxiways: Yankee, Delta
SID's: November 2, Romeo 1, Golf 5
Tower frequency: 118.3
Approach frequency: 120.2
Rexbury Area Control: 128.9

En route
New County Upper Control: 135.9
Valley Control: 128.5
Meadow Control: 126.3

Winton Airport
Runways: 07, 12, 25, 30
Taxiways: Inner/Outer

Tower frequency: 118.1
Winton Radar frequency: 121.1
Approach frequency: 121.3
Ground frequency: 121.7
VOR–RED (Redhill)

Reporting points
RIV (River)
BCK (Blackrock)
LAK (Lake)
RED (Redhill)

Listen and Read You are flying from Rexbury to Winton. Your callsign is Sunair 367, your stand is 19. The time is 13.40. The recording begins with ATIS information, and then asks you to make initial contact with Rexbury Ground.
Listen and Speak Follow the instructions on the CD, and reply to the controller.
Check Check your answers, page 52.

1.7.3 Flight from Dublin to Paris (initial contact to line-up)

Listen and Read Flight plan details:
callsign: SF309
reporting points:
Liffy
Wallasey
Telba
Midhurst
Runways at Dublin: 11, 17 and 23.
Note that the callsign letters Sierra Foxtrot are often abbreviated to Sierra Fox.
Listen and Speak Take the pilot's part, follow the instructions on the CD and reply to the controller. The exercise contains route clearance, so you must be ready to copy (have pencil and paper ready). The exercise starts with initial contact with Dublin Ground Control.
Check Check your answers, page 53.

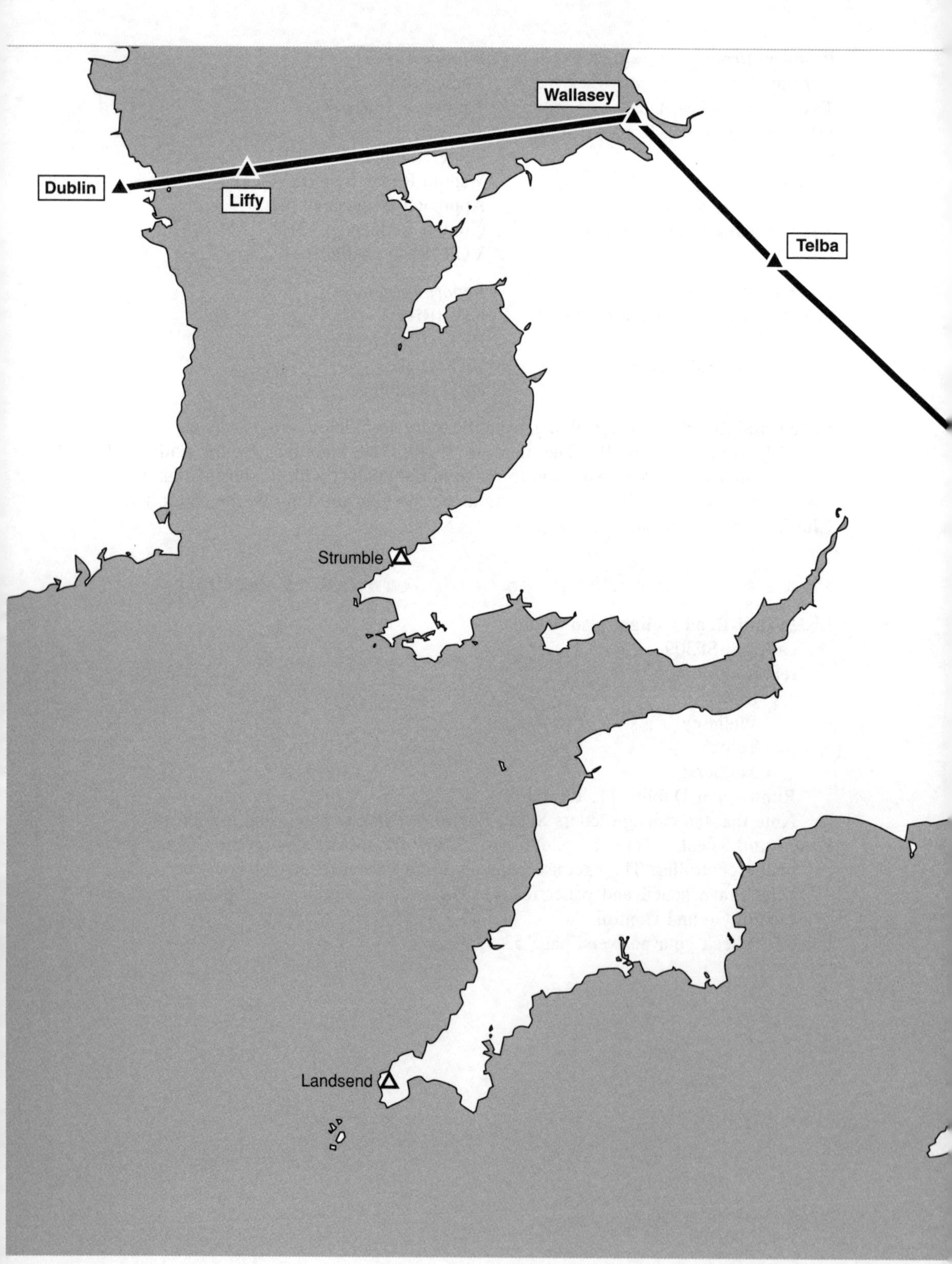
Wallasey
Dublin
Liffy
Telba
Strumble
Landsend

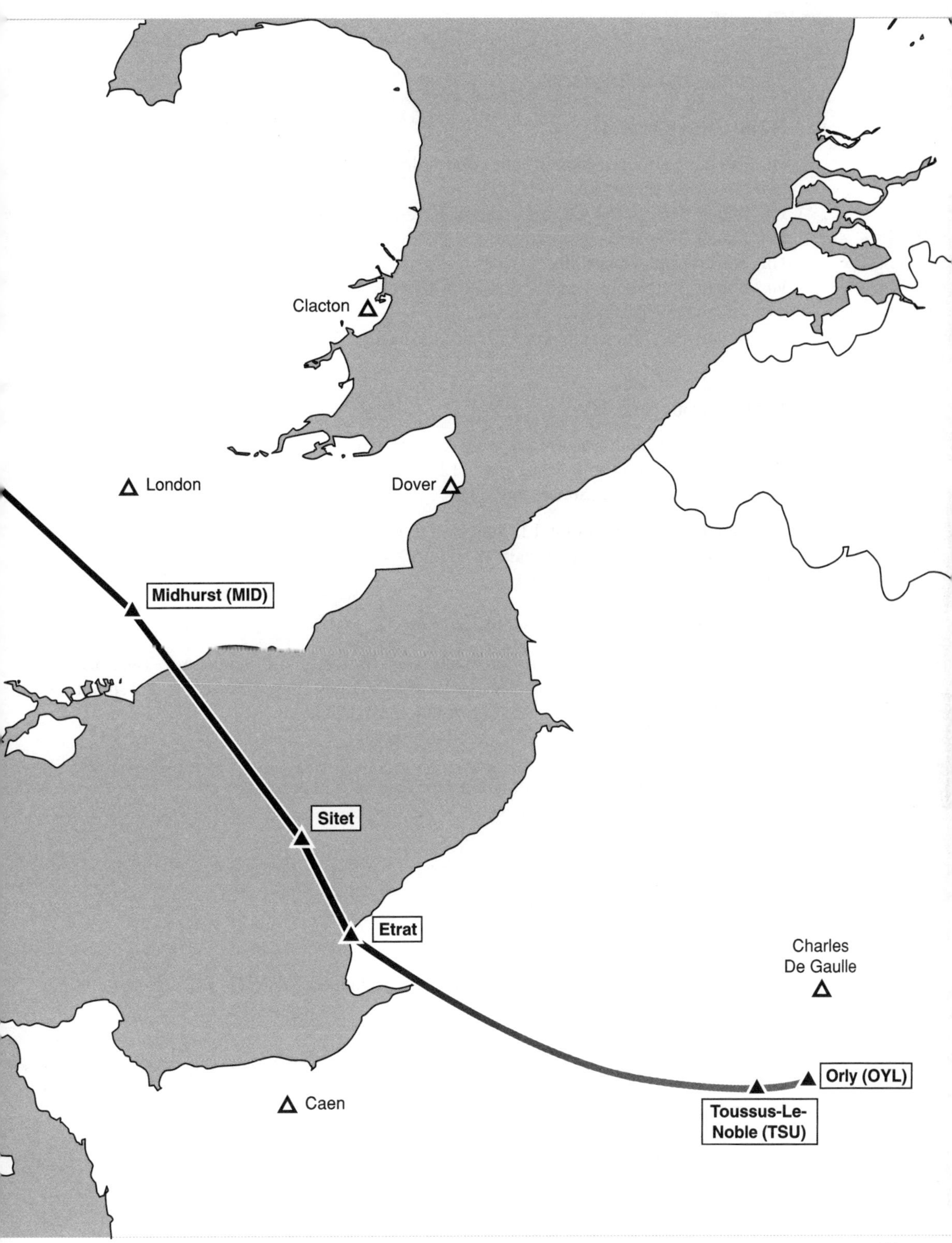
Clacton
London
Dover
Midhurst (MID)
Sitet
Etrat
Charles
De Gaulle
Orly (OYL)
Toussus-Le-
Noble (TSU)
Caen

CHECK

Start-up and push-back

1.7.1 **Write** (from page 48)

PIL Rexbury Ground, Sunair 369, good morning. (8)
CTL Go ahead Sunair 369. (7)
PIL Sunair 369, Stand C6, information F, request start-up for Winton. (3)
CTL Sunair 369, start-up approved. (5)
PIL Starting up, Sunair 369. (2)
PIL Sunair 369, request push-back from C6. (1)
CTL Sunair 369, push-back approved. (4)
CTL Sunair 369, hold position, I'll call you back. (6)

Taxi and line-up

1.7.1 **Write** (from page 48)

PIL Winton Ground, Sunair 369 ready to taxi. (3)
CTL Sunair 369, taxi to holding point 12. (6)
PIL Holding point 12, Sunair 369. (1)

PIL Reaching holding point 12, Sunair 369. (5)
CTL Sunair 369, line up and wait. (2)
PIL Lining up, Sunair 369. (4)

1.7.2 **Listen and Speak** (from page 49)

ATIS This is Rexbury departure information Foxtrot at 13.30 Zulu time. Take-off and landing runway 29, wind 260° 12 knots, CAVOK, temperature 14, dew point 11, QNH 1023, no sig. This was information Foxtrot.
PIL Rexbury Ground, Sunair 367, good afternoon.
CTL ....
PIL Sunair 367, stand 19, information Fox received, request start-up.
CTL ....
PIL Stand 19, Sunair 367.
CTL ....
PIL Starting up, Sunair 367.
CTL ....
PIL Ready to copy, Sunair 367.
CTL ....
PIL Sunair 367 is cleared to Winton via flight planned route, Golf 5 departure, climb to FL110 initially, level change en route.
CTL ....
PIL Sunair 367, request push-back
CTL ....
PIL Holding point 29, taxiway D, Sunair 367.
CTL ....
PIL Tower on 118.3, goodbye.
PIL Rexbury Tower, Sunair 367, good afternoon, reaching holding point 29.
CTL ....

PIL Sunair 367, 727 in sight.

CTL . . . .

PIL Behind the landing 727 line up, Sunair 367.

1.7.3 Listen and Speak (from page 49)

PIL Dublin Ground, SF309.

CTL . . . .

PIL We'll be ready to start-up in 20 minutes, SF309.

CTL . . . .

PIL SF309, What is the departure runway?

CTL . . . .

PIL Runway 17, 110° 20 knots.

CTL . . . .

PIL Ready to copy, SF309.

CTL . . . .

PIL SF309, cleared to Paris Orly, via Liffy Blue 1, flight planned route, FL230 to request level change.

CTL . . . .

PIL Backtrack runway 11, Dublin Tower 118.6, SF309, goodbye.

PIL Dublin Tower, SF309, good morning.

CTL . . . .

PIL Backtrack 11, expediting, approved to line up and wait runway 17.

CTL . . . .

1.8 SUPPLEMENTARY VOCABULARY

1.8.1 Phases of flight

Write Put the different phases of flight in the correct sequence, filling in the table below.

climb	push-back
take-off	final approach
descent	taxi
start-up	take-off roll
approach	touch-down
cruise	line-up

no.	phase of flight
1	start-up
2	
3	
4	
5	
6	
7	
8	
9	
10	
11	
12	

Check Check your answers, page 57.

1.8.2 Airport words

Look and Write Look at the pictures and write down the number that corresponds to these words.

No.		*No.*	
___	terminal building	___	holding bay/area
___	intersection	___	high-speed turn-off
___	satellite	___	runway
___	tower	___	holding point
___	jetway	___	passenger steps
___	taxiway	___	threshold

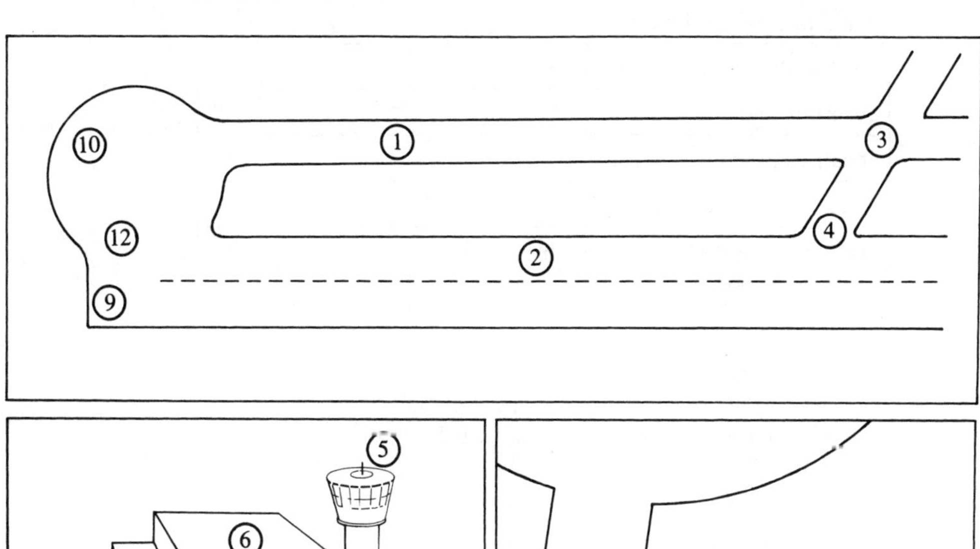

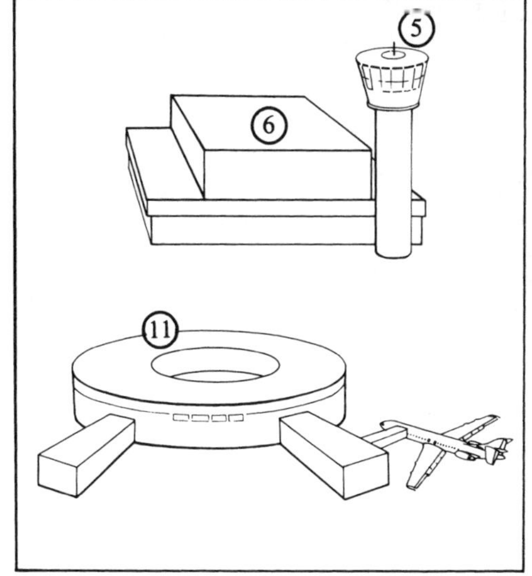

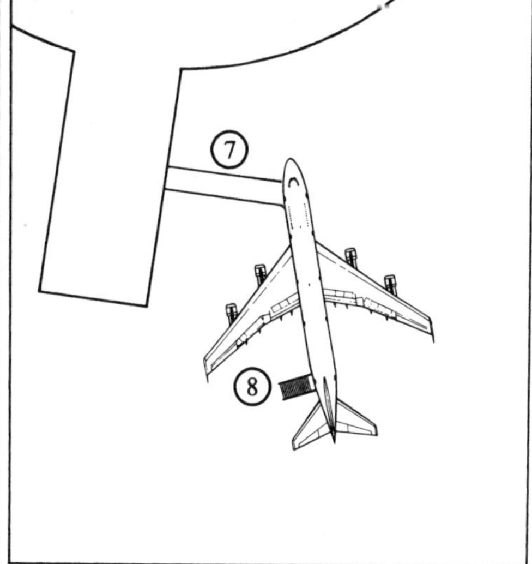

Check Check your answers, page 57.

1.8.3 Airport vehicles

Read and Write Look at the list of phrases in the table which describe different vehicles found at an airport. Match them with the list of vehicles under the table, and write in the names of each vehicle.

it helps you not to get lost	
used at push-back	
used for electrical power at the parking stand	
for extinguishing fires	
to clear the tarmac on winter days	
it carries fuel	
it carries food	
it takes passengers to the plane	
like a huge bus which rises to the level of the door	

shuttle bus
fuel tanker
GPU (ground power unit)
FOLLOW ME van
mobile lounge
catering truck
snow plough
fire truck
tug

Check Check your answers, page 57.

CHECK

1.8.1 **Write** (from page 54)

1	start-up
2	push-back
3	taxi
4	line-up
5	take-off roll
6	take-off
7	climb
8	cruise
9	descent
10	approach
11	final approach
12	touch-down

1.8.2 **Look and Write** (from page 55)

No.		*No.*	
6	terminal building	10	holding area/bay
3	intersection	4	high-speed turn-off
11	satellite	2	runway
5	tower	12	holding point
7	jetway	8	passenger steps
1	taxiway	9	threshold

1.8.3 **Read and Write** (from page 56)

it helps you not to get lost	FOLLOW ME van
used at push-back	tug
used for electrical power at the parking stand	GPU
for extinguishing fires	fire truck
to clear the tarmac on winter days	snow plough
it carries fuel	fuel tanker
it carries food	catering truck
it takes passengers to the plane	shuttle bus
like a huge bus which rises to the level of the door	mobile lounge

Part Two

Take-off to top of climb

2.1 DISTRESS AND URGENCY MESSAGES

NOTE: Each incident in real life is different and must be evaluated separately. The exercises in this section are designed to practise *language*, not procedure.

Read Study the following definitions:

Distress: a dangerous situation requiring immediate assistance.

Urgency: a condition concerning the safety of an aircraft or other vehicle, or of someone on board or within sight, but which does not require immediate assistance.

For example:

Uncontrollable *engine fire* is a *distress* situation.

A *passenger taken seriously ill* is an *urgency* situation.

Read and Write Classify these incidents into the 'distress' or 'urgency' category, and write them in the table below.

total electrical failure
depressurisation
fire in the hold
fire in the toilets
fuel endurance 10 minutes at initial approach phase
a bomb scare
injuries among passengers and cabin crew after severe turbulence
engine flameout
bird ingestion at initial climb, one engine shut down
wheel well fire
passenger with a heart attack

Distress	Urgency

Check Check your answers, page 64.

Read and Write Look at this list of possible incidents during flight. Think of actions you might take to solve each problem.

Problem	Possible action
1. total electrical failure	
2. depressurisation	
3. fire in the hold	
4. fire in the toilets	
5. fuel endurance very low	
6. a bomb scare	
7. severe icing	
8. injuries among passengers and cabin crew after severe turbulence	
9. engine flameout	
10. bird ingestion after take-off	
11. wheel well fire	
12. passenger with heart attack	

Now look at this list of possible actions to solve the problems. Choose an action for each problem and write it in the table above. The same answer may be used several times.

- look for a doctor on board and land as soon as possible
- put on oxygen mask and make an emergency descent
- land immediately
- release fire bottle and land immediately
- ask for priority landing
- change level
- look for VMC conditions and land
- return to the airport
- try to extinguish the fire and land immediately
- land immediately
- try to make an airstart

Check Check your answers, page 64.

Read Distress messages should consist of:

1. MAYDAY, MAYDAY, MAYDAY
2. Name of ground station being called OR 'All stations, all stations'
3. aircraft identification
4. description of the emergency
5. intention of the pilot
6. position, level and heading
7. other information

Urgency messages should have the same elements, with 'MAYDAY' replaced by 'PAN PAN, PAN PAN, PAN PAN.'

1. PAN PAN, PAN PAN, PAN PAN
2. Name of ground station being called OR 'All stations, all stations'
3. aircraft identification
4. description of the emergency
5. intention of the pilot
6. position, level and heading
7. other information

Listen and Read Listen to the recorded examples of distress and urgency messages.

Read You are flying from Rexbury to Winton on a twin engined jet aircraft. The flight time is about 2½ hours; alternate for Winton is Overby, situated 75 miles North-West of Winton. Newbridge airport is 50 miles South-East of Rexbury. Winton is 1200 miles East of Rexbury.

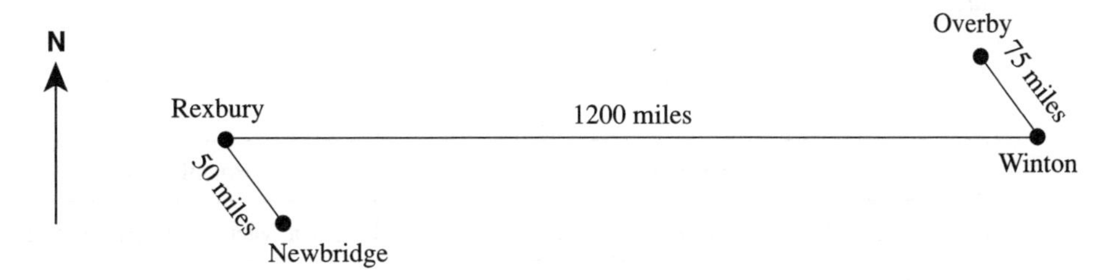

Listen and Speak Look at the following flight details and situations. Decide on the appropriate action, and call control. You will hear a version of each call after you speak.

1 Sunair 664 — 60 miles West of Winton — FL310 — depressurisation
2 Sunair 967 — 40 miles East of Rexbury — FL280 — bomb scare
3 Sunair 663 — 20 miles East of Rexbury — FL190 — bird ingestion — one engine shut down
4 Sunair 525 — 15 miles North East of Rexbury — FL140 — wheel well fire

Check Check your answers, page 65. (There are no 'right answers' because there are so many variables in real life, but you can compare the possible answers with your own.)

CHECK

2.1 **Read and Write** (from page 61)

Distress	Urgency
total electrical failure fire in the hold fire in the toilets wheel well fire depressurisation	fuel endurance 10 minutes at initial approach a bomb scare injuries among passengers and cabin crew engine flameout bird ingestion passenger with a heart attack

(Remember, each real situation is different so the 'answers' to this exercise may be different)

2.1 **Read and Write** (from page 62)

Problem	Possible Action
1. total electrical failure	look for VMC conditions and land
2. depressurisation	put on oxygen mask and make an emergency descent
3. fire in the hold	land immediately
4. fire in the toilets	try to extinguish the fire and land immediately
5. fuel endurance very low	ask for priority landing
6. a bomb scare	land immediately
7. severe icing	change level
8. injuries among passengers and cabin crew after severe turbulence	look for a doctor on board and land as soon as possible
9. engine flameout	try to make an airstart
10. bird ingestion after take-off	return to the airport
11. wheel well fire	release fire bottle and land immediately
12. passenger with heart attack	look for a doctor on board and land as soon as possible

2.1 **Listen and Speak** (from page 63)

1. MAYDAY, MAYDAY, MAYDAY, Sunair 664.
   Emergency descent due to depressurisation.
   Squawking A7700.
   Position 60 miles west of Winton.
   Leaving flight level 310 descending to flight level 100 over.

2. PAN PAN, PAN PAN, PAN PAN, Sunair 967.
   We are coming back to Rexbury. There seems to be a bomb on board.
   Position 40 miles East of Rexbury, heading 270, flight level 280.
   Request priority landing and emergency services.

3. Sunair 663, Rexbury Control 20 miles East of Rexbury. Flight level 190, we are coming back. We have shut down one engine due to bird ingestion. Request descent and landing data at Rexbury.

4. MAYDAY MAYDAY MAYDAY, Sunair 525.
   We have a fire warning on the main gear.
   Request emergency landing at Rexbury.
   Our position is 15 miles North East of Rexbury, flight level 140.

2.2 TAKE-OFF

2.2.1 Take-off (routine)

Key words and phrases

Check that you understand all the words in this list. Look up any new words in an aviation dictionary.

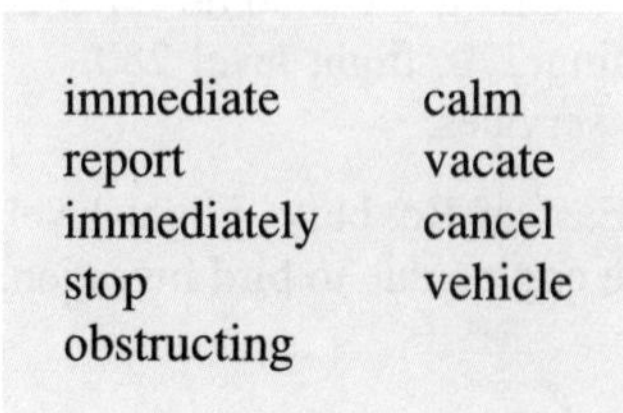

immediate	calm
report	vacate
immediately	cancel
stop	vehicle
obstructing	

Typical exchange

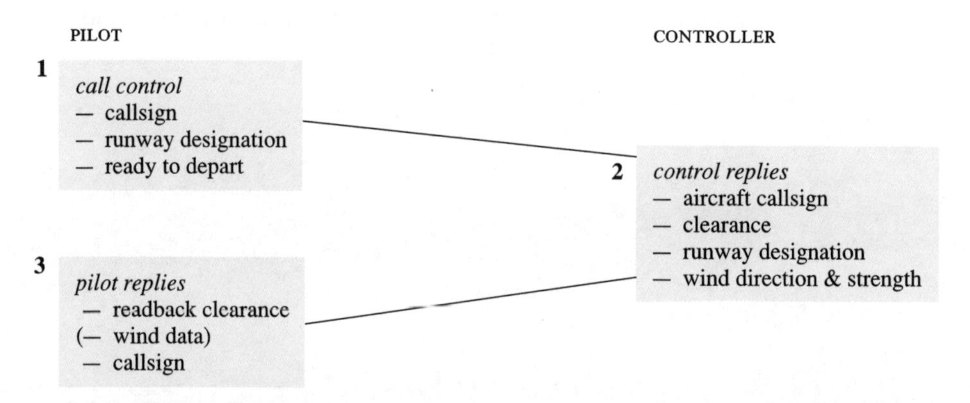

NOTES

— The pilot can omit the wind data in the reply.

Phraseology practice 1

Listen Listen to the dialogue on the CD.

Listen and Repeat Listen and repeat the pilot's words.

Write Complete the dialogue below by writing in the pilot's words.
Check with the CD if necessary.

Check Check your answers, page 71.

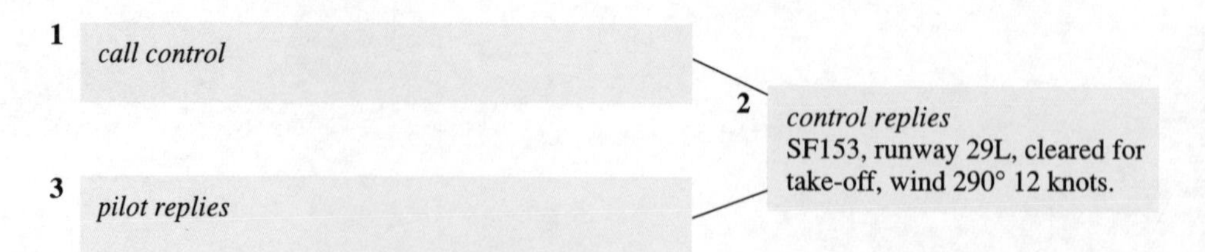

1
call control
2
control replies
SF153, runway 29L, cleared for take-off, wind 290° 12 knots.
3
pilot replies

Listen and Speak Get take-off clearance for the flights below, and reply to the controller's instructions. Listen to the example and then continue in the same way, starting with the example again.

No.	*Callsign*	*Runway*
1	SF153	29L
2	FBG	18
3	AG235	31
4	ESQ	07

Check Check your answers, page 71.

Typical exchange

If the controller wants to stop the departure or vacate the runway quickly, the exchange looks like this:

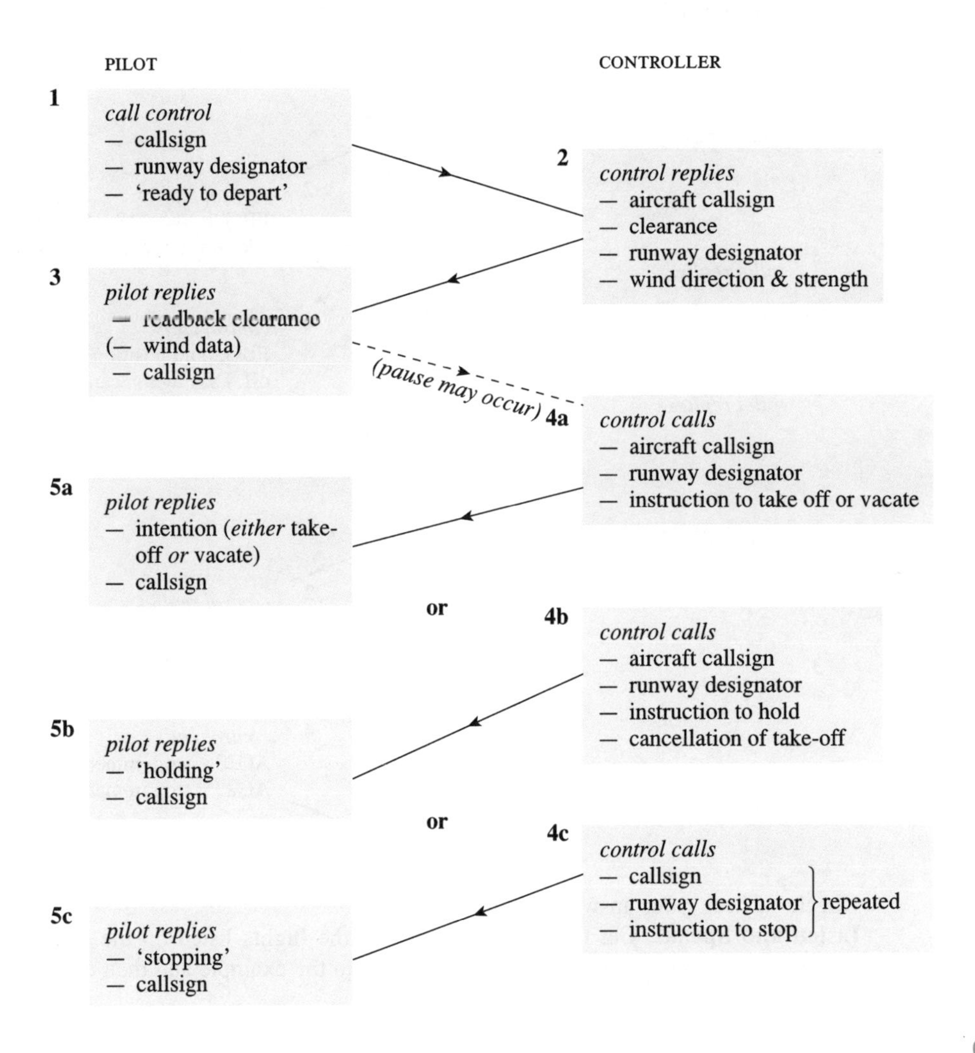

Phraseology practice 2

Listen If the controller wants to stop the departure, or vacate the runway quickly, the instructions may be slightly different. Listen to the examples on the CD.

Listen and Repeat Listen and repeat the pilot's words.

Write Complete the dialogues below by writing in the pilot's words.
Listen to the CD again if necessary.

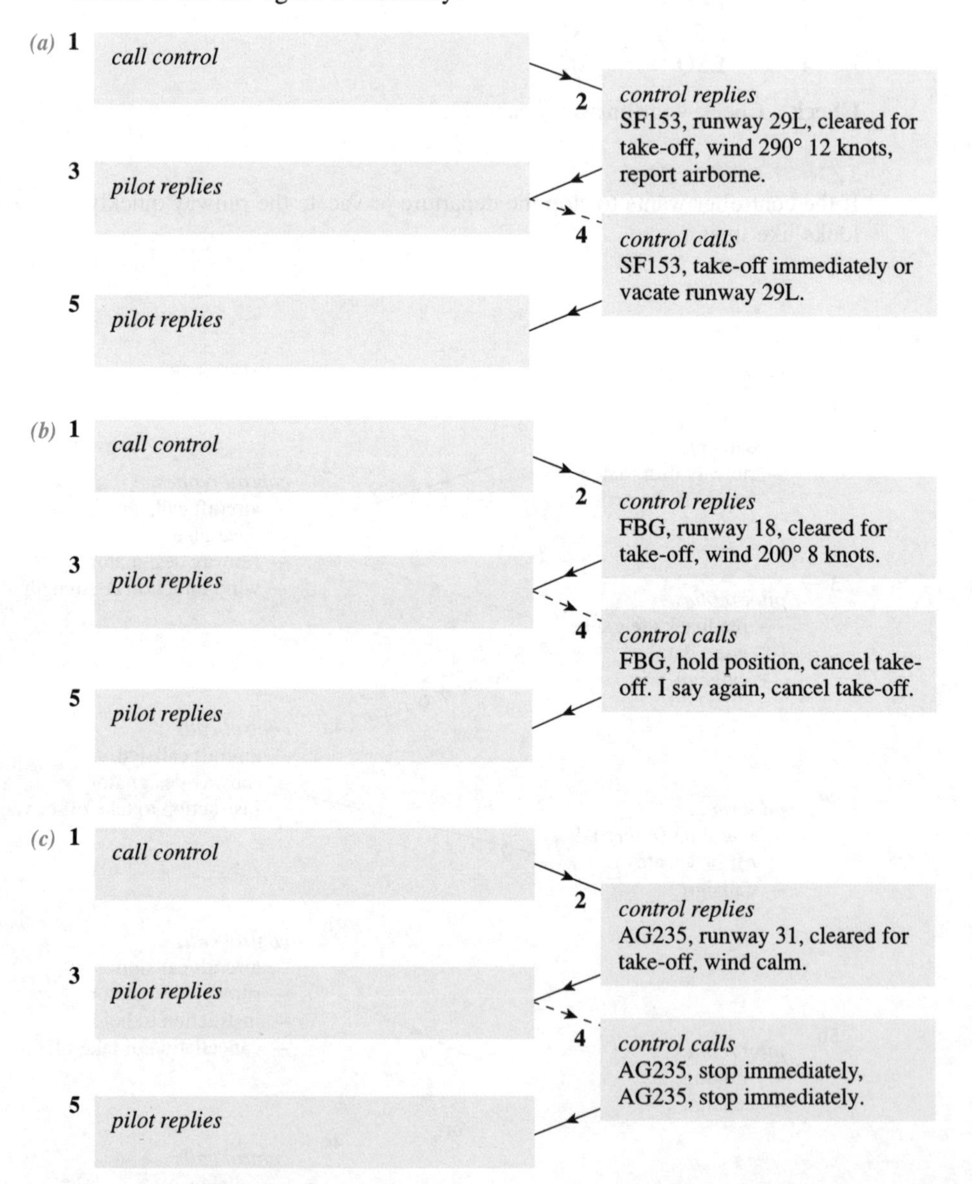

(a) 1
call control
2
control replies
SF153, runway 29L, cleared for take-off, wind 290° 12 knots, report airborne.
3
pilot replies
4
control calls
SF153, take-off immediately or vacate runway 29L.
5
pilot replies
(b) 1
call control
2
control replies
FBG, runway 18, cleared for take-off, wind 200° 8 knots.
3
pilot replies
4
control calls
FBG, hold position, cancel take-off. I say again, cancel take-off.
5
pilot replies
(c) 1
call control
2
control replies
AG235, runway 31, cleared for take-off, wind calm.
3
pilot replies
4
control calls
AG235, stop immediately, AG235, stop immediately.
5
pilot replies

Check Check your answers, page 71.

Listen and Speak Get take-off clearance for the flights listed on the next page and reply to the controller's instructions. Listen to the example and then continue in the same way, starting with the example again.

No.	Callsign	Runway	No.	Callsign	Runway
1	SF153	29L	**5**	MPH	07
2	FBG	18	**6**	RST	26
3	AG235	31	**7**	DNO	12
4	JDI	07	**8**	UCQ	25

Check Check your answers, page 72.

2.2.2 Take-off: (non-routine)

Listen and Answer Listen to the dialogues and write down the answers to these questions. There is one question for each dialogue.

1. Why was the take-off abandoned?

   . . . .

2. Why did the controller stop the take-off?

   . . . .

3. Why was the take-off aborted?

   . . . .

Check Check your answers, page 73.

Listen and Write Listen again and complete the texts below.

1 CTL Sunair 332, runway 25, cleared to take-off, ____________ ____________.

PIL Taking off, Sunair 332.

PIL Sunair 332 ____________. Take-off abandoned, due to ____________.

CTL Do you request taxi to the ____________ Sunair 332?

PIL ____________, request return to parking area.

2 PIL Sunair 596, runway 25, ready for departure.

CTL Sunair 596, runway 25, cleared to take-off, ____________.

PIL Sunair 596, taking off.

(*pause*)

CTL Sunair 596, ____________, ____________, ____________, ____________ coming from left main gear.

PIL Sunair 596 stopping.

PIL Sunair 596, ____________ ____________, request ____________.

3 PIL Sunair 879, take-off ____________ due to ____________. We ____________ slightly off the runway.

CTL Sunair 879, are you able to __________?

PIL Negative, the right gear is __________. Request __________ __________ and __________ to take the passengers to the __________.

CTL Roger, Sunair 879, we'll get a __________ to come out to you as well.

Check Check your answers, page 74.

Your word list

Write down any words in the dialogues you do not understand, or are not sure about. Try to guess the meaning in English or in your own language, and write it down. Then check with a dictionary.

CHECK

2.2.1 **Listen and Write** (from page 66)

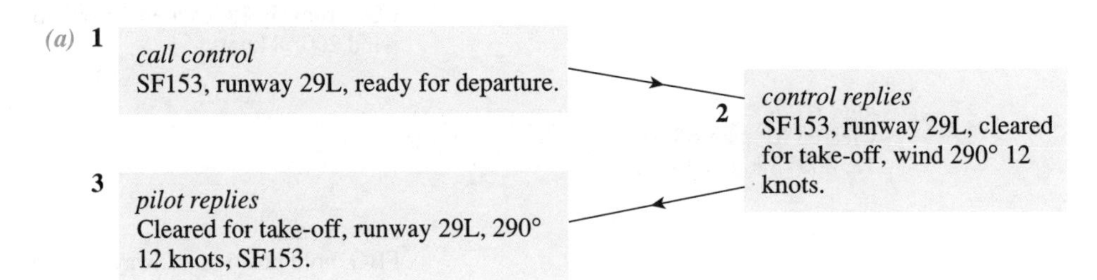

2.2.1 **Listen and Speak** (from page 67)

1 PIL SF153, runway 29L, ready for departure.
CTL . . . .
PIL Cleared for take-off, runway 29L, 290° 12 knots, SF153.

2 PIL FBG, runway 18, ready for departure.
CTL . . . .
PIL Cleared for take-off, runway 18, 200°, 8 knots, FBG.

3 PIL AG235, runway 31, ready for departure.
CTL . . . .
CTL . . . .
PIL Cleared for take-off, runway 31, wind calm, AG235.

4 PIL ESQ, runway 07, ready for departure.
CTL . . . .
PIL Cleared for take-off, runway 07, 005°, 19 knots, ESQ.

2.2.1 **Write** (from page 68)

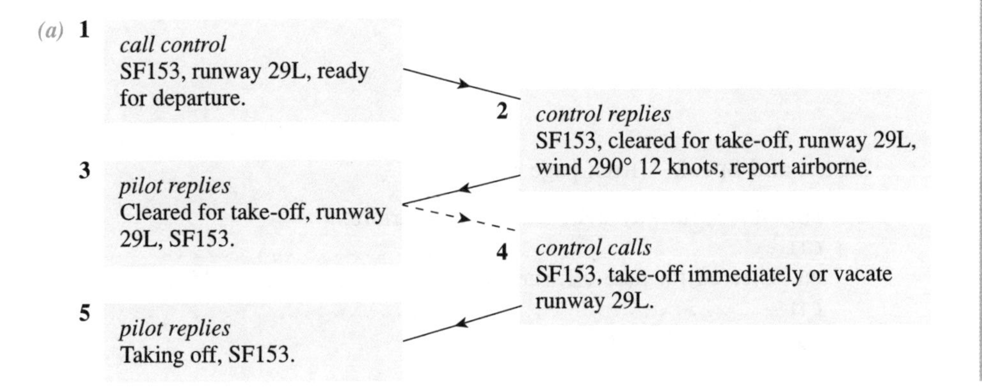

(a) 1
call control
SF153, runway 29L, ready for departure.
2
control replies
SF153, cleared for take-off, runway 29L, wind 290° 12 knots, report airborne.
3
pilot replies
Cleared for take-off, runway 29L, SF153.
4
control calls
SF153, take-off immediately or vacate runway 29L.
5
pilot replies
Taking off, SF153.

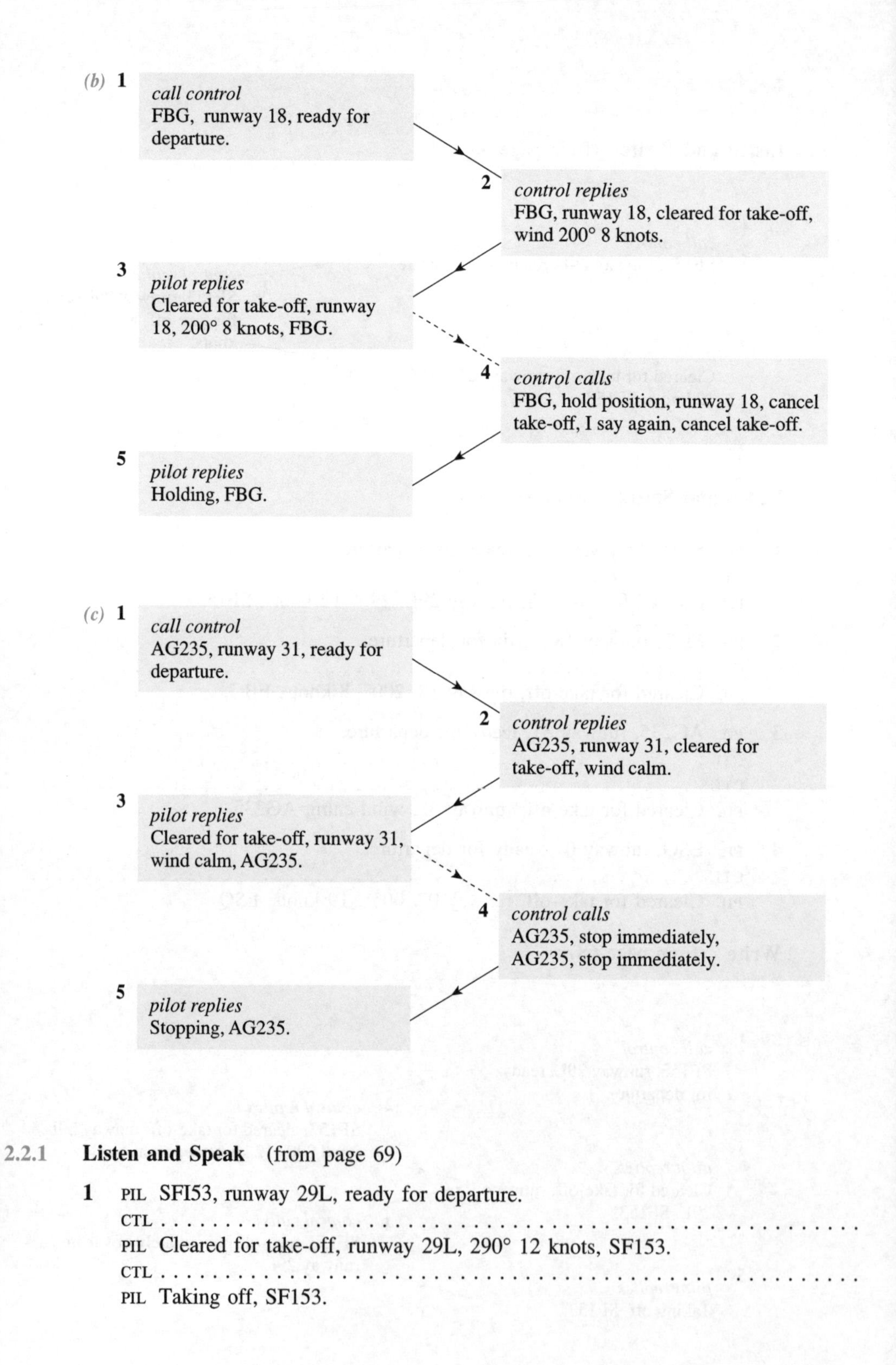

(b) 1
call control
FBG, runway 18, ready for departure.
2
control replies
FBG, runway 18, cleared for take-off, wind 200° 8 knots.
3
pilot replies
Cleared for take-off, runway 18, 200° 8 knots, FBG.
4
control calls
FBG, hold position, runway 18, cancel take-off, I say again, cancel take-off.
5
pilot replies
Holding, FBG.
(c) 1
call control
AG235, runway 31, ready for departure.
2
control replies
AG235, runway 31, cleared for take-off, wind calm.
3
pilot replies
Cleared for take-off, runway 31, wind calm, AG235.
4
control calls
AG235, stop immediately, AG235, stop immediately.
5
pilot replies
Stopping, AG235.

2.2.1 Listen and Speak (from page 69)

1 PIL SFI53, runway 29L, ready for departure.

CTL . . . .

PIL Cleared for take-off, runway 29L, 290° 12 knots, SF153.

CTL . . . .

PIL Taking off, SF153.

2 PIL FBG, runway 18, ready for departure.
CTL . . . .
PIL Cleared for take-off, runway 18, 200° 8 knots, FBG.
CTL . . . .
PIL Holding FBG.

3 PIL AG235, runway 31, ready for departure.
CTL . . . .
PIL Cleared for take-off, runway 31, wind calm, AG235.
CTL . . . .
PIL Stopping, AG235.

4 PIL JDI, runway 07, ready for departure.
CTL . . . .
PIL Cleared for take-off, runway 07, 120° 16 knots, JDI.
CTL . . . .
PIL Stopping JDI.

5 PIL MPH, runway 07, ready for departure.
CTL . . . .
PIL Cleared for take-off, runway 07, 150° 11 knots, MPH.
CTL . . . .
PIL Taking off (*or* 'vacating runway'), MPH.

6 PIL RST, runway 26, ready for departure.
CTL . . . .
PIL Cleared for take-off, runway 26, 340° 5 knots, RST.
CTL . . . .
PIL Holding, RST.

7 PIL DNO, runway 12, ready for departure.
CTL . . . .
PIL Cleared for take-off, runway 12, 090° 7 knots, DNO.
CTL . . . .
PIL Stopping, DNO.

8 PIL UCQ, runway 25, ready for departure.
CTL . . . .
PIL Cleared for take-off, runway 25, 170° 13 knots, UCQ.
CTL . . . .
PIL Holding, UCQ.

2.2.2 **Listen and Answer** (from page 69)

1. Why was the take-off abandoned?
   It was abandoned because of engine failure.
2. Why did the controller stop the take-off?
   He stopped the take-off because of fire in the left main gear.
3. Why was the take-off aborted?
   It was aborted due to a tyre blow-out.

2.2.2 **Listen and Write** (from page 69)

1 CTL Sunair 332, runway 12, cleared to take-off, wind 340° 16 knots.
PIL Taking off, Sunair 332.
PIL Sunair 332 stopping. Take-off abandoned, due to engine failure.
CTL Do you request taxi to the parking area Sunair 332?
PIL Affirm, request return to parking area.

2 PIL Sunair 596, runway 12, ready for departure.
CTL Sunair 596, runway 12, cleared for take-off, wind calm.
PIL Sunair 596, taking off.
(*pause*)
CTL Sunair 596, stop immediately, I say again, stop immediately, flames coming from left main gear.
PIL Sunair 596 stopping.
PIL Sunair 596, activating escape slides, request emergency services.

3 PIL Sunair 879, take-off aborted due to tyre blow-out. We slid slightly off the runway.
CTL Sunair 879, are you able to taxi off the runway?
PIL Negative, the right gear is bogged down. Request passenger steps and buses to take the passengers to the terminal.
CTL Roger, Sunair 879, we'll get a tug to come out to you as well.

2.3 INITIAL CLIMB

2.3.1 Initial climb (routine)

Key words and phrases

Check that you understand all the words and phrases in this list.

present heading	on track
so as to cross . . .	expedite
continue climb	report reaching
change	report passing
until	correction

Typical exchange

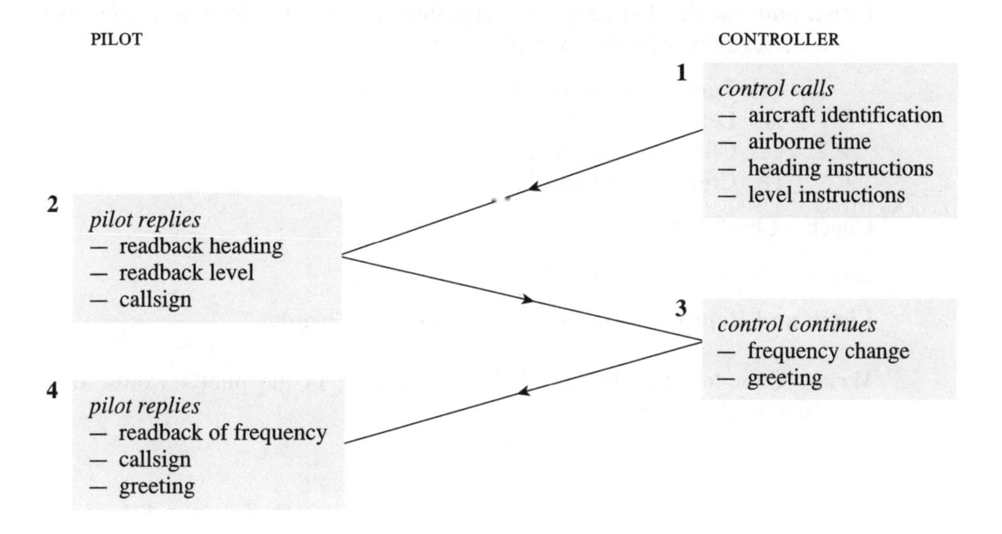

NOTE

— There may be a pause, or/and communication with other traffic between *pilot reply* **2** and *control call* **3**. In this case, of course, control starts with the aircraft callsign, as a new exchange is starting.

Phraseology practice

Write Here is a list of various instructions given during the climb. Listen to the CD, identify each instruction on the list, and write the number beside it.

Instruction	Number on CD
A Climb to flight level 190.	
B Climb on present heading.	
C Climb straight ahead.	
D Climb on track to Delta.	
E Turn right, heading 190.	
F Turn left, heading 190.	
G Climb so as to cross Delta at flight level 190.	
H Continue present heading until flight level 150.	
I Expedite climb to flight level 190.	

Check Check your answers, page 79.

Listen and Speak Listen to the instructions on the CD. Reply to the instructions like this, begining with the examples again.

1. CTL Turn left heading 190.
   PIL Left heading 190.
2. CTL Climb to flight level 220.
   PIL Climbing to flight level 220.

Check Check your answers, page 79.

Listen Listen to the dialogue on the CD.

Listen and Repeat Listen and repeat the pilot's words.

Write Complete the dialogue below by writing in the pilot's words. If necessary, listen to the CD again.

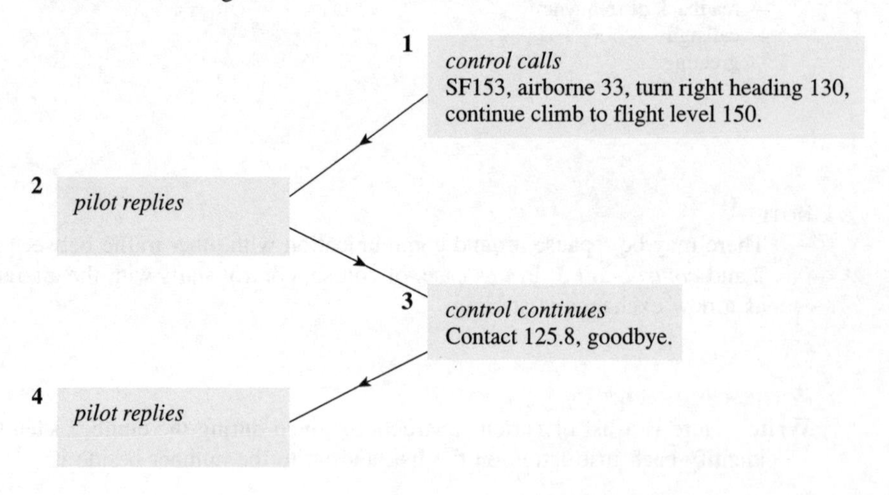

1
control calls
SF153, airborne 33, turn right heading 130, continue climb to flight level 150.
2
pilot replies
3
control continues
Contact 125.8, goodbye.
4
pilot replies

Check Check your answers, page 79.

Listen and Speak Reply to the instructions given to the following flights. Listen to the example, then continue in the same way, starting with the example again.

Callsigns

1	SF153	**4**	OPR
2	AG235	**5**	DNO
3	YFL	**6**	ZE692

Check Check your answers, page 80.

2.3.2 Initial climb (non-routine)

Listen and Answer Listen to the three dialogues and write down the answers to these questions. There is one question for each dialogue.

1. Why have they shut down an engine?

   . . . .

2. Why are they returning?

   . . . .

3. What must they do before returning to Rexbury?

   . . . .

Check Check your answers, page 80.

Listen and Write Listen again and complete the texts below.

1 PIL Sunair 670, Rexbury Approach, we've ____________ no. 1 engine after a ____________. We're ____________.

CTL Do you require ____________, Sunair 670?

PIL Negative, there is no ____________, Sunair 670.

CTL Roger, Sunair 670, turn left heading 250.

2 PIL Sunair 539, we're returning. We seem to have a ____________ the ____________ has just ____________. Request ____________ ____________ and ____________ ____________.

CTL Roger, Sunair 539, I'll call you back.

CTL Sunair 539, you're ____________ ____________, call Tower on 118.5.

PIL 118.5, Sunair 539.

3 PIL Sunair 281, we have an ____________. We intend to ____________ to Rexbury, but we ____________ 40 tons of fuel first.

CTL Roger, Sunair 281, ____________ ____________, at 5000 ft, right ____________ over Forest. ____________ ____________.

PIL Sunair 281, 5000 ft over Forest.

(*pause*)

PIL Sunair 281, reaching Forest, ready to dump fuel.

CTL Roger, go ahead Sunair 281, break.

All aircraft, Rexbury Control, ____________ in progress, DC8, ____________ Forest VOR, ____________ ____________, ____________ flight below 5000 ft ____________ 10 nautical miles of ____________ ____________.

PIL Sunair 281, fuel dumping completed, request approach to Rexbury.

Check Check your answers, page 80.

Your word list

Write down any words in the dialogues you do not understand, or are not sure about. Try to guess the meaning, in English or in your own language, and write it down. Then check with a dictionary.

CHECK

2.3.1 **Listen and Write** (from page 76)

Instruction	No.
A	5
B	6
C	1
D	7
E	2
F	4
G	3
H	8
I	9

2.3.1 **Listen and Speak** (from page 76)

1. Left heading 190.
2. Climbing flight level 220.
3. Climbing straight ahead.
4. Left heading 260.
5. Climbing on track to Papa.
6. Climbing to flight level 270.
7. Right heading 310.
8. Climbing to cross Zulu at 150.
9. Present heading until flight level 190.
10. Climbing on track to Zulu.
11. Expediting climb to flight level 170.

2.3.1 **Write** (from page 76)

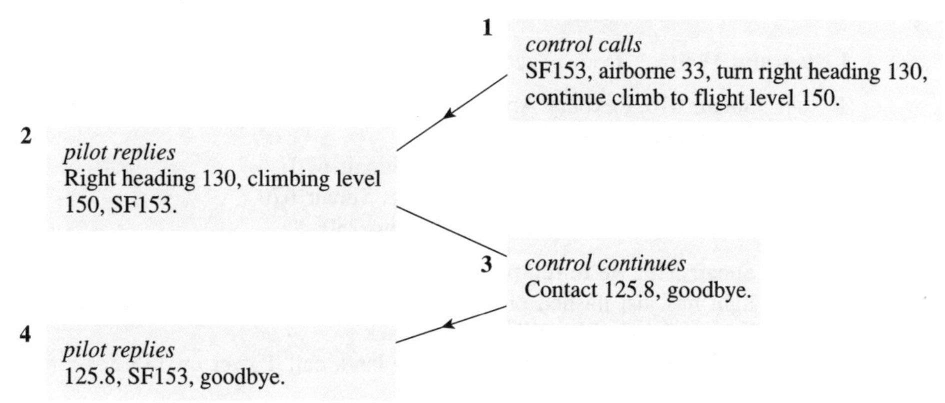

1
control calls
SF153, airborne 33, turn right heading 130, continue climb to flight level 150.
2
pilot replies
Right heading 130, climbing level 150, SF153.
3
control continues
Contact 125.8, goodbye.
4
pilot replies
125.8, SF153, goodbye.

SECTION 2.3

2.3.1 Listen and Speak (from page 77)

1 CTL . . . .
PIL Right heading 130, climbing to 150, SF153.
CTL . . . .
PIL 125.8, SF153, goodbye.

2 CTL . . . .
PIL Climbing on present heading to FL110, AG235.
CTL . . . .
PIL 129.6, AG235, goodbye.

3 CTL . . . .
PIL Left heading 230, expediting to FL70, YFL.
CTL . . . .
PIL 129.7, YFL, goodbye.

4 CTL . . . .
PIL Climbing to cross November at FL90, OPR.
CTL . . . .
PIL 128.6, OPR, goodbye.

5 CTL . . . .
PIL Right heading 190, climbing to FL130, DNO.
CTL . . . .
PIL 132.9, DNO, goodbye.

6 CTL . . . .
PIL Climbing on present heading to FL130, ZE692.
CTL . . . .
PIL 134.2, ZE 692, goodbye.

2.3.2 Listen and Answer (from page 77)

1. Why have they shut down an engine?
   Because of a bird strike/bird ingestion.
2. Why are they returning?
   There is a wheel well fire.
3. What must they do before returning to Rexbury?
   They must dump fuel.

2.3.2 Listen and Write (from page 77)

1 PIL Sunair 670, Rexbury Approach, we've shut down no. 1 engine after a bird strike. We're coming back.
CTL Do you require landing priority, Sunair 670?
PIL Negative. There is no fire warning, Sunair 670.
CTL Roger, Sunair 670, turn left heading 250.

2 PIL Sunair 539, we're returning. We seem to have a wheel well fire — the warning light has just flashed on. Request priority landing and emergency services.
CTL Roger, Sunair 539, I'll call you back.
CTL Sunair 539, you're number one to land, call Tower on 118.5.
PIL 118.5, Sunair 539.

3 PIL Sunair 281, we have an engine failure. We intend to return to Rexbury, but we have to dump 40 tons of fuel first.

CTL Roger, Sunair 281, proceed to fuel dumping area, at 5000 ft, right pattern over Forest. Report when reaching.

PIL Sunair 281, 5000 ft over Forest.

(*pause*)

PIL Sunair 281, reaching Forest, ready to dump fuel.

CTL Roger, go ahead Sunair 281, break.

All aircraft Rexbury Control, fuel dumping in progress, DC8, on radial 240 Forest VOR, ranging 14 to 20 nm, avoid flight below 5000 ft within 10 nautical miles of fuel dumping track.

PIL Sunair 281, fuel dumping completed, request approach to Rexbury.

2.4 CLIMB

2.4.1 Climb (routine)

Key words and phrases

Check that you understand all the words in this list. Look up any new words in a dictionary.

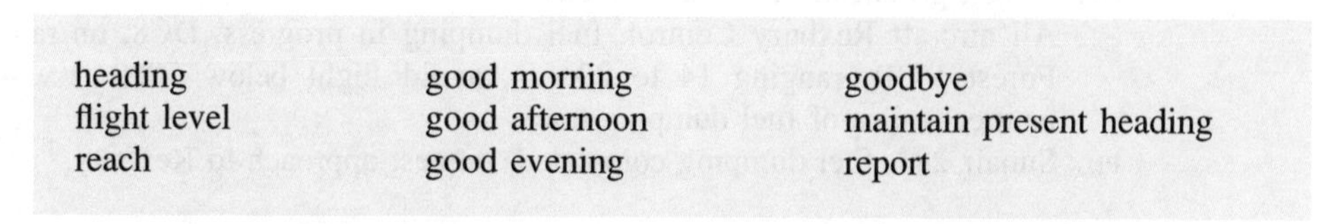

heading	good morning	goodbye
flight level	good afternoon	maintain present heading
reach	good evening	report

Typical exchange sequences

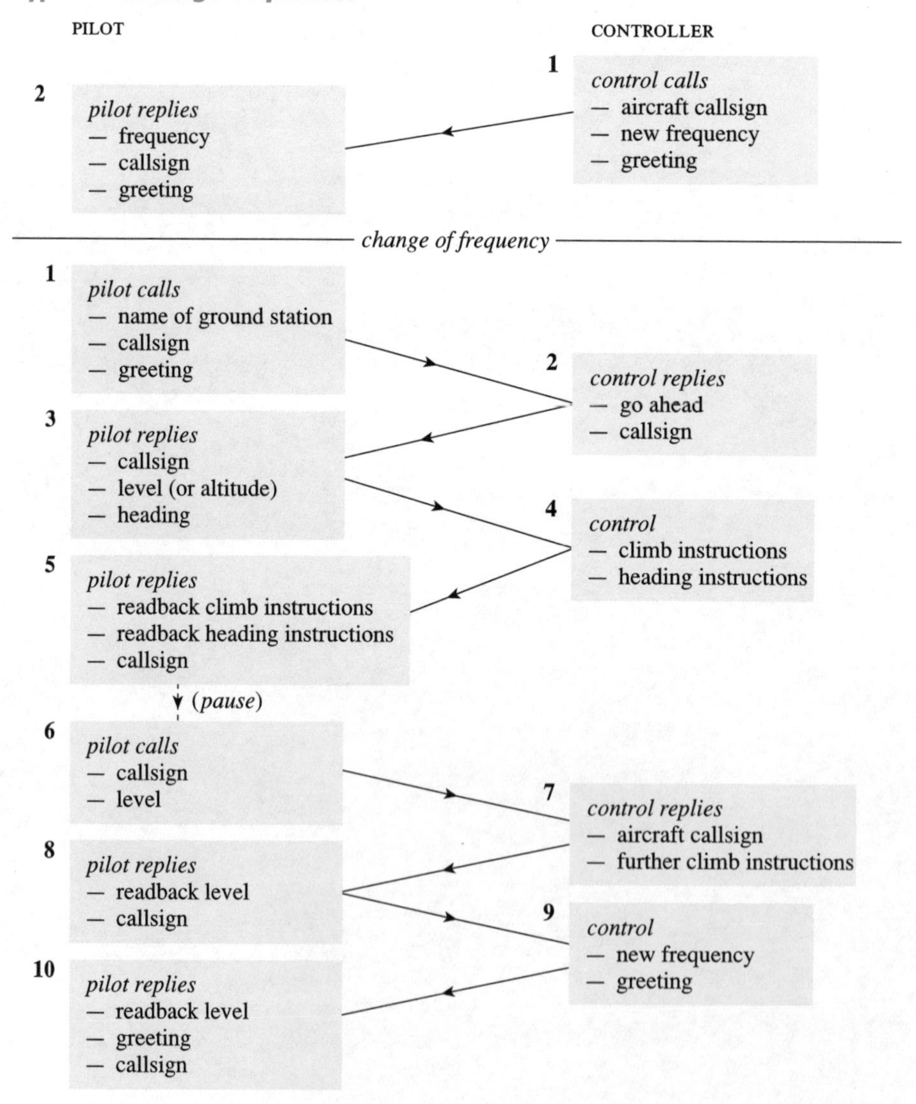

NOTES

— *Greetings:* Greetings like 'good morning', 'good afternoon' in the first call, and 'goodbye' at the end of an exchange are very commonly used. They do not appear in official phraseologies, but 'good morning', 'good afternoon' or 'good evening' replaces 'how do you read?' at initial contact; and 'goodbye' replaces 'over' or 'over and out'. The greetings are a little bit of human exchange, and quite often the speaker will translate them into the language of the receiver ('bonjour') to a French person, 'buenas dias' to a Spaniard, etc.).
— *Use of callsigns:* In *control reply* **2**, the controller may use: aircraft callsign, name of ground station, greeting; *or* name of ground station, greeting, aircraft callsign.

Once contact is made, the callsign can be omitted until the end of the exchange, so numbers **4** and **9** have no callsigns here.

At initial contact, the pilot says the name of the ground station first, then the aircraft callsign, as in *pilot call* **1**.

When the pilot calls a ground station another time, the aircraft callsign comes first, and the name of the ground station is normally unnecessary (*pilot call* **6**).

At the end of an exchange, when the pilot is 'signing off', the callsign is at the end, e.g. *pilot replies* **5** and **10**.
— *Order of items in readbacks:* In readbacks there is a strong tendency for the pilot to put the most important (the most immediate) instruction first. So in *pilot reply* **5**, the readback of heading instructions may come first, followed by the readbacks of climb instructions.

Phraseology practice

Listen Listen to the dialogue.
Listen and Repeat Listen and repeat the pilot's words.
Write Complete the dialogue below by filling in the pilot's words. Check with the CD if necessary.

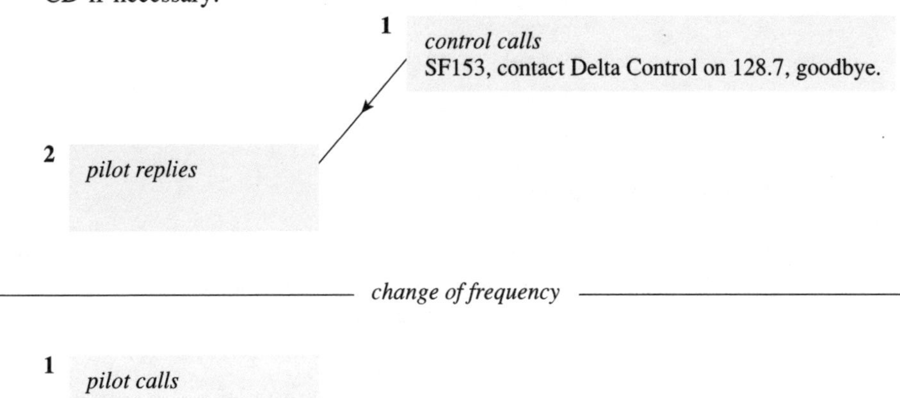
1
control calls
SF153, contact Delta Control on 128.7, goodbye.
2
pilot replies

change of frequency

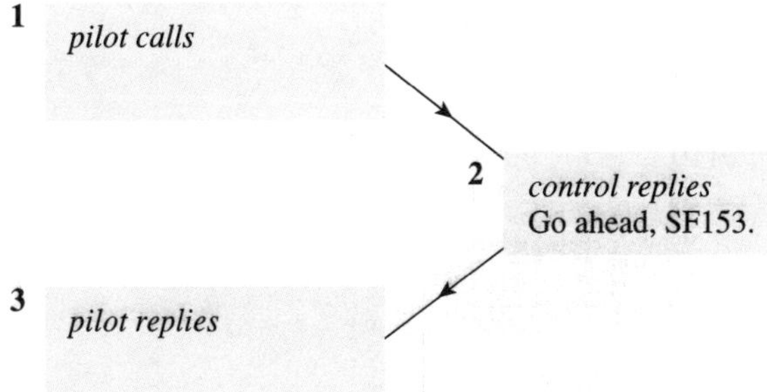
1
pilot calls
2
control replies
Go ahead, SF153.
3
pilot replies

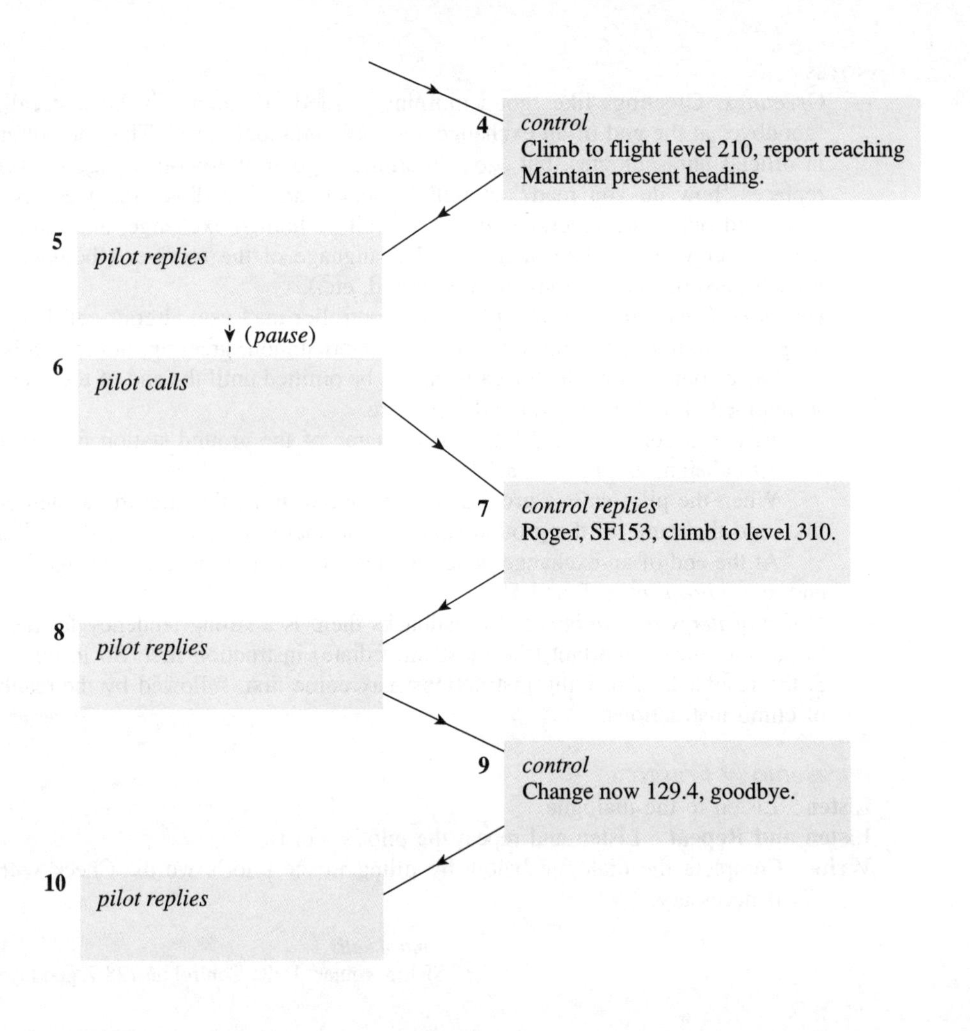
4 control
Climb to flight level 210, report reaching
Maintain present heading.
5 pilot replies
(pause)
6 pilot calls
7 control replies
Roger, SF153, climb to level 310.
8 pilot replies
9 control
Change now 129.4, goodbye.
10 pilot replies

Check Check your answers, page 86.

Listen and Speak Take the pilot's part and reply to the controller's instructions on the CD. Listen to the example, then reply in the same way using the data for the following flights. Start with the example again.

	Callsign	Present flight level	Heading
1	SF153	90	130
2	AG235	110	250
3	YFL	70	230
4	OPR	80	180
5	DNO	90	190
6	ZE692	80	090

Check Check your answers, page 87.

2.4.2 Climb (non-routine)

Listen and Answer Listen to the dialogues and write down the answers to these questions. There is one question for each dialogue.

1. What was the cause of the turbulence?

   . . . .

2. Why does the controller want the pilot to change his rate of climb?

   . . . .

3. What is the emergency, and what immediate action are they taking?

   . . . .

Check Check your answers, page 88.
Listen and Write Listen again and complete the texts below.

1 PIL Sunair 928, we've just come through some ___________. What kind of traffic is there ___________?

CTL It must've been ___________, there's a 747 ___________, although ___________ ___________ was provided.

2 CTL Sunair 596, ___________ ___________?

PIL ___________ ___________.

CTL ___________ traffic, ___________ ___________ ___________ FL180 at the ___________?

PIL ___________ FL180 ___________, ___________ Sunair 596.

3 PIL MAYDAY MAYDAY MAYDAY, Winton Control, Sunair 165, we have ___________ ___________, we are ___________ ___________ ___________ to FL30, leaving FL310, left of Green 4, ___________ Newbridge for ___________ ___________, please ___________. ___________ ___________, ___________ 040, ___________ Winton VOR.

Check Check your answers, page 88.

Your word list

Write down any words in the dialogues you do not understand or are not sure about. Try to guess the meaning, in English or in your own language and write it down. Then check with a dictionary.

CHECK

2.4.1 Listen and Write (from page 84)

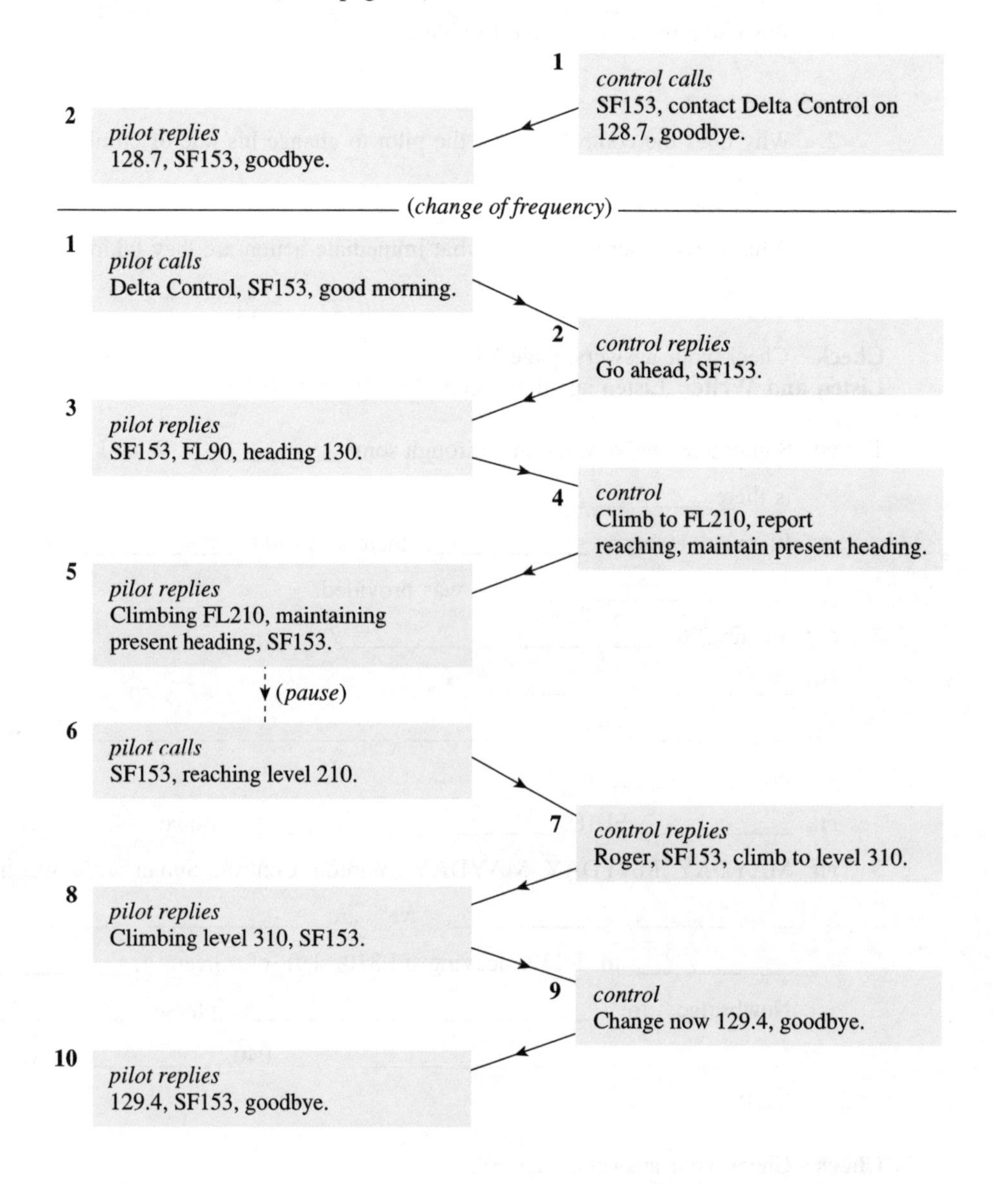

1
control calls
SF153, contact Delta Control on 128.7, goodbye.
2
pilot replies
128.7, SF153, goodbye.
(change of frequency)
1
pilot calls
Delta Control, SF153, good morning.
2
control replies
Go ahead, SF153.
3
pilot replies
SF153, FL90, heading 130.
4
control
Climb to FL210, report reaching, maintain present heading.
5
pilot replies
Climbing FL210, maintaining present heading, SF153.
(pause)
6
pilot calls
SF153, reaching level 210.
7
control replies
Roger, SF153, climb to level 310.
8
pilot replies
Climbing level 310, SF153.
9
control
Change now 129.4, goodbye.
10
pilot replies
129.4, SF153, goodbye.

2.4.1 **Listen and Speak** (from page 84)

1
CTL . . . .
PIL 128.7, Sierra Foxtrot 153, goodbye.
PIL Delta Control, Sierra Foxtrot 153, good morning.
CTL . . . .
PIL Sierra Foxtrot 153, FL90, heading 130.
CTL . . . .
PIL Climbing level 210, maintaining present heading, Sierra Foxtrot 153.
PIL Sierra Foxtrot 153, reaching level 210.
CTL . . . .
PIL Climbing level 310.
CTL . . . .
PIL 129.4, Sierra Foxtrot 153, goodbye.

2
CTL . . . .
PIL 132.4, goodbye Alpha Golf 235.
PIL Foxtrot Control, Alpha Golf 235, good morning.
CTL . . . .
PIL Alpha Golf 235, FL110, heading 250.
CTL . . . .
PIL Climbing to level 210, report passing level 180. Alpha Golf 235.
PIL Alpha Golf 235, passing level 180.
CTL . . . .
PIL Right turn heading 330, climbing to level 280. Alpha Golf 235.
CTL . . . .
PIL 131.7, Alpha Golf 235, goodbye.

3
CTL . . . .
PIL 126.5, goodbye.
PIL Mike Control, Yankee Foxtrot Lima, good morning.
CTL . . . .
PIL Yankee Foxtrot Lima, FL70, heading 230.
CTL . . . .
PIL Climbing to FL250, expediting until passing level 150. Yankee Foxtrot Lima.
CTL . . . .
PIL Left turn heading 180. Yankee Foxtrot Lima.
CTL . . . .
PIL 128.9, goodbye. Yankee Foxtrot Lima.

4
CTL . . . .
PIL 127.3 goodbye
PIL November Control, Oscar Papa Romeo, good morning.
CTL . . . .
PIL Oscar Papa Romeo, FL80, heading 180.
CTL . . . .
PIL Right turn heading 230, climbing to FL240. Oscar Papa Romeo.
PIL Oscar Papa Romeo, reaching level 240.
CTL . . . .
PIL Climbing to FL290. Oscar Papa Romeo.
CTL . . . .
PIL 129.5, goodbye. Oscar Papa Romeo.

5 CTL . . . .
PIL 133.2, goodbye.
PIL Whisky Control, Delta November Oscar, good morning.
CTL . . . .
PIL Delta November Oscar, FL90, heading 190.
CTL . . . .
PIL Climbing level 250, report passing level 150.
PIL Delta November Oscar, passing level 150.
CTL . . . .
PIL Left turn heading 160, climbing level 270.
CTL . . . .
PIL 129.5, goodbye. Delta November Oscar.

6 CTL . . . .
PIL 126.9, goodbye.
PIL Foxtrot Control, Zulu Echo 692, good morning.
CTL . . . .
PIL Zulu Echo 692, FL80, heading 090.
CTL . . . .
PIL Right turn heading 130, climbing to level 210, expediting until passing level 150. Zulu Echo 692.
CTL . . . .
PIL Wilco.
PIL Zulu Echo 692, reaching level 210.
CTL . . . .
PIL 128.2, goodbye. Zulu Echo 692.

2.4.2 Listen and Answer (from page 85)

1. What was the cause of the turbulence?
   It was wake turbulence caused by a 747.
2. Why does the controller want the pilot to change his rate of climb?
   Due to traffic, he wants the plane to climb quickly to FL180.
3. What is the emergency and what immediate action are they taking?
   There is a fire in the hold. They are making an emergency descent to FL30.

2.4.2 Listen and Write (from page 85)

1 PIL Sunair 928, we've just come through some severe turbulence. What kind of traffic is there ahead of us?
CTL It must've been wake turbulence, there's a 747 ahead, although normal separation was provided.

2 CTL Sunair 596, what is your rate of climb?
PIL 700 ft per minute.
CTL Due to traffic, can you adjust your rate of climb to be above flight level 180 at the FIR boundary?
PIL Above flight level 180 at the FIR boundary, wildo, Sunair 596.

3 PIL MAYDAY MAYDAY MAYDAY, Winton Control, Sunair 165, we have fire in the hold, we are making an emergency descent to FL30, leaving FL310, left of Green 4, heading to Newbridge for emergency landing, please advise. Present position, radial 040, 50 miles from Winton VOR.

2.5 END OF CLIMB

2.5.1 End of climb (routine)

Key words and phrases

Check that you understand all the words and phrases in this list.

available	can you accept?
negative	not at the moment
further climb	unavailable
heavy traffic	

Typical exchange

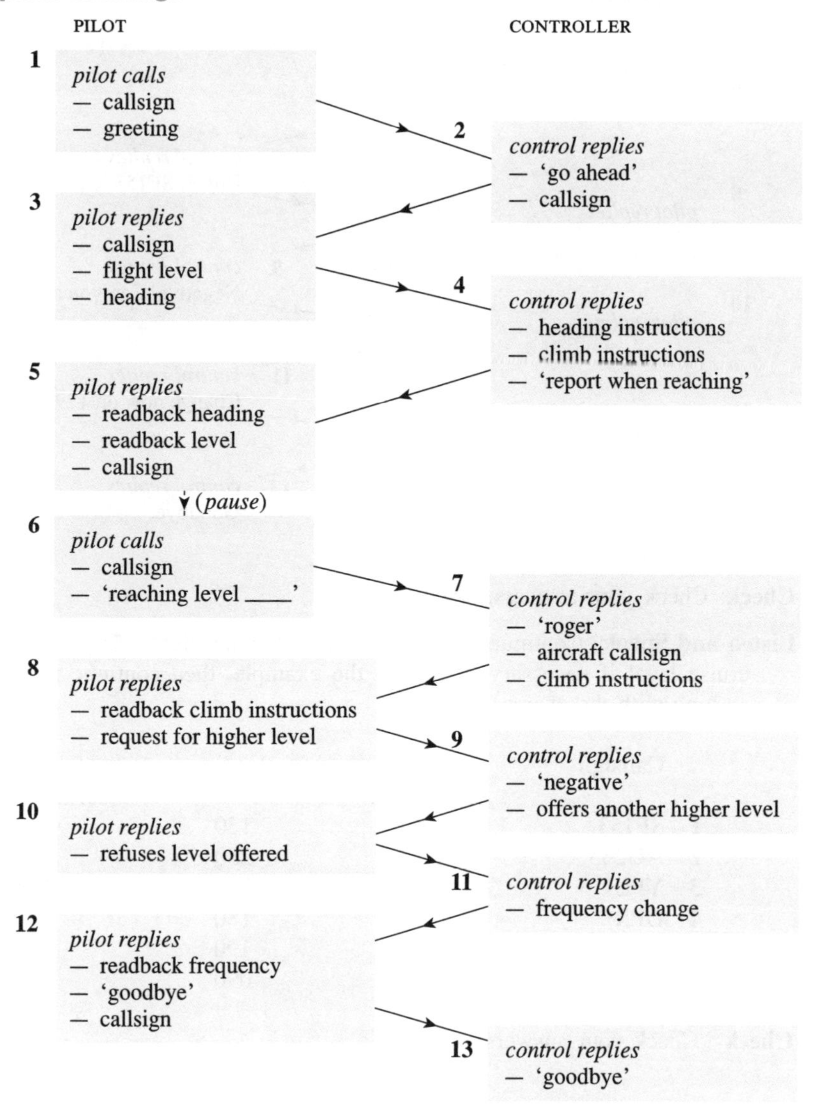

Phraseology practice

Listen Listen to the recorded dialogue.

Listen and Repeat Listen and repeat the pilot's words.

Write Complete the text below by writing in the pilot's words. Check with the recording if necessary.

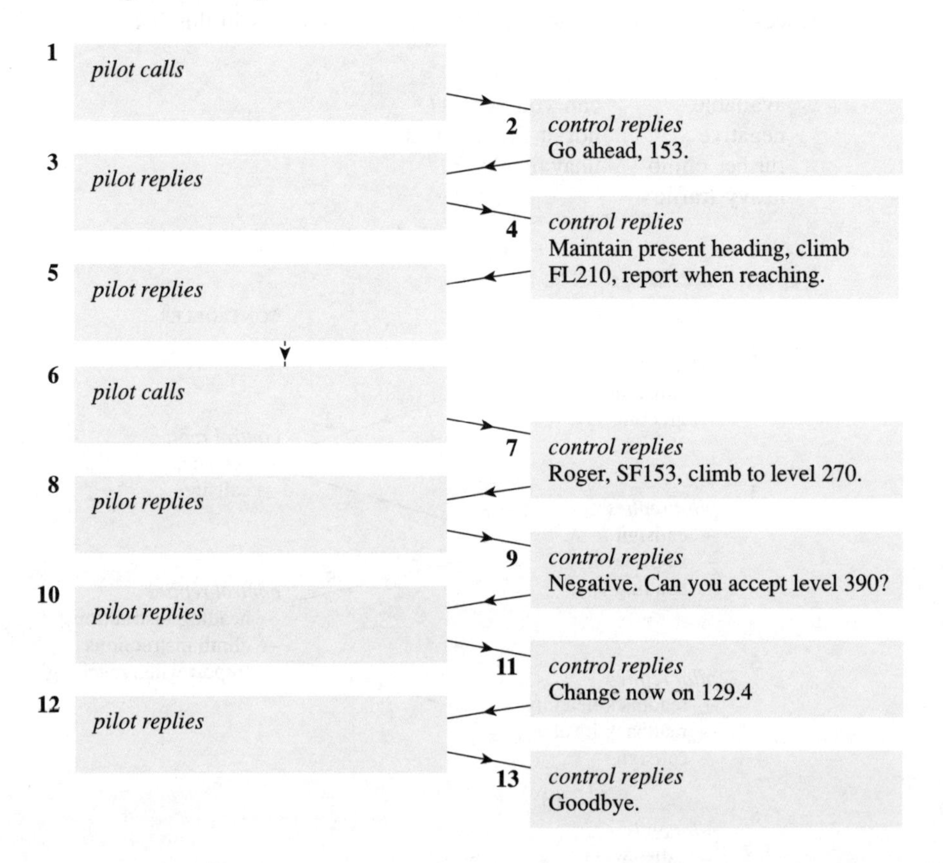

1 pilot calls
2 control replies
Go ahead, 153.
3 pilot replies
4 control replies
Maintain present heading, climb FL210, report when reaching.
5 pilot replies
6 pilot calls
7 control replies
Roger, SF153, climb to level 270.
8 pilot replies
9 control replies
Negative. Can you accept level 390?
10 pilot replies
11 control replies
Change now on 129.4
12 pilot replies
13 control replies
Goodbye.

Check Check your answers, page 92.

Listen and Speak Continue for each of the following flights. Try to negotiate a good cruise level if necessary. Listen to the example, then continue in the same way, starting with the example again.

	Callsign	Present flight level	Heading	Preferred cruise level
1	SF153	90	130	310
2	AG235	110	250	330
3	YFL	70	230	330
4	OPR	80	180	290
5	DNO	90	190	210
6	ZE692	100	090	330

Check Check your answers, page 93.

2.5.2 End of climb (non-routine)

Listen and Answer Listen to the three dialogues and write down the answers to these questions. There is one question for each dialogue.

1. What is the problem and what action is being taken?

   . . . .

2. Why does the pilot want a lower level?

   . . . .

3. Why does the pilot change her route?

   . . . .

Check Check your answers, page 94.

Listen and Write Listen again and complete the texts below.

1 PIL Winton Control, Sunair 883, ____________ ____________ ____________, ____________ is rising fast, ____________ ____________ to FL120.

CTL Roger, descend to FL120, ____________.

PIL Descending to FL120, Sunair 883.

PIL Sunair 883, reaching FL120.

CTL Roger, Sunair 883, ____________ ____________?

PIL Request ____________ to Rexbury ____________ this level.

2 PIL Sunair 596, could we have a ____________ ____________? We're ____________ ____________ at this level.

CTL Sunair 596, call you back.

CTL Sunair 596, ____________ to FL280.

PIL ____________ to FL280, Sunair 596.

3 PIL Sunair 725, request ____________ to Overby, a passenger is ____________, probably a ____________.

CTL Roger Sunair 725, turn right heading 290, I'll tell Overby you ____________ ____________.

PIL Turning right 290, Sunair 725.

Check Check your answers, page 94.

Your word list

Write down any words in the dialogues you do not understand, or are not sure about. Try to guess the meaning, in English or in your own language, and write it down. Then check with a dictionary.

CHECK

2.5.1 **Write** (from page 90)

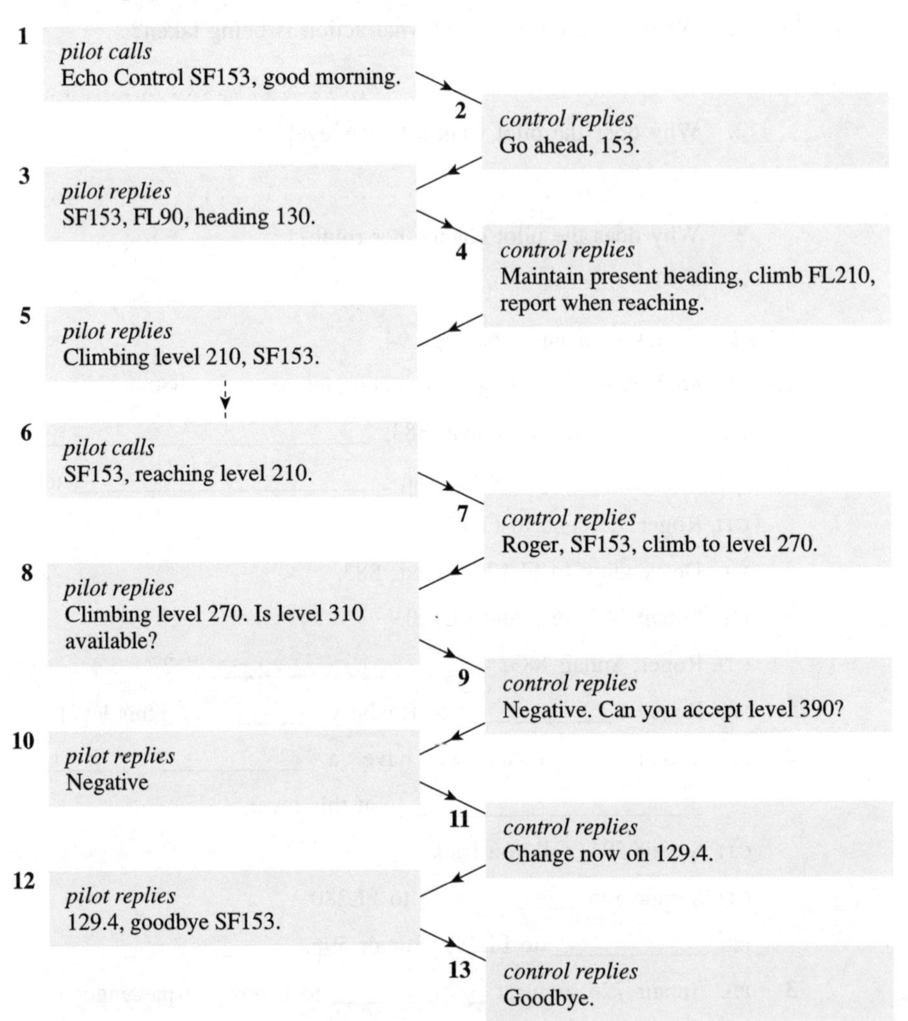

1
pilot calls
Echo Control SF153, good morning.
2
control replies
Go ahead, 153.
3
pilot replies
SF153, FL90, heading 130.
4
control replies
Maintain present heading, climb FL210, report when reaching.
5
pilot replies
Climbing level 210, SF153.
6
pilot calls
SF153, reaching level 210.
7
control replies
Roger, SF153, climb to level 270.
8
pilot replies
Climbing level 270. Is level 310 available?
9
control replies
Negative. Can you accept level 390?
10
pilot replies
Negative
11
control replies
Change now on 129.4.
12
pilot replies
129.4, goodbye SF153.
13
control replies
Goodbye.

NOTE

If the pilot wanted to accept the much higher level offered, there would be an additional exchange:

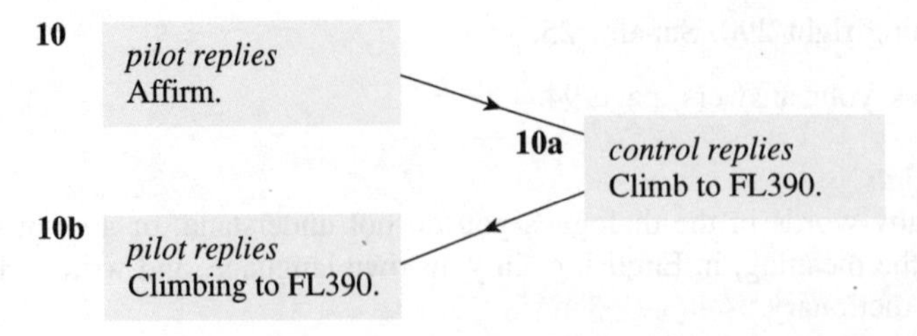

10
pilot replies
Affirm.
10a
control replies
Climb to FL390.
10b
pilot replies
Climbing to FL390.

SECTION 2.5

2.5.1 **Listen and Speak** (from page 90)

1 PIL Echo Control, Sierra Foxtrot 153, good morning.
CTL . . . .
PIL Sierra Foxtrot 153, FL90, heading 130.
CTL . . . .
PIL Climbing level 210, Sierra Foxtrot 153.
PIL SF153, reaching level 210.
CTL . . . .
PIL Climbing level 270. Is 310 available?
CTL . . . .
PIL Negative.
CTL . . . .
PIL 129.4, goodbye.

2 PIL Echo Control, Alpha Golf 235, good morning.
CTL . . . .
PIL Alpha Golf 235, FL110, heading 250.
CTL . . . .
PIL Right turn 290. Alpha Golf 235.
CTL . . . .
PIL Climbing level 280, Alpha Golf 235. Is 330 available?
CTL . . . .
PIL Negative.
CTL . . . .
PIL 131.7, goodbye.
CTL . . . .

3 PIL Echo Control, Yankee Foxtrot Lima, good morning.
CTL . . . .
PIL Yankee Foxtrot Lima, FL70, heading 230.
CTL . . . .
PIL Climbing level 190. Yankee Foxtrot Lima.
CTL . . . .
PIL Yankee Foxtrot Lima, reaching level 190.
CTL . . . .
PIL Climbing level 330.
CTL . . . .
PIL 126.8, goodbye. Yankee Foxtrot Lima.
CTL . . . .

4 PIL Echo Control, Oscar Papa Romeo, good morning.
CTL . . . .
PIL Flight level 80, heading 180.
CTL . . . .
PIL Left turn heading 160.
CTL . . . .
PIL Climbing level 250, OPR, is level 290 available?
CTL . . . .
PIL Negative.
CTL . . . .
PIL Climbing level 250 OPR.

PIL OPR, reaching 250.
CTL . . . .
PIL 132.9, goodbye.

5 PIL Echo Control, Delta November Oscar, good morning.
CTL . . . .
PIL Reaching level 90, heading 190.
CTL . . . .
PIL Climbing 170.
PIL DNO, reaching level 170.
CTL . . . .
PIL Climbing 210.
CTL . . . .
PIL 129.3, goodbye. Delta November Oscar.
CTL . . . .

6 PIL Echo Control, Zulu Echo 692, good morning.
CTL . . . .
PIL Reaching level 100, heading 90.
CTL . . . .
PIL Left turn, 010, climbing level 170, report 150.
PIL ZE 692, passing 150.
CTL . . . .
PIL Climbing level 290. Is 330 available?
CTL . . . .
PIL Negative.
CTL . . . .
PIL 133.2, goodbye. ZE 692.

2.5.2 Listen and Answer (from page 91)

1. What is the problem and what action is being taken?
   There is a pressurisation problem. They are descending to FL120, to continue their flight.
2. Why does the pilot want a lower level?
   There is moderate turbulence at their present level.
3. Why does the pilot change her route?
   A passenger has had a heart attack.

2.5.2 Listen and Write (from page 91)

1 PIL Winton Control, Sunair 883, we are unable to control pressurisation, cabin altitude is rising fast, request immediate descent to flight level 120.
CTL Roger, descend to flight level 120, report reaching.
PIL Descending to FL120, Sunair 883.
PIL Sunair 883, reaching FL120.
CTL Roger, Sunair 883, what are your intentions?
PIL Request resume our flight to Rexbury at this level.

2 PIL Sunair 596, could we have a slightly lower flight level? We're experiencing moderate turbulence at this level.
CTL Sunair 596, call you back.
CTL Sunair 596, descend to FL280.
PIL Descending to FL280, Sunair 596.

3 PIL Sunair 725, request divert to Overby, a passenger is seriously ill, probably a heart attack.

CTL Roger Sunair 725, turn right heading 290, I'll tell Overby you require medical assistance on landing.

PIL Turning right 290, Sunair 725.

2.6 REVIEW OF PART TWO

2.6.1 Flight from Rexbury to Winton (take-off and climb)

Listen and Read Flight plan details:
ATC clearance: Golf 5 departure, climb initially to FL110
Flight planned cruising level 290
Route: reporting points RIV (River) then BCK (Blackrock)

For further details, turn to page 48.

Listen and Speak You are flying from Rexbury to Winton, callsign Sunair 367. Follow the instructions on the CD and reply to the controller. The exercise starts with the aircraft lined up on runway 29 and ready for departure.

Check Check your answers, page 98.

2.6.2 Flight from Dublin to Paris (take-off and climb)

Listen and Read Flight plan details:
Callsign SF309
reporting points:
Liffy
Wallasey
Telba
Midhurst

Listen and Speak Take the pilot's part, follow the instructions on the CD and reply to the controller. The exercise starts with the aircraft lined up on runway 17 ready for departure.
NOTE: You will hear communications with other traffic on your frequency.

Check Check your answers, page 98.

CHECK

2.6.1 **Listen and Speak** (from page 96)

PIL Ready for departure, runway 29, Sunair 367.
CTL . . . .
PIL Cleared for take-off, runway 29, Sunair 367.
CTL . . . .
PIL Climbing to FL110, Rexbury Control on 128.8, Sunair 367, goodbye.
PIL Rexbury Control, Sunair 367, good afternoon.
CTL . . . .
PIL Right turn, heading 050, climbing to FL220, Sunair 367.
CTL . . . .
PIL Climbing to FL270, direct to Romeo India Victor VOR, Sunair 367.
PIL Sunair 367, is FL330 available?
CTL . . . .
CTL . . . .
PIL Negative, Sunair 367.
CTL . . . .
PIL Climbing to FL270, Sunair 367.
PIL Sunair 367, reaching FL270.
CTL . . . .
PIL 135.9, Sunair 367, goodbye.

2.6.2 **Listen and Speak** (from page 96)

PIL SF309 ready to depart.
CTL . . . .
PIL Cleared to take-off runway 17, left turn-out direct Liffy, 100 20 knots.
CTL . . . .

CTL . . . .
PIL Dublin 128.0, SF309, goodbye.

PIL Dublin, SF309, good afternoon.
CTL . . . .
PIL Direct Liffy, climbing FL230, SF309.

CTL . . . .
PIL FL100, SF309.
CTL . . . .
PIL Climbing to FL230, London 128.05, SF309.

PIL London, SF309, good afternoon.
CTL . . . .
PIL Maintain 230 on reaching, squawking 5260.

CTL . . . .
PIL Climbing to FL290, SF309.

CTL . . . .
PIL Climbing to FL330, SF309.

2.7 SUPPLEMENTARY VOCABULARY

2.7.1 Words for planes

Read and Write Look at these six groups of words about planes. Choose the correct heading for each group from the list of headings below.

Group 1 ___________
aeroplane
aircraft
plane
airplane

Group 2 ___________
helicopter
balloon
glider
airship

Group 3 ___________
long haul
short haul
medium haul
STOL*
VTOL*

Group 4 ___________
fighter
airliner
freighter
bomber
tanker
business jet
executive aircraft
seaplane

Group 5 ___________
twin jet
single-engined aircraft
tri-jet
four engined aircraft
jet
turbo prop

Group 6 ___________
narrow-bodied plane
wide-bodied plane
a jumbo

Headings: Range / Power
Purpose / Flying machines
Size / Plane words

Check Check your answers, page 105.

---

* STOL — short take-off and landing
* VTOL — vertical take-off and landing

Read and Write The same six groups of words are organised here into a 'word tree', but one word from each group is missing. Write in the missing words.

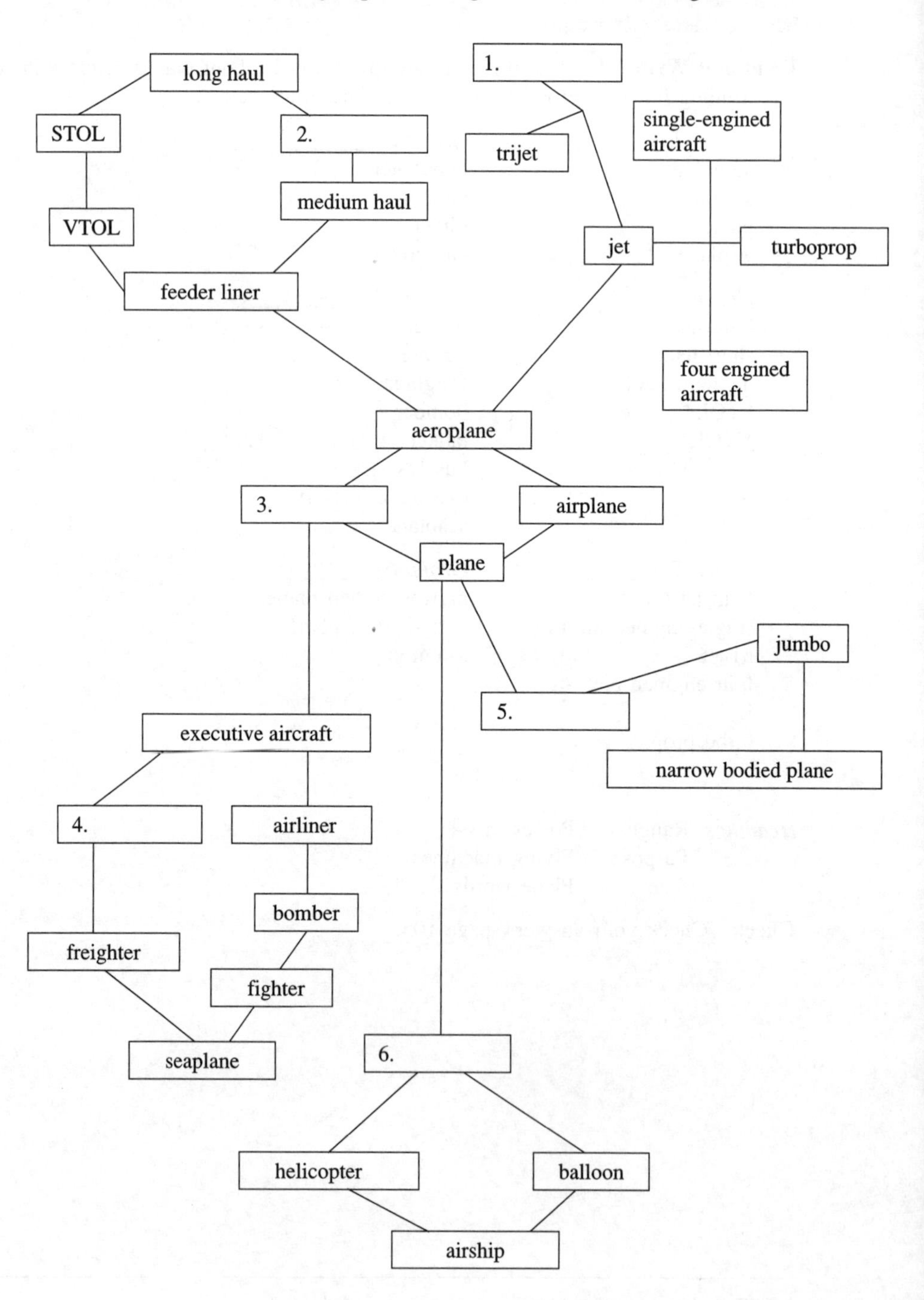

Check Check your answers, page 105.

2.7.2 Parts of a plane

Look and Think Look at the pictures on this page. There is a word which corresponds to each number. Decide which of the words you know.

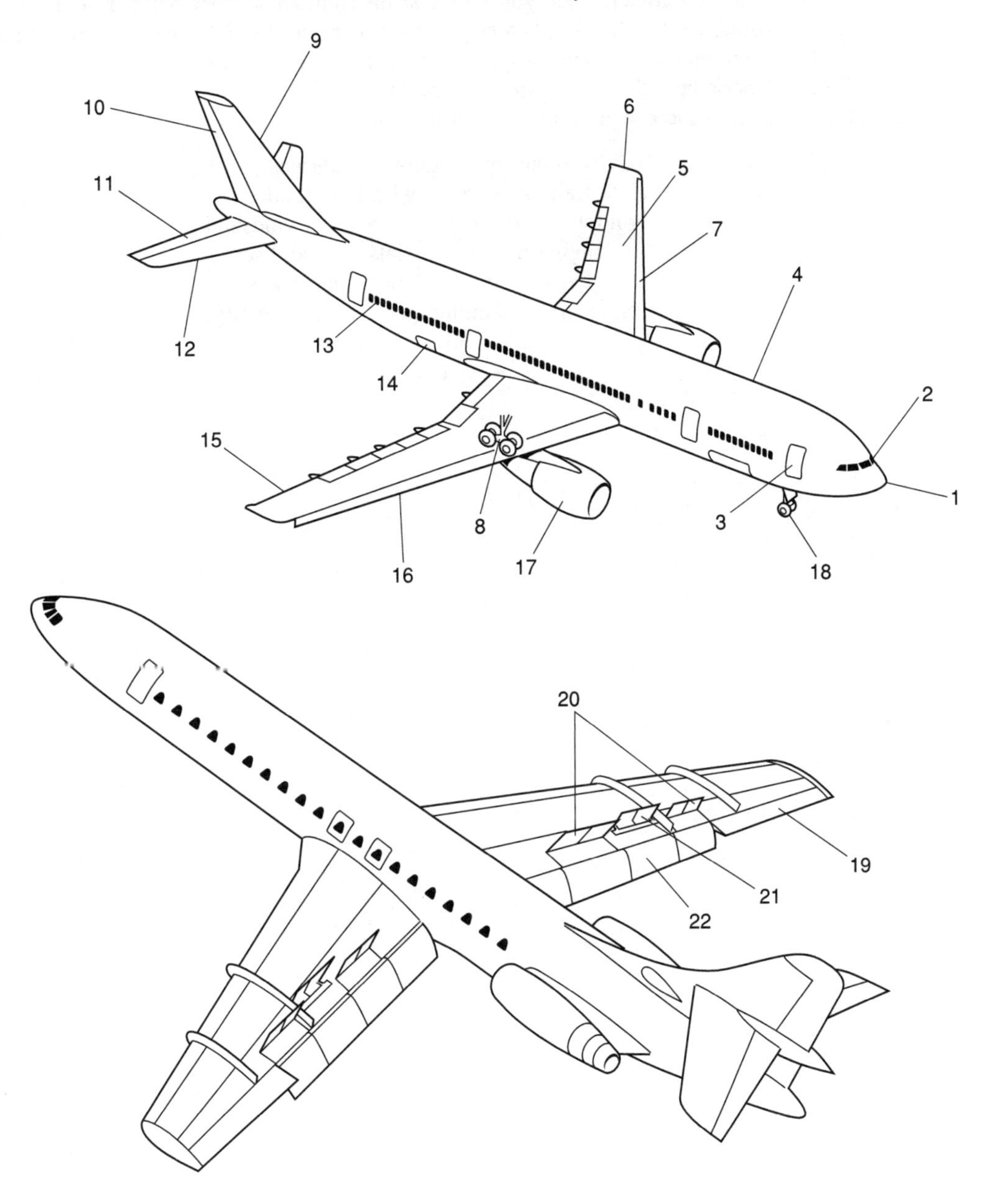

Look, Listen and Repeat Look at the picture, listen to the CD and repeat the words.

Look, Listen and Speak Now test yourself. How many of the words do you remember? Listen to the CD, look at the picture and say the correct word when you hear the number. Then you will hear the right answer. Remember, don't repeat the words; try to say them *before* you hear them on the CD. Listen to an example. Now continue in the same way. Start with the example again.

Check Check how the words are written, page 105.

Read Look at these words for parts of a plane.

wing tip door ailerons
trailing edge wheel rudder
window fuselage nose windshield
engine nacelle slats stabiliser
flaps tyre tail airbrakes
elevators landing gear leading edge
wing tail-fin nose gear
spoilers

Write Now fill in the 'word tree' below by putting a term in each box. (Some words are filled in for you.) Try to give some kind of organisation to the tree. There is no right or wrong answer here. It is an exercise to help you to remember the words by thinking about them.

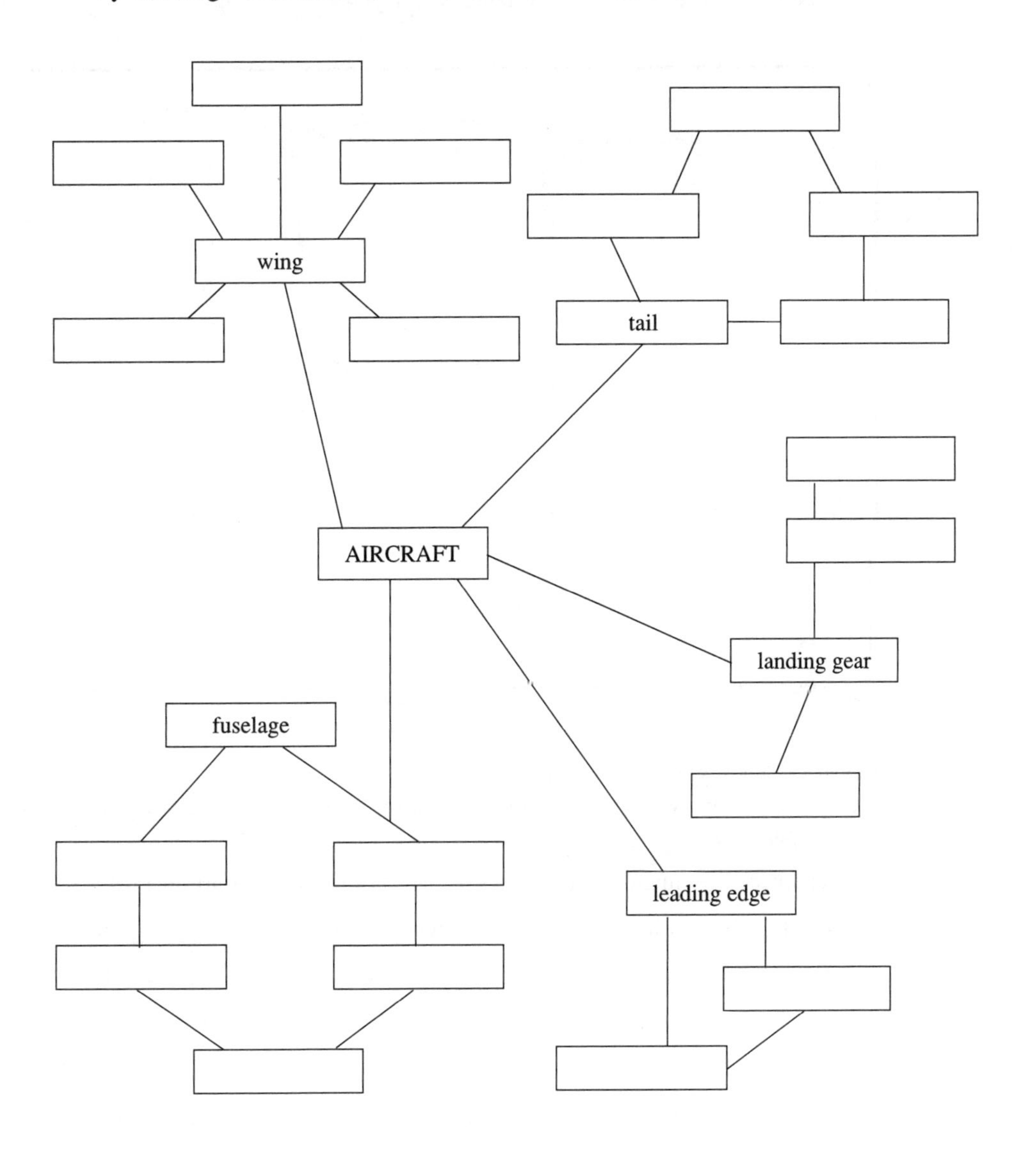

Write Now try to make the same word tree, but this time, *do not look* at the tree you filled in or the list of words.

Check Check your version of the tree with the version given on page 106.
(NOTE: There is no single right answer – this is just one possibility.)

2.7.3 Cockpit instruments

Listen and Write Listen to the description of the main control panel and write in the abbreviations for the names of the instruments in the correct place on the diagram. The first two instruments are labelled for you.

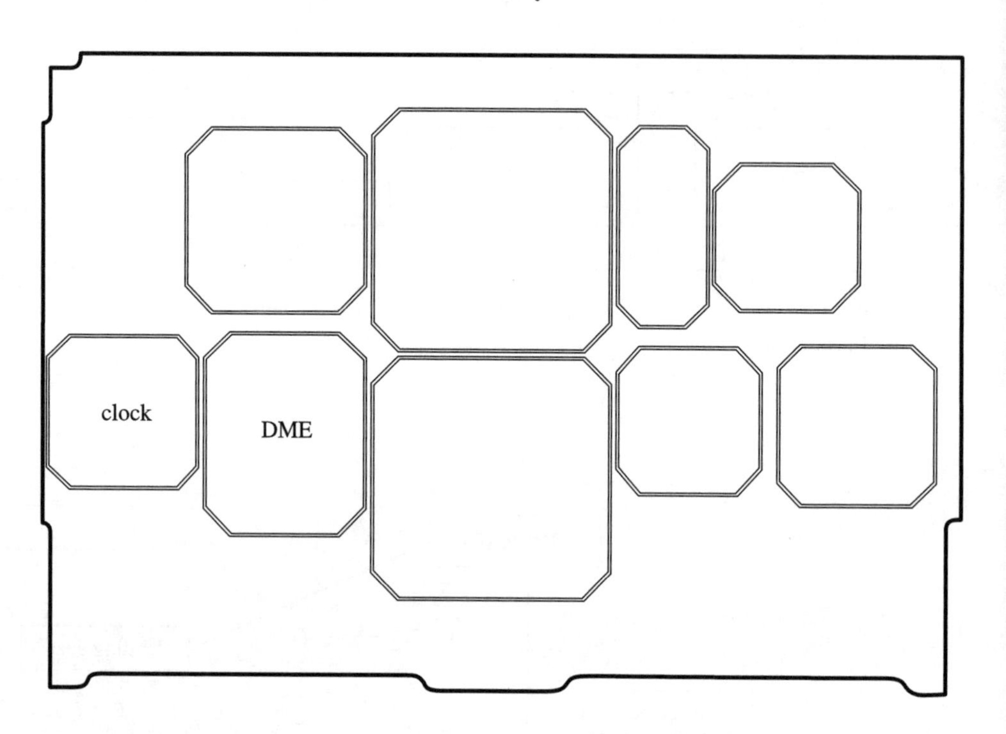

Check Cheek your answers, page 107.

Complete Complete the text below so that the description corresponds to the diagram on page 107.

The captain's main control panel on the Airbus 300B. Starting in the bottom left-hand corner, on the ____________ there is a clock. ____________ the clock is the DME (Distance Measuring Equipment) and ____________ the DME you find the Air Speed Indicator. ____________ of the Air Speed Indicator is the Attitude Director Indicator (the ADI). ____________ the ADI there is the Horizontal Situation Indicator (HSI). On the bottom row, ____________, is the Automatic Direction Finder, the ADF. ____________ the ADF and the HSI is an altimeter, and ____________ it is a radio altimeter. ____________ of the radio altimeter, ____________ the ADF, is the vertical speed indicator.

Check Check your answers, page 107.

CHECK

2.7.1 **Read and Write** (from page 99)

Group 1: Plane Words
Group 2: Flying Machines
Group 3: Range
Group 4: Purpose
Group 5: Power
Group 6: Size

2.7.1 **Read and Write** (from page 100)

1. twin jet
2. short haul
3. aircraft
4. business jet
5. wide-bodied plane
6. glider

2.7.2 **Look, Listen and Speak** (from page 102)

1. nose
2. windshield (or windscreen)
3. door
4. fuselage
5. wing
6. wing tip
7. slats
8. landing gear (or undercarriage)
9. tail fin
10. rudder
11. elevators
12. stabiliser
13. window
14. hold (or cargo compartment) door
15. trailing edge
16. leading edge
17. engine nacelle
18. nose gear
19. ailerons
20. spoilers
21. airbrakes
22. flaps

2.7.2 **Write** (from page 103)

Compare your tree with this one. There are many equally good ways to organise the words.

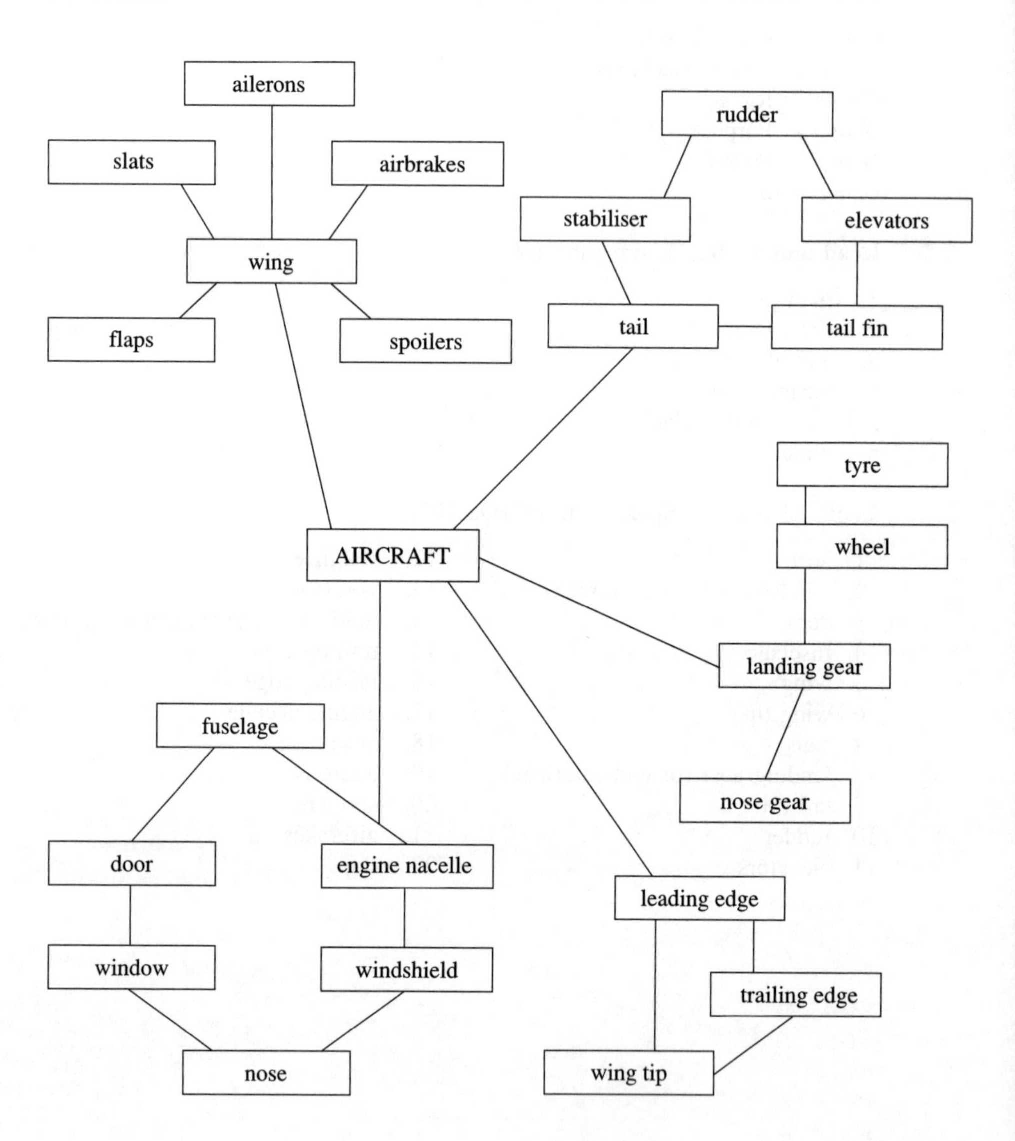

2.7.3 **Listen and Write** (from page 104)

2.7.3 **Complete** (from page 104)

The captain's main control panel on the Airbus 300B. Starting in the bottom left-hand corner, on the left there is a clock. Next to the clock is the DME (Distance Measuring Equipment) and above the DME you find the Air Speed Indicator. On the right of the Air Speed Indicator is the Attitude Director Indicator (the ADI). Below the ADI there is the Horizontal Situation Indicator (HSI). On the bottom row, on the right, is the Automatic Direction Finder, the ADF. Between the ADF and the HSI is an altimeter, and above it is a radio altimeter. On the right of the radio altimeter, above the ADF, is the vertical speed indicator.

Part Three

Cruise to descent

3.1 VOLMETS

Key words and phrases

Check that you understand all the words and phrases in this list. Look up any new words in an aviation dictionary.

mist	thin
bcmg (becoming)	scattered
rain	more than
tempo	less than
drizzle	ceiling
visibility	overcast
freezing rain	haze
recent	RVR = Runway Visual Range

Typical volmets

These recorded broadcasts follow the same pattern at each station. There is a little variation in some of the items from station to station, but the order is very similar to ATIS weather reports.

— airport name
— wind data: direction and strength
— visibility (in metres or kilometres)
— present weather (rain, mist, snow, drizzle, etc.)
— cloud cover (sky clear, few, scattered, broken, overcast)
— ceiling (in feet or metres)
— temperature
— dew point
(— QNH)
— trend: no sig
or bcmg (plus expected change)
or tempo (plus possible temporary conditions)

NOTE: Some countries (e.g. Russia, Poland) give wind strength in metres per second.

Phraseology practice

Listen and Write Listen to the met. reports and note the details in the table below. You may have to listen several times.

1	Berlin Tegel	
2	Berlin Schönefeld	
3	Berlin Tempelhof	
4	Dresden	
5	Frankfurt	
6	Gander	
7	Warsaw	
8	Potsdam	
9	Gdansk	
10	Moscow Sheremetyeva	
11	Budapest	
12	Praha	
13	Paris De Gaulle	
14	Frankfurt	
15	Catania Fontanarossa	
16	Palermo Puntaraisi	
17	Athenai	
18	Thessaloniki	
19	Benson	
20	Brize Norton	
21	East Midlands	
22	Madrid Barajas	

Check Check your notes using the texts on page 114.

CHECK

3.1 **Listen and Write** (from page 112)

1. Berlin Tegel 2020 320° 4 knots, 10 kms or more, few 1100 ft, temperature 13, dew point 11, QNH 1021, trend no sig.
2. Berlin Schönefeld 2020 290° 5 knots CAVOK, temperature 13, dew point 10, QNH 1021, trend no sig.
3. Berlin Tempelhof 2020 330° 5 knots, 10 kms or more, scattered 1100 ft, temperature 13, dew point 11, QNH 1022, trend no sig.
4. Dresden 2020 290° 3 knots CAVOK, temperature 13, dew point 11, QNH 1021, trend no sig.
5. Frankfurt 1620 340° 15 knots, 10 kms or more, few 4800 ft, temperature 23, dew point 14, QNH 1024 trend no sig.
6. This is Gander radio time 1750 Zulu, Gander Gander, valid 1800 Zulu until 1800 Zulu. Wind 010° 15 knots gusting 25 knots, visibility more than 6 miles, light snow showers, 2000 broken 10000 overcast.
7. Warsaw 1700 Zulu, wind 170° 5 metres per second, visibility 7 kms, light snow, few 700 ft broken 1000 ft, temperature 0, dew point — 0, QNH 1009 hectopascal, no sig.
8. Potsdam 1700Z wind 250° 3 metres per second, visibility 4000 metres mist, overcast 1300 ft, temperature 4, dew point 3, QNH not available trend forecast not available.
9. Gdansk 1700Z wind 250° 4 metres per second, visibility 3000 metres, mist, broken 400 ft, temperature 1, dew point 0, QNH 1005 hectopascal trend forecast not available.
10. Moscow Sheremetyevo 1700Z wind 250° 4 metres per second, visibility 1400 metres RVR 25R more than 1500 metres no change moderate shower with snow, overcast cumulo nimbus 1100 ft, temperature –1, dew point –2, QNH 1007 hectopascal, tempo, vis 400 metres, heavy shower with snow.
11. Budapest 1700Z wind 220° 10 knots, visibility 10 kms, light rain, few 1200 ft, scattered 2700 ft overcast 6700 ft, temperature 3, dew point 2, QNH 1017 hectopascal no sig.
12. Praha 1700Z wind 230° 8 knots, visibility 10 kms, scattered 2000 ft, broken 3000 ft, temperature 6, dew point 4, QNH 1013 hectopascal, no sig.

    All stations this is **Paris radio**

13. De Gaulle 0800 wind 220° 17 knots, visibility 4000 metres light rain, mist, clouds broken at 600 ft, clouds broken at 1000 ft, temperature 11, dew point 11, QNH 1008 no sig.
14. Frankfurt 0620 110° 2 knots CAVOK, temperature 14, dew point 11, QNH 1017 trend no sig.
15. Catania Fontanarossa, 04.50 Z. Wind calm, visibility 8 kms, mist, temperature 21, dew point 20, ONH 1009.
16. Palermo Puntaraisi, 04.50 Z. Wind calm, visibility 7 kms, mist, temperature 25, dew point 23.

17. 05.50 Athenai. Calm, visibility 8 kms, mist, sky clear, temperature 24, dew point 19, no sig.
18. 05.50 Thessaloniki. Calm, visibility 7 kms, mist sky clear, temperature 22, dew point 20, no sig.
19. Benson no report.
20. Brize Norton at 0950 wind 270° 6 knots CAVOK, temperature 9, dew point 5, QNH 1001, no sig.
21. East Midlands at 0950 wind 260° 11 knots, visibility 10 kms or more cloud, few 2000 ft scattered 3000 ft broken 4200 ft, temperature 8, dew point 6, QNH 999.
22. Madrid Barajas forecast Madrid Barajas between 1000 and 1900 190° 12 knots, visibility 10 kms, scattered at 2000 ft broken at 4000 ft tempo between 1000 and 1900 240° 12 knots maximum 22 knots, visibility 6 kms drizzle, rain scattered at 1000 ft broken at 2000 ft.

3.2 EN ROUTE: POSITION REPORTS

3.2.1 En route: position reports (routine)

Key words and phrases

Check that you understand the words and phrases in this list. Look up any new words in an aviation dictionary.

omit	radial
position reports	resume
intercept	VOR

Phraseology practice 1

Listen and Write Listen to the controller's instructions about position reports. Identify each instruction on the list below, and write its number in the box. The first one is done for you.

	A	Report passing Alpha.
	B	Next report at Alpha.
	C	Omit position reports until Alpha.
1	D	Omit position reports this frequency.
	E	Report intercepting the 210 radial of the Alpha VOR.
	F	Report 15 miles from Alpha DME.
	G	Resume position reporting.
	H	Report intercepting the 120 radial of the Alpha VOR.
	I	Report 5 miles from Alpha DME.
	J	Report passing the Alpha VOR 342 radial.

Check Check your answers, page 120.

Typical exchange

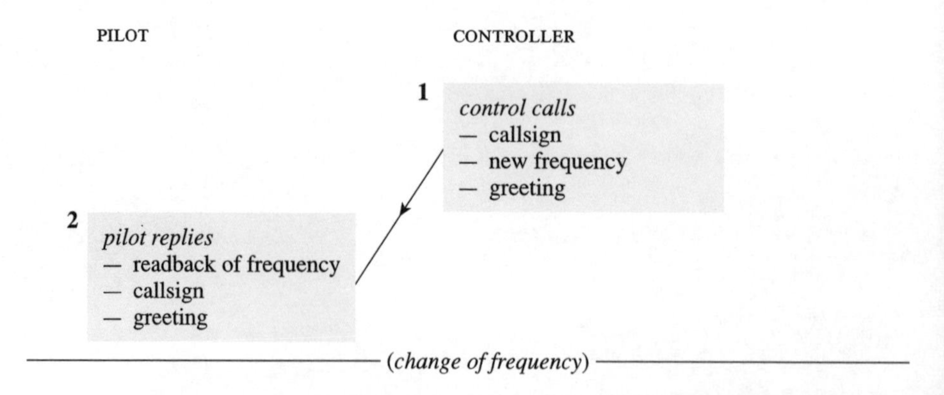

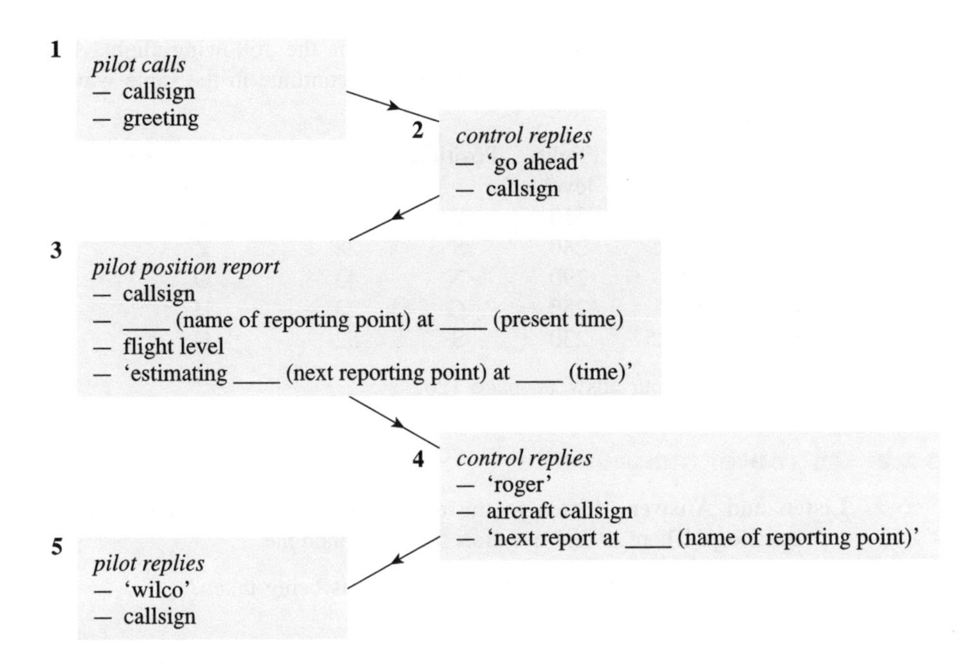

1
pilot calls
— callsign
— greeting
2
control replies
— 'go ahead'
— callsign
3
pilot position report
— callsign
— ____ (name of reporting point) at ____ (present time)
— flight level
— 'estimating ____ (next reporting point) at ____ (time)'
4
control replies
— 'roger'
— aircraft callsign
— 'next report at ____ (name of reporting point)'
5
SF153, contact 129.4, goodbye.
pilot replies
— 'wilco'
— callsign

Phraseology practice 2

Listen Listen to the dialogue on the CD.

Listen and Repeat Listen again and repeat the pilot's words.

Write Complete the dialogue below by writing in the pilot's words. Check with the CD if necessary.

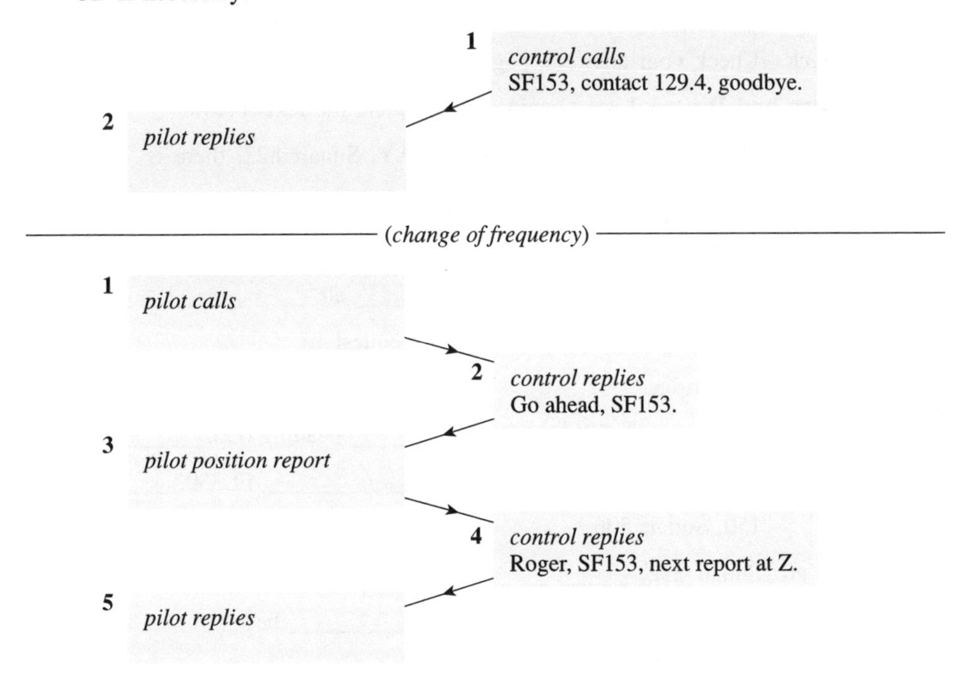

Check Check your answers, page 120.

Listen and Speak Make position reports for the following flights using the data given below. Listen to the example, then continue in the same way, starting with the example again.

No.	Callsign	Flight level	Position	Time	Next reporting point	Estimated time
1	SF153	310	R	35	Y	+10′
2	AG235	280	S	28	Z	+12′
3	BI196	290	N	43	O	+15′
4	NJ342	250	G	23	H	+16′
5	MO725	230	S	52	U	+10′

Check Check your answers, page 120.

3.2.2 En route: (non-routine)

Listen and Answer Listen to the dialogues and write down the answers to these questions. There is one question for each dialogue.

1. What is the problem and what action is being taken?

   . . . .

2. What is the problem and what action is being taken?

   . . . .

3. Why does the pilot ask for a change of heading?

   . . . .

Check Check your answers, page 121.

Listen and Write Listen again and complete the texts below.

1 PIL MAYDAY, MAYDAY, MAYDAY, Sunair 822, there is ___________, we ___________ an ___________ ___________ to FL25, ___________ to Overby for ___________ ___________.

2 PIL Sunair 506, we have ___________ all ___________, ___________ the ___________ ___________. Request to ___________ ___________ to Newbridge.

CTL Roger, Sunair 506, turn ___________ heading 030, ___________ to FL150.

PIL ___________ left heading 030, ___________ FL330, ___________ to level 150, Sunair 506.

3 PIL Sunair 312, ___________ ___________ to avoid ___________.

CTL Roger, Sunair 312, what will ___________ be?

PIL Heading 250°, Sunair 312.

PIL Sunair 312, we're clear of ________ now.

CTL Roger, Sunair 312, turn left heading 230 ________ ________.

Check Check your answers, page 121.

Your word list

Write down any words in the dialogues you do not understand or are not sure about. Try to guess the meaning, in English or in your own language and write it down. Then check with a dictionary.

CHECK

3.2.1 Listen and Write (from page 116)

7	A	Report passing Alpha.
2	B	Next report at Alpha.
8	C	Omit position reports until Alpha.
1	D	Omit position reports this frequency.
9	E	Report intercepting the 210 radial of the Alpha VOR.
10	F	Report 15 miles from Alpha DME.
3	G	Resume position reporting.
4	H	Report intercepting the 120 radial of the Alpha VOR.
5	I	Report 5 miles from Alpha DME.
6	J	Report passing the Alpha VOR 342 radial.

3.2.1 Write (from page 117)

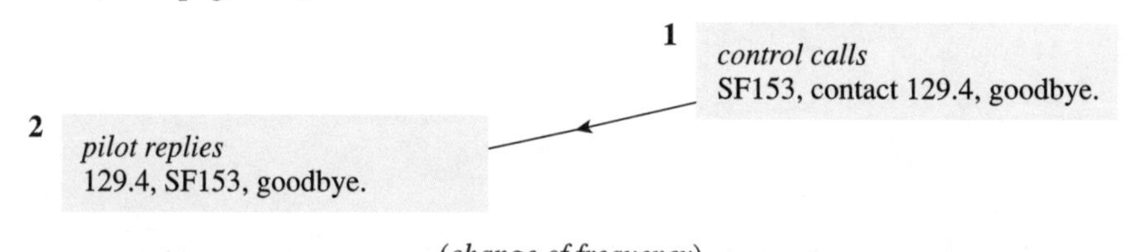

(change of frequency)

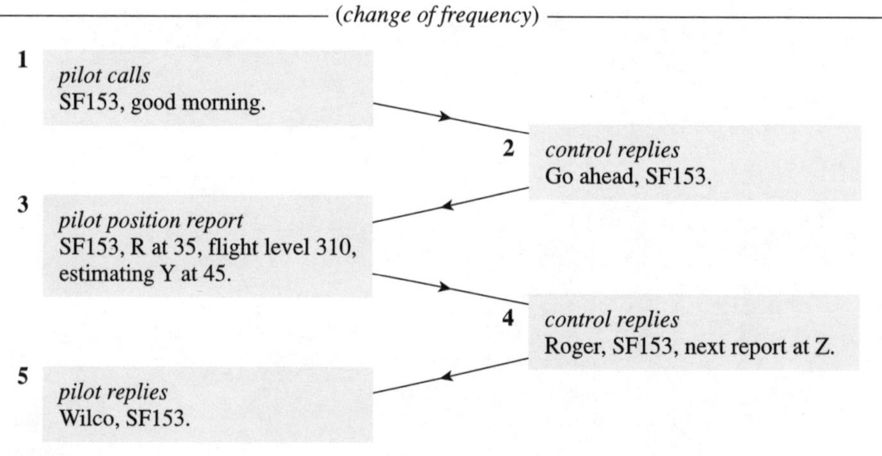

1
pilot calls
SF153, good morning.
2
control replies
Go ahead, SF153.
3
pilot position report
SF153, R at 35, flight level 310, estimating Y at 45.
4
control replies
Roger, SF153, next report at Z.
5
SF153, contact 129.4, goodbye.
pilot replies
Wilco, SF153.

3.2.1 Listen and Speak (from page 118)

1 CTL . . . .
PIL Sierra Foxtrot, Romeo at 35, FL310, estimating Yankee at 45.
CTL . . . .
PIL Wilco, Sierra Foxtrot 153.

2 CTL . . . .
PIL Alpha Golf 235, Sierra at 28, FL280, estimating Zulu at 40.
CTL . . . .
PIL Wilco, Alpha Golf 235.

3 CTL . . . .
PIL Bravo India 196, November at 43, FL290, estimating Oscar at 58.
CTL . . . .
PIL Wilco, Bravo India 196.

4 CTL . . . .
PIL November Juliet 342, Golf at 23, FL250, estimating Hotel at 39.
CTL . . . .
PIL Wilco, November Juliet 342.

5 CTL . . . .
PIL Mike Oscar 725, Sierra at 52, FL230, estimating Uniform at 02.
CTL . . . .
PIL Wilco, Mike Oscar 725.

3.2.2 **Listen and Answer** (from page 118)

1. What is the problem and what action is being taken?
   There is depressurisation, and they are making an emergency descent.
2. What is the problem and what action is being taken?
   They have lost all electrical power except the emergency circuit, so they are diverting to Newbridge.
3. Why does the pilot ask for a change of heading?
   To avoid a build-up (or CB's).

3.2.2 **Listen and Write** (from page 118)

1 PIL MAYDAY, MAYDAY, MAYDAY, Sunair 822, there is depressurisation, we are making an emergency descent to FL25, heading to Overby for emergency landing.

2 PIL Sunair 506, we have lost all electrical power, except the emergency circuit. Request to divert immediately to Newbridge.
CTL Roger, Sunair 506, turn left heading 030, descend to FL150.
PIL Turning left heading 030, leaving FL330, descending to level 150, Sunair 506.

3 PIL Sunair 312, request 10° heading change right of track to avoid build-up.
CTL Roger, Sunair 312, what will your heading be?
PIL Heading 250°, Sunair 312.
PIL Sunair 312, we're clear of CBs now.
CTL Roger, Sunair 312, turn left heading 230 to come back on track.

3.3 EN ROUTE: TRAFFIC INFORMATION

3.3.1 En route: traffic information (routine)

Key words and phrases

Check that you understand all the words and phrases in this list. Look up any new words in an aviation dictionary.

unknown	vectors
same direction	resume own navigation
moving	direct
fast moving	magnetic track
parallel	distance
descend	at your 10 o'clock position
negative contact	opposite direction

Phraseology practice 1

Listen and Write Listen to the items of traffic information on the CD, and look at the diagrams. Identify the diagram which corresponds to each item in the table below. (Y = the plane receiving the information
X = the unknown traffic)

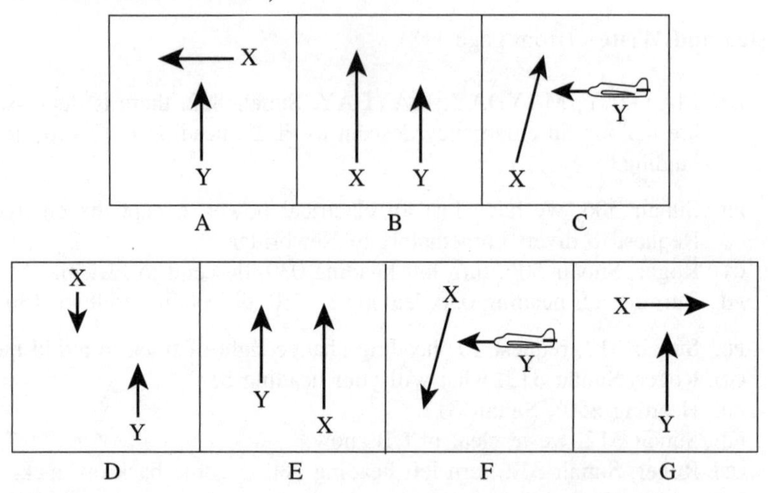

Item no.	Diagram
1	
2	
3	
4	
5	
6	
7	

Check Check your answers, page 127.

Typical exchange

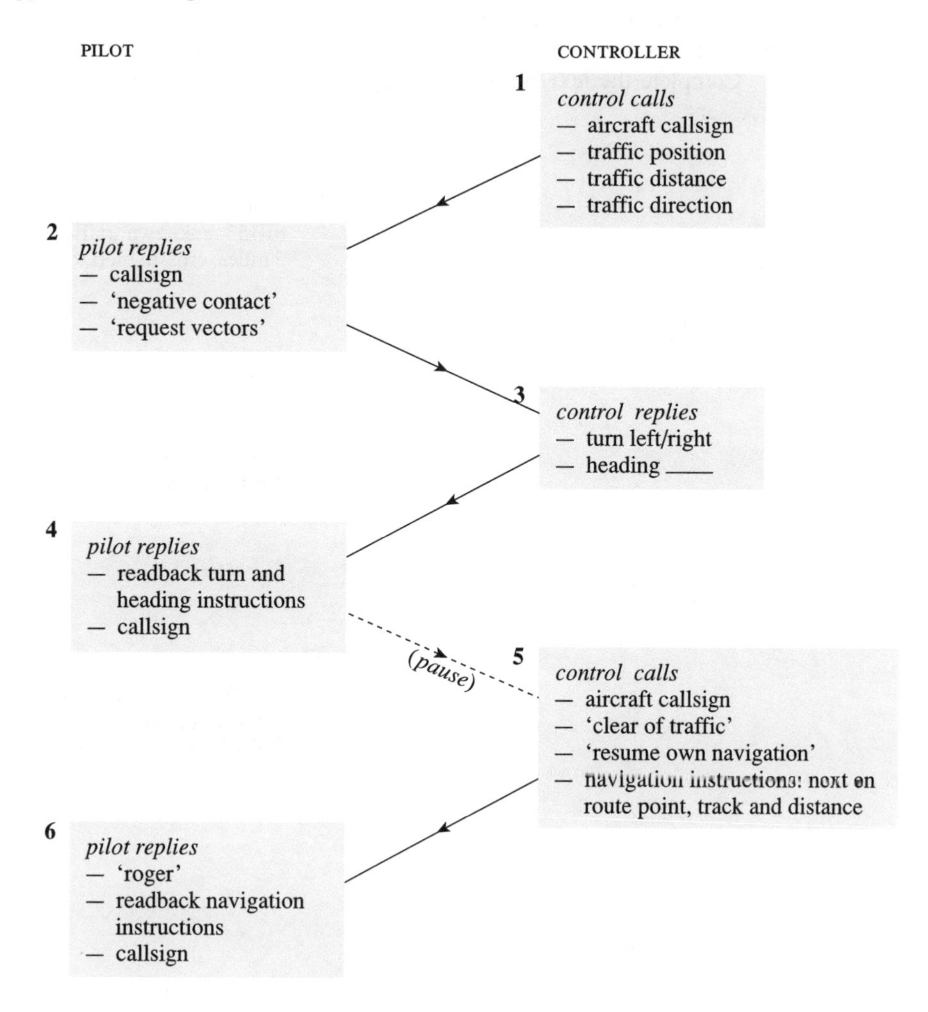
PILOT
CONTROLLER
1
control calls
— aircraft callsign
— traffic position
— traffic distance
— traffic direction
2
pilot replies
— callsign
— 'negative contact'
— 'request vectors'
3
control replies
— turn left/right
— heading ____
4
pilot replies
— readback turn and heading instructions
— callsign
(pause)
5
control calls
— aircraft callsign
— 'clear of traffic'
— 'resume own navigation'
— navigation instructions: next en route point, track and distance
6
pilot replies
— 'roger'
— readback navigation instructions
— callsign

Phraseology practice 2

Listen Listen to the recorded dialogue.
Listen and Repeat Listen to the same dialogue and repeat the pilot's words.
Write Complete the text below by filling in the pilot's words. Check with the CD if necessary.

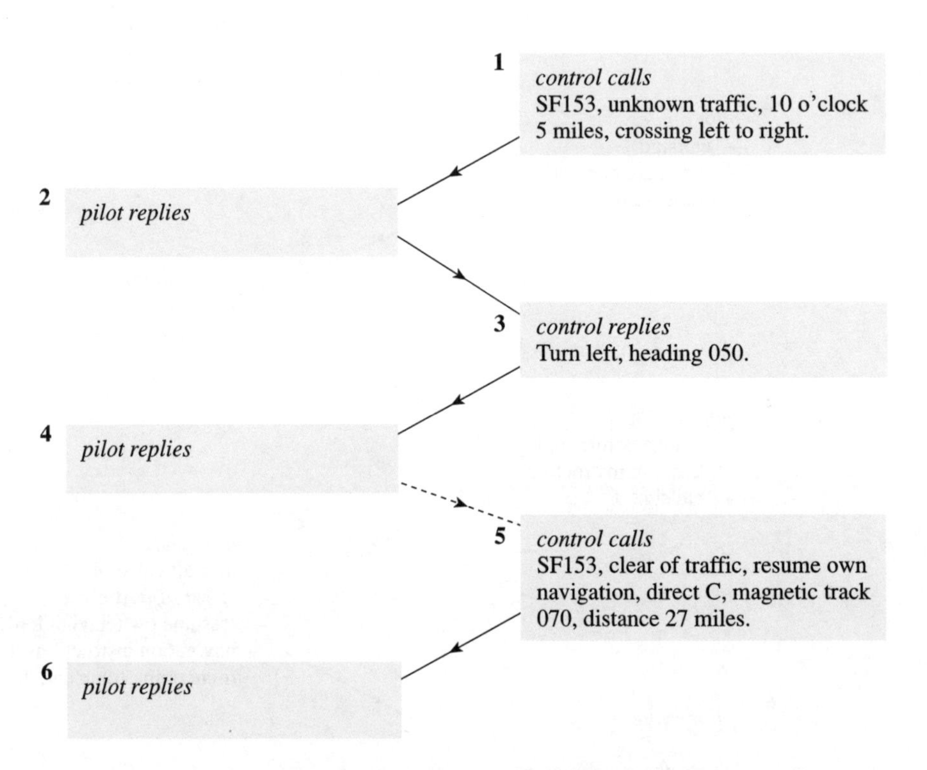

1
control calls
SF153, unknown traffic, 10 o'clock 5 miles, crossing left to right.
2
pilot replies
3
control replies
Turn left, heading 050.
4
pilot replies
5
control calls
SF153, clear of traffic, resume own navigation, direct C, magnetic track 070, distance 27 miles.
6
pilot replies

Check Check your answers, page 127.

Listen and Speak Listen and respond to the traffic information on the CD. Your callsign is SF153.
Check Check your answers, page 127.

Phraseology practice 3

Listen Listen to the recorded dialogue.
Listen and Repeat Listen and repeat the pilot's words.
Write Mark the position of the 'unknown traffic' on the diagram below.

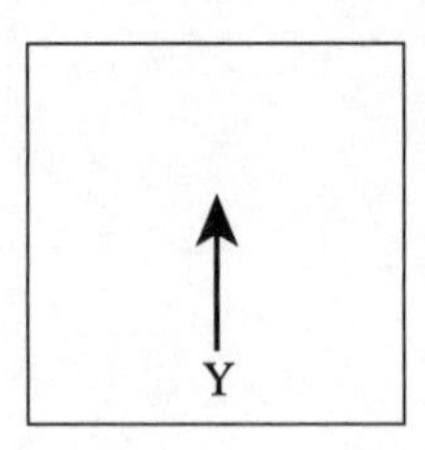

Listen and Write Complete the diagrams below.

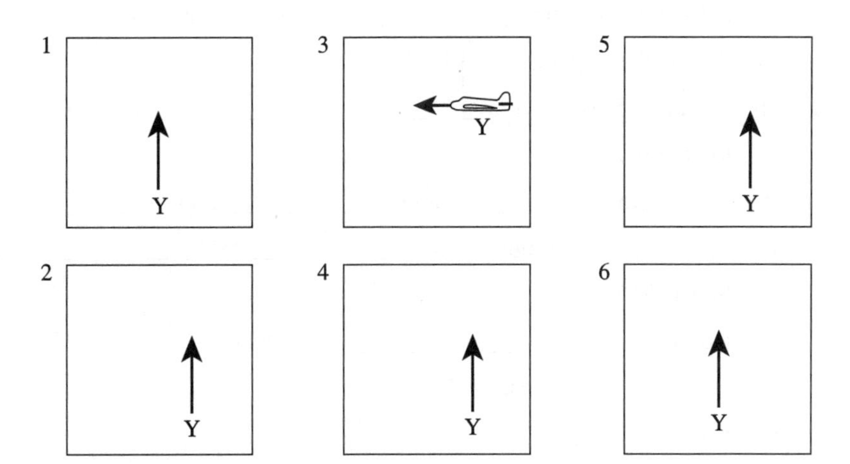

Check Check your answers, page 128.

3.3.2 En route: (non-routine)

Listen and Answer Listen to the dialogues and write down the answers to these questions. There is one question for each dialogue.

1. What evasive action did the pilot take, and with what results?

   . . . .

2. What is the problem, and what action is the pilot taking?

   . . . .

3. What is the problem, and what action is the pilot taking?

   . . . .

Check Check your answers, page 128.

Listen and Write Listen again and complete the texts below.

1 PIL Sunair 593, ____________ ____________ to avoid ____________ with ____________ ____________.

CTL Do you have any other ____________? Did you see the ____________ or ____________?

PIL It was a ____________, that's all we know.

CTL Do you ____________ an ____________?

PIL ____________. It was a very close thing. ____________ if the ____________ are OK.

PIL Sunair 593, ___________ passengers have been ___________ ___________, but there's a doctor ___________, so we'll continue our ___________.

CTL Roger, Sunair 593.

2 PIL Sunair 715, we have a ___________ ___________, request ___________ to Overby.

CTL Sunair 715, ___________ now, ___________ 280, ___________ to FL110.

PIL ___________ right 280, ___________ 180, ___________ to FL110, Sunair 715.

CTL Do you ___________ ___________ at Overby?

PIL ___________, Sunair 715.

CTL Roger, will ___________.

3 CTL Sunair 177, Winton Control, your company ___________ us you ___________ have a ___________.

PIL Do you have any ___________ about ___________?

CTL Negative.

PIL ___________ ___________ to Newbridge, request ___________ ___________ on ___________, Sunair 177.

Check Check your answers, page 128.

Your word list

Write down any words in the dialogues you do not understand, or are not sure about. Try to guess the meaning in English or your own language, and write it down. Then check with a dictionary.

CHECK

3.3.1 **Listen and Write** (from page 122)

Item no.	Diagram
1	G
2	B
3	D
4	A
5	C
6	E
7	F

3.3.1 **Write** (from page 124)

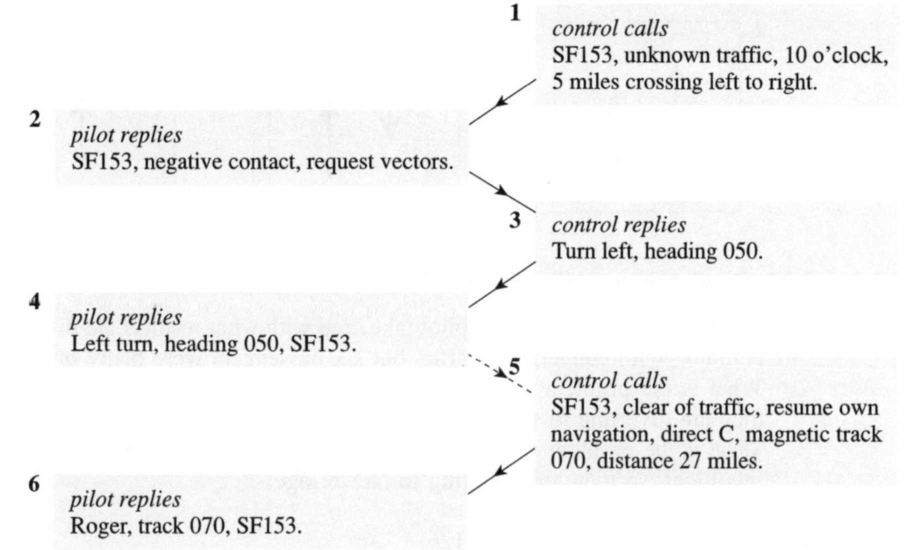

1
control calls
SF153, unknown traffic, 10 o'clock, 5 miles crossing left to right.
2
pilot replies
SF153, negative contact, request vectors.
3
control replies
Turn left, heading 050.
4
pilot replies
Left turn, heading 050, SF153.
5
control calls
SF153, clear of traffic, resume own navigation, direct C, magnetic track 070, distance 27 miles.
6
pilot replies
Roger, track 070, SF153.

3.3.1 **Listen and Speak** (from page 124)

1 CTL . . . .
PIL SF153, negative contact, request vectors.
CTL . . . .
PIL Left turn heading 050, SF153.
CTL . . . .
PIL Roger, track 070, SF153.

2 CTL . . . .
PIL SF153, negative contact, request vectors.
CTL . . . .
PIL Right turn heading 170, SF153.
CTL . . . .
PIL Roger, track 149, SF153.

3 CTL . . . .
PIL SF153, negative contact, request vectors.
CTL . . . .
PIL Right turn heading 250, SF153.
CTL . . . .
PIL Roger, track 227, SF153.

3.3.1 **Listen, Speak and Write** (from page 125)

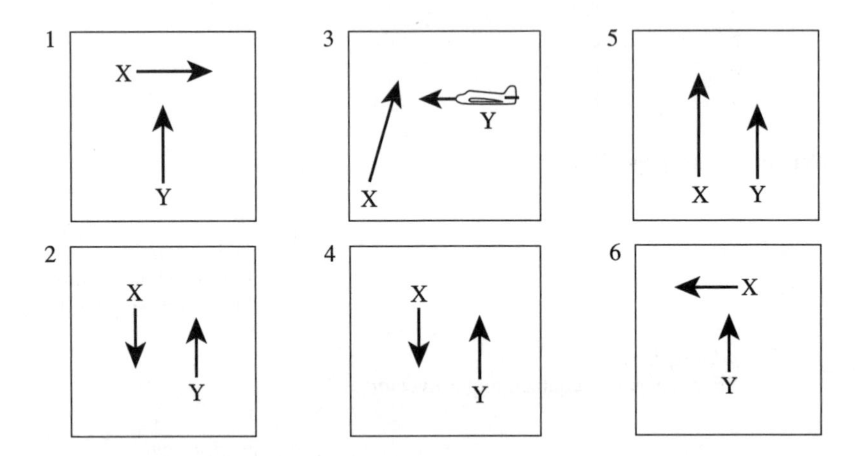

3.3.2 **Listen and Answer** (from page 125)

1. What evasive action did the pilot take, and with what results? He dived and avoided colliding with converging traffic, but six passengers were badly bruised.
2. What is the problem and what action is the pilot taking? There is a fuel leak, so they are diverting to Overby.
3. What is the problem and what action is the pilot taking? There is a bomb scare on this flight, so they are diverting to Newbridge.

3.3.2 **Listen and Write** (from page 126)

1 PIL Sunair 593, we've just had to dive to avoid colliding with converging traffic.
CTL Do you have any other details? Did you see the type or the markings?
PIL It was a white jet, that's all we know.
CTL Do you wish to file an air miss report?
PIL Affirm. It was a very close thing. I'll check if the passengers are OK.
PIL Sunair 593, six passengers have been badly bruised, but there's a doctor on board, so we'll continue on our route.
CTL Roger, Sunair 593.

2 PIL Sunair 715, we have a serious fuel leak, request divert to Overby.
CTL Sunair 715, turn right now, heading 280, descend to FL110.
PIL Turning right 280, leaving level 180, descending to FL110, Sunair 715.
CTL Do you require emergency assistance at Overby?
PIL Affirm, Sunair 715.
CTL Roger, will advise.

3 CTL Sunair 177, Winton Control, your company has informed us you may have a bomb on board.

PIL Do you have any information about the type of bomb?

CTL Negative.

PIL Diverting immediately to Newbridge, request emergency services on landing, Sunair 177.

3.4 DESCENT

3.4.1 Descent (routine)

Key words and phrases

Check that you understand all the words and phrases in the list below. Look up any new words in an aviation dictionary.

squawk ident	affirm
radar contact	increase
leave	rate of descent
confirm	

Typical exchange

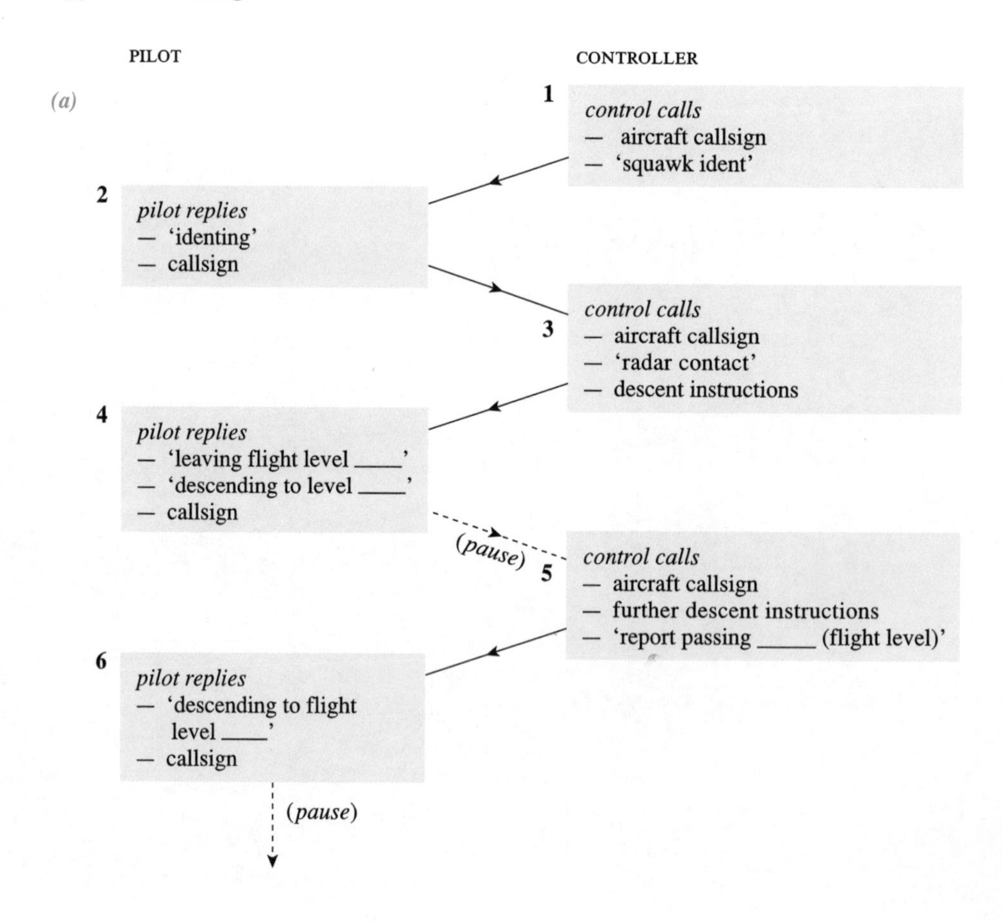

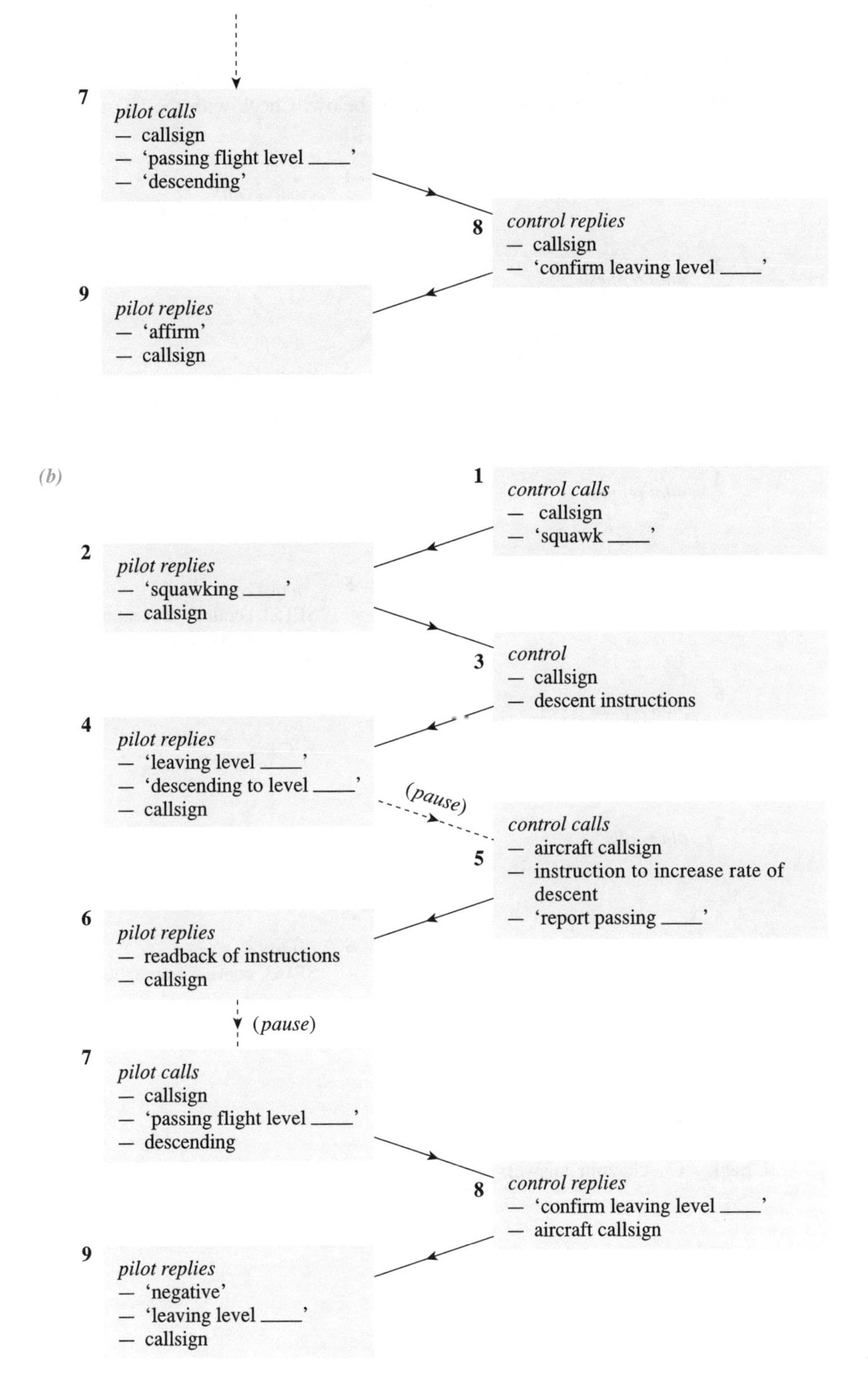

7
pilot calls
— callsign
— 'passing flight level ____'
— 'descending'
8
control replies
— callsign
— 'confirm leaving level ____'
9
pilot replies
— 'affirm'
— callsign
(b)
1
control calls
— callsign
— 'squawk ____'
2
pilot replies
— 'squawking ____'
— callsign
3
control
— callsign
— descent instructions
4
pilot replies
— 'leaving level ____'
— 'descending to level ____'
— callsign
(pause)
5
control calls
— aircraft callsign
— instruction to increase rate of descent
— 'report passing ____'
6
pilot replies
— readback of instructions
— callsign
(pause)
7
pilot calls
— callsign
— 'passing flight level ____'
— descending
8
control replies
— 'confirm leaving level ____'
— aircraft callsign
9
pilot replies
— 'negative'
— 'leaving level ____'
— callsign

Phraseology practice

Listen Listen to dialogue (***a***).

Listen and Repeat Listen again and repeat the pilot's words.

Write Complete the text of dialogue (***a***) below. Check with the CD if necessary.

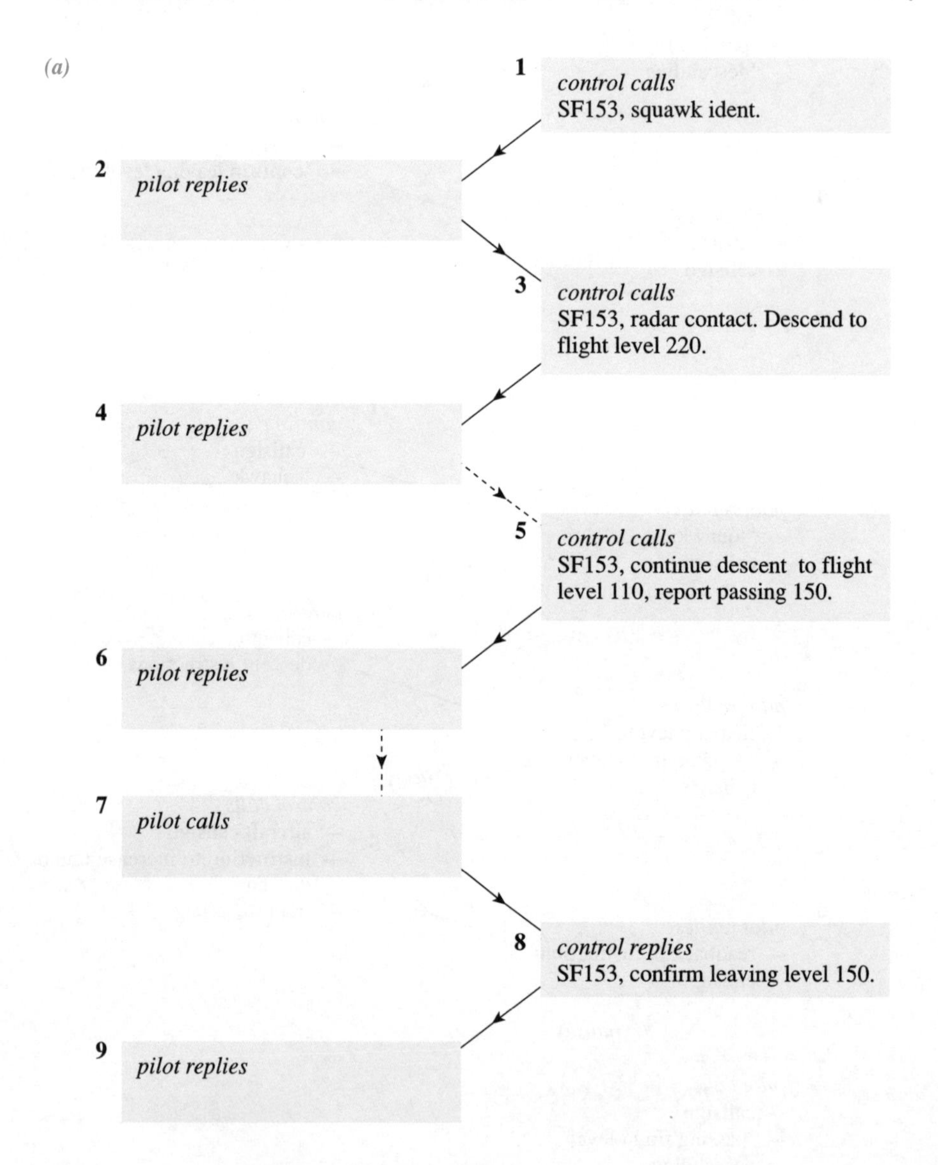

(a)
1
control calls
SF153, squawk ident.
2
pilot replies
3
control calls
SF153, radar contact. Descend to flight level 220.
4
pilot replies
5
control calls
SF153, continue descent to flight level 110, report passing 150.
6
pilot replies
7
pilot calls
8
control replies
SF153, confirm leaving level 150.
9
pilot replies

Check Check your answers, page 135.

Listen Listen to dialogue (***b***).

Listen and Repeat Listen again and repeat the pilot's words.

Write Complete the text below by writing in the pilot's words. Check with the CD if necessary.

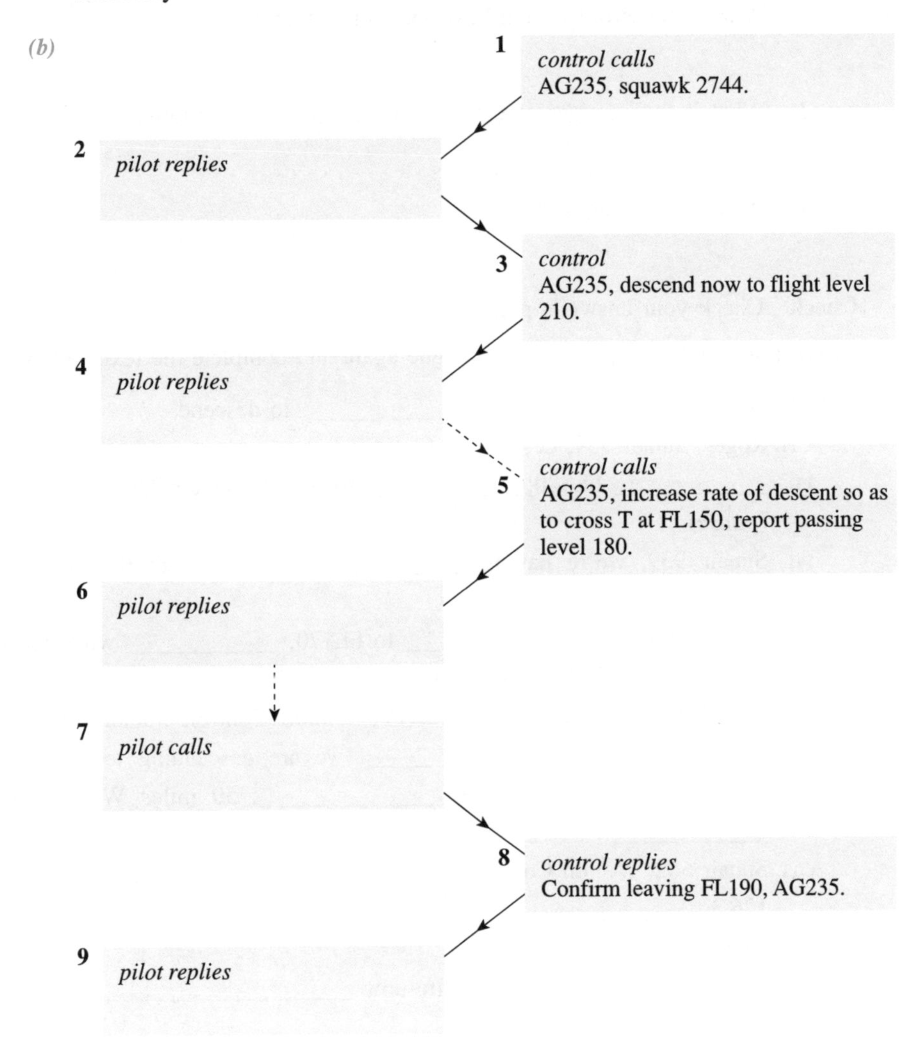

(b)
1
control calls
AG235, squawk 2744.
2
pilot replies
3
control
AG235, descend now to flight level 210.
4
pilot replies
5
control calls
AG235, increase rate of descent so as to cross T at FL150, report passing level 180.
6
pilot replies
7
pilot calls
8
control replies
Confirm leaving FL190, AG235.
9
pilot replies

Check Check your answers, page 135.

Listen and Speak Reply to the instructions for the following flights.

No.	Callsign	Cruising level
1	SF153	310
2	AG235	280
3	BI196	290
4	NJ342	250
5	MO725	230

Check Check your answers, page 136.

3.4.2 Descent (non-routine)

Listen and Answer Listen to the dialogues and write down the answers to these questions. There is one question for each dialogue.

1. What is the problem and how does this affect descent?

   . . . .

2. What is the emergency and what are the pilot's intentions?

   . . . .

3. What is the problem?

   . . . .

Check Check your answers, page 137.

Listen and Write Listen to the dialogue again and complete the texts below.

1 PIL Winton Control, Sunair 939, ____________ to descend.

CTL Roger, Sunair 939, descend to FL190.

PIL ____________ FL320, ____________ to FL190, Sunair 939.

(*pause*)

PIL Sunair 939, we're having ____________________ with the pressurisation, ____________ ____________.

CTL Roger, Sunair 939, ____________ to FL170, ____________ when reaching.

PIL Descending to FL170, Sunair 939.

2 PIL MAYDAY, MAYDAY, MAYDAY, Winton Control, Sunair 662, we have ______________ ______________, we are descending to FL30, request ______________ at Winton, ______________, 50 miles West of Winton, ____________ 75°.

CTL Sunair 662, Winton Control, roger Mayday, ____________, ____________ on 126.3 ____________ ____________, Mayday.

(*pause*)

PIL Mayday Winton. Sunair 662, fire now ____________, ____________.

CTL Roger, Sunair 662.

Mayday all stations ____________ ____________.

3 PIL Sunair 779, ____________ ____________ due to ____________ ____________. Sunair 779, FL290, heading 110. ____________ Plaintree VOR this time, ____________ ____________ FL100 over RIV ____________, ____________ next for landing runway 32 at Winton.

Check Check your answers, page 137.

Your word list

Write down any words in the dialogues you do not understand, or are not sure about. Try to guess the meaning in English or in your own language, and write it down. Then check with a dictionary.

CHECK

3.4.1 **Write** (from pages 132 and 133)

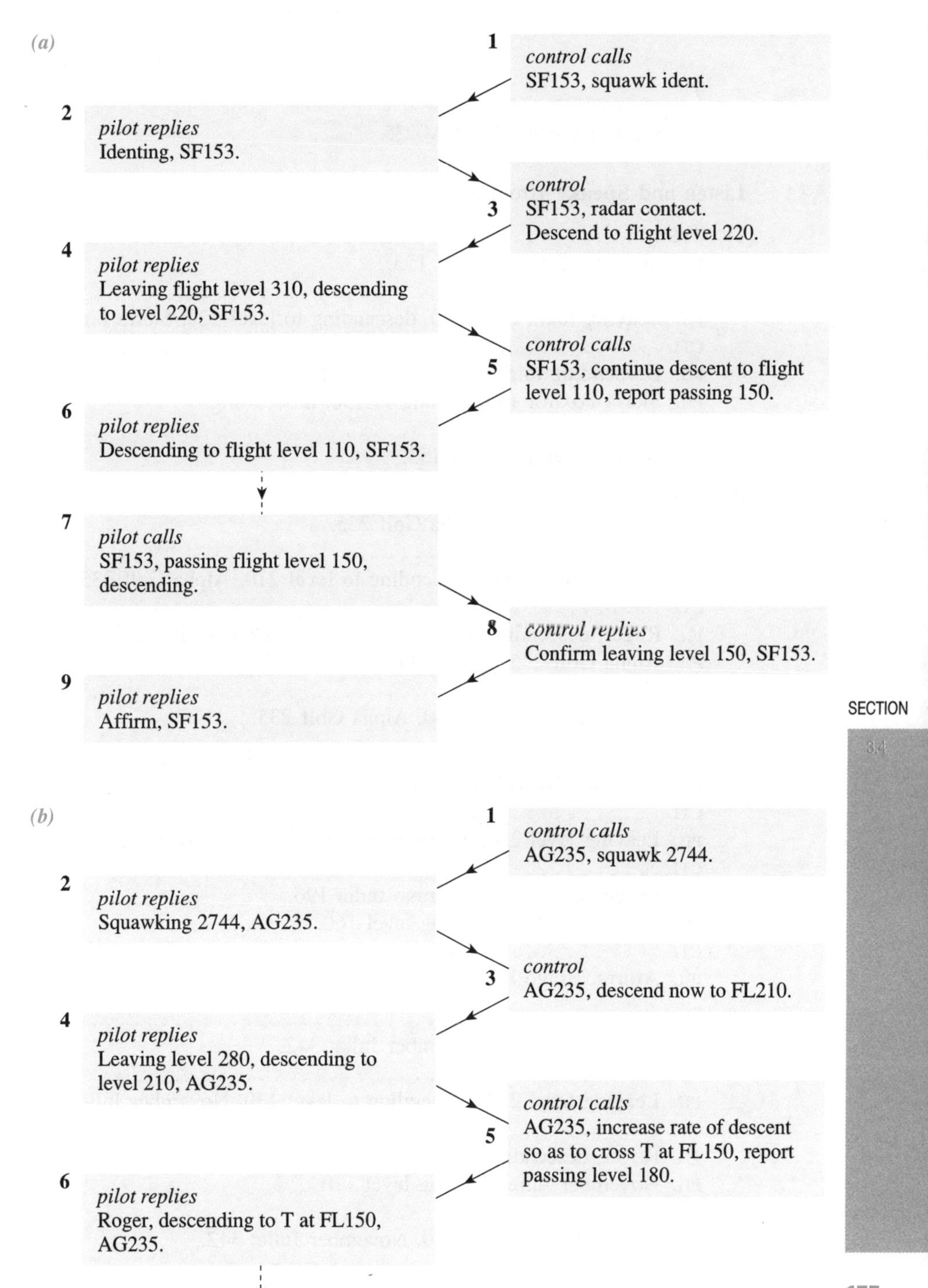

(a)
1
control calls
SF153, squawk ident.
2
pilot replies
Identing, SF153.
control
3
SF153, radar contact.
Descend to flight level 220.
4
pilot replies
Leaving flight level 310, descending to level 220, SF153.
control calls
5
SF153, continue descent to flight level 110, report passing 150.
6
pilot replies
Descending to flight level 110, SF153.
7
pilot calls
SF153, passing flight level 150, descending.
8
control replies
Confirm leaving level 150, SF153.
9
pilot replies
Affirm, SF153.
(b)
1
control calls
AG235, squawk 2744.
2
pilot replies
Squawking 2744, AG235.
control
3
AG235, descend now to FL210.
4
pilot replies
Leaving level 280, descending to level 210, AG235.
control calls
5
AG235, increase rate of descent so as to cross T at FL150, report passing level 180.
6
pilot replies
Roger, descending to T at FL150, AG235.

7 *pilot calls*
AG235, passing FL180, descending.

8 *control replies*
Confirm leaving FL190, AG235.

9 *pilot replies*
Negative, leaving FL180, AG235.

3.4.1 **Listen and Speak** (from page 133)

1 CTL . . . .
PIL Identing, Sierra Foxtrot 153.
CTL . . . .
PIL Leaving flight level 310, descending to level 220, Sierra Foxtrot 153.
CTL . . . .
PIL Descending to flight level 110, SF153.
PIL Sierra Foxtrot 153, passing FL150, descending.
CTL . . . .
PIL Affirm, Sierra Foxtrot 153.

2 CTL . . . .
PIL Squawking 2744, Alpha Golf 235.
CTL . . . .
PIL Leaving level 280, descending to level 210, Alpha Golf 235.
CTL . . . .
PIL Roger, descending to Tango at FL150, Alpha Golf 235.
PIL Alpha Golf 235, passing FL180, descending.
CTL . . . .
PIL Negative, leaving FL180, Alpha Golf 235.

3 CTL . . . .
PIL Identing, Bravo India 196.
CTL . . . .
PIL Leaving level 290, descending to level 190, Bravo India 196.
CTL . . . .
PIL Descending to FL90, Bravo India 196.
PIL Bravo India 196, passing level 160.
CTL . . . .
PIL Affirm, Bravo India 196.

4 CTL . . . .
PIL Squawking 4526, November Juliet 342.
CTL . . . .
PIL Leaving level 250, descending to level 130, November Juliet 342.
CTL . . . .
PIL Roger, descending to cross Sierra at 80, November Juliet 342.
PIL November Juliet, passing level 110.
CTL . . . .
PIL Negative, leaving FL110, November Juliet 342.

5 CTL . . . .
PIL Identing, Mike Oscar 725.
CTL . . . .
PIL Leaving level 230, descending to level 170, Mike Oscar 725.
CTL . . . .
PIL Roger, descending to cross Delta at level 90, Mike Oscar 725.
PIL Mike Oscar 725, passing level 140.
CTL . . . .
PIL Affirm, Mike Oscar 725.

3.4.2 Listen and Answer (from page 134)

1. What kind of problem is there and how does this affect descent?
   There is a pressurisation problem so they have to descend slowly.
2. What is the emergency and what are the pilot's intentions?
   There is a fire in the rear toilets. The pilot intends to make an emergency landing at Winton.
3. What is the problem?
   They have a receiver failure.

3.4.3 Listen and Write (from page 134)

1 PIL Winton Control, Sunair 939, ready to descend.
CTL Roger, Sunair 939, descend to FL190.
PIL Leaving FL310, descending to FL190, Sunair 939.
(*pause*)
PIL Sunair 939, we're having problems with the pressurisation, we'll have to descend slowly.
CTL Roger, Sunair 939, recleared to FL170, call me back when reaching.
PIL Descending to FL170, Sunair 939.

2 PIL MAYDAY MAYDAY MAYDAY, Winton Control, Sunair 662, we have fire in the rear toilets, we are descending to FL30, request an emergency landing at Winton, position, 50 miles West of Winton, heading 75°.
CTL Sunair 662, Winton Control, roger Mayday, break.
All stations on 126.3 stop transmitting, Mayday.
(*pause*)
PIL Mayday Winton. Sunair 662, fire now under control, cancel distress.
CTL Roger, Sunair 662.
Mayday all stations distress traffic ended.

3 PIL Sunair 779, transmitting blind due to receiver failure.
Sunair 779, FL290, heading 110. Over Plaintree VOR this time, descending to be at FL100 over RIV intersection, standard arrival procedure next for landing runway 32 at Winton.
(NOTE: This message should be transmitted twice.)

3.5 REVIEW OF PART THREE

3.5.1 Flight from Rexbury to Winton (en route)

Listen and Read Flight plan details:
Blackrock (BCK) beacon, estimated 48
Lake (LAK) VOR, estimated 15

You are flying from Rexbury to Winton, callsign Sunair 367. You are cruising at FL270. You are being handed over from Rexbury Control to New County Upper Control. After the handover you tune in to the Volmets for the area. You are 55 nm from Blackrock, the next reporting point.

Listen and Speak Follow the instructions on the CD, and reply to the controller.

Check Check your answers, page 140.

3.5.2 Flight from Dublin to Paris (en route)

Listen and Read Flight plan details:
Callsign SF309
reporting points: Wallesey, Telba, Midhurst, Sitet, Etrat. Route maps are on pages 50 and 51.

Listen and Speak Take the pilot's part. Follow the instructions and reply to the controllers; SF309 is now climbing to FL330.

Check Check your answers, page 140.

CHECK

3.5.1 **Listen and Speak** (from page 138)

PIL New County Upper Control, Sunair 367, good afternoon.

CTL . . . .

PIL Continue to Blackrock, report reaching, Sunair 367.

This is Winton Volmet. This is Winton Volmet.
Winton airport at 14.30, 280° 10 knots, 8000 metres, temperature 12, dew point 11, QNH 1020, no sig.

Overby at 14.30, 240° 12 knots, 10 kms or more, temperature 8, dew point 6, QNH 1020, no sig.

Newbridge at 14.30, 250° 4 knots, 3000 metres, mist, temperature 6, dew point 4, QNH 1016, no sig.

CTL . . . .

PIL Roger, traffic in sight, Sunair 367.

CTL . . . .

CTL . . . .

PIL 128.5, Sunair 367, goodbye.

PIL Valley Control, Sunair 367, good afternoon, estimating BCK at 48.

CTL . . . .

PIL Roger, continue to Blackrock.

PIL Sunair 367, over Blackrock this time, estimating LAK at 15.

CTL . . . .

PIL Roger.

PIL Sunair 367, request turn right 30° to avoid build-up.

CTL . . . .

PIL 025°, Sunair 367.

CTL . . . .

PIL Turning right heading 050, Sunair 367.

PIL Sunair 367, we have passed the build-up, are now back on track.

CTL . . . .

PIL Proceeding to Lake, Sunair 367.

PIL Over LAK this time, Sunair 367.

CTL . . . .

PIL To RED, Sunair 367.

3.5.2 **Listen and Speak** (from page 138)

CTL . . . .

PIL Heading 100, SF309.

CTL . . . .

PIL Turning right, heading 125.

PIL SF309, reaching FL330.

CTL . . . .

PIL Own navigation to Honiley, SF309.

CTL . . . .

PIL Direct to Midhurst, SF309.

CTL . . . .

PIL London 133.7, SF309, good day.

PIL London, SF309, good afternoon.

CTL . . . .

PIL Maintaining FL330, direct Midhurst, SF309.

CTL . . . .

PIL London 127.7, SF309.

PIL London, SF309, good afternoon.

CTL . . . .

PIL Maintaining FL330, SF309.

CTL . . . .

PIL Go ahead SF309.

CTL . . . .

PIL Descending to FL310.

CTL . . . .

PIL Paris 132.0.

PIL Paris, SF309, good afternoon.

CTL . . . .

PIL Maintaining FL310, cleared to Reymy, squawking 0444.

3.6 SUPPLEMENTARY VOCABULARY

3.6.1 Weather words

Listen and Write Listen to the recording and write the weather words you recognise under the correct heading below. For example, *rain* goes under *precipitation.*

WIND	PRECIPITATION	VISIBILITY

SURFACES	CLOUD	STORMS

Listen and Check Listen to the categories and words read out on the recording, then check the words you don't know. (You can read the words on page 146). Note that some words fit into more than one category, e.g. CB's fits under both *clouds* and *storms*.

Write Choose from these words to complete the 'weather word tree' below. There is no right or wrong answer here. It is an exercise to help you to remember the words by thinking about them. Try to choose some words that you do not know very well.

sandstorm wet CAVOK drizzle broken headwind
CBs hail damp gusts fog-bound tornado pools of water
snow dispersing clear air turbulence black ice slush
a build-up (thick/dense) fog light rain snow
snow drifts hailstones ceiling turbulence haze
(in and out of) the tops crosswind flooded
freezing rain a rainbow storm cells fog patches

overcast heavy rain water spout
strong wind snow ruts down/up-draught frost
sleet icy patches cirrus closing in
VMC conditions a flash of lightning

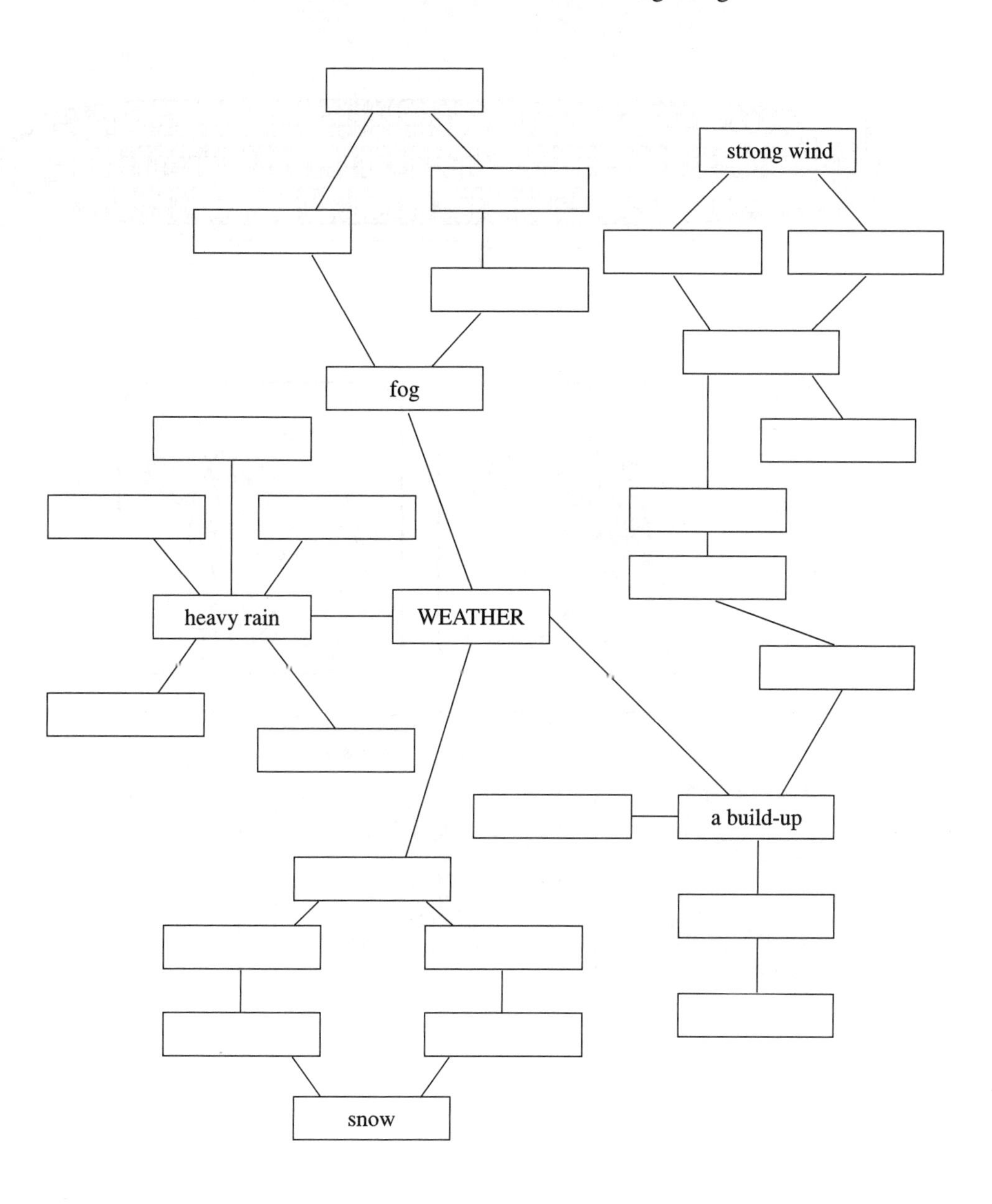

Write Now try to make the same word tree, but this time, *do not look* at the tree you filled in or the list of words.

Check Compare your version of the tree with the version given on page 147.
(NOTE: It is not a 'right answer' — only one possible answer.)

3.6.2 Cabin and safety equipment words

Look and Think Look at the diagrams on this page. Do you know the words which correspond to the numbers?

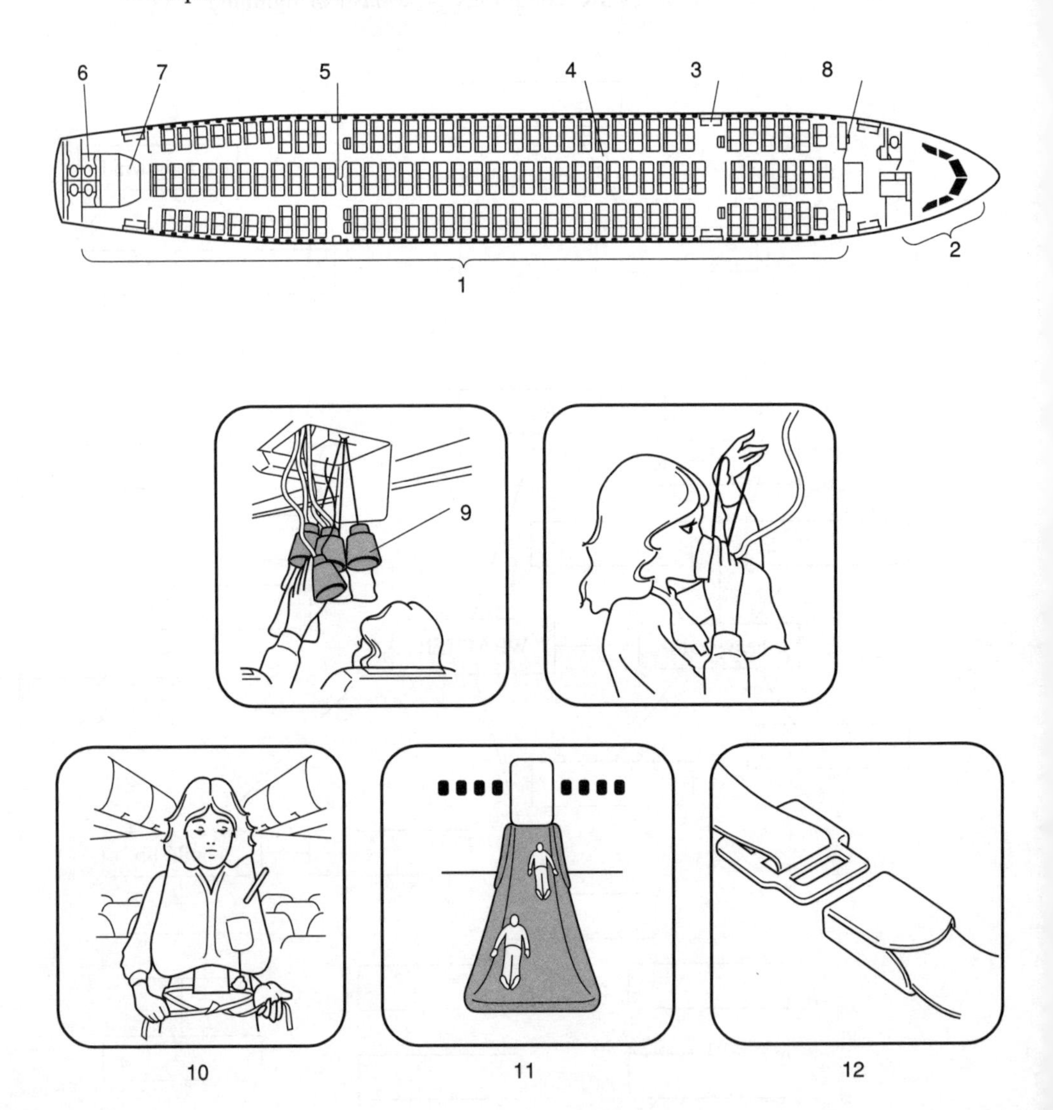

Look, Listen and Repeat Look at the diagrams, listen to the CD and repeat the words.

Look, Listen and Write Look at the diagrams and listen to the CD. Write down the words which correspond to each number, below.

1	7 ....
2	8 ....
3	9 ....
4	10 ....
5	11 ....
6	12 ....

Check Check your answers, page 147.

Look, Listen and Speak Now test yourself. Look at the diagrams only. Do not look at the words. Listen to the CD and say the correct word when you hear the number. Then you will hear the right answer.

CHECK

3.6.1 Listen and Check (from page 142)

WIND
calm
headwind
tailwind
crosswind
drift
gusts
strong wind
light wind
turbulence
clear air turbulence
severe/moderate turbulence
windshear
down/up draught

PRECIPITATION
rain
drizzle
scattered showers
heavy rain
light rain
sleet
snow
hail
hailstones
freezing rain
icing
frost
a rainbow

VISIBILITY
CAVOK
VMC conditions
mist
(thick/dense) fog
fog patches
haze
dispersing
closing in
fog-bound

SURFACES
wet
damp
flooded
icy patches
standing water
pools of water
snow ruts
snow banks
snow drifts
black ice
slush

CLOUDS
broken
overcast
CBs
(in and out of) the tops
ceiling
cirrus
a bank of clouds
storm cells
a build-up

STORMS
sandstorm
tornado
hurricane
typhoon
water spout
thunder
lightning
a flash of lightning
to be struck by lightning
CB's

3.6.1 **Write** (from page 143)

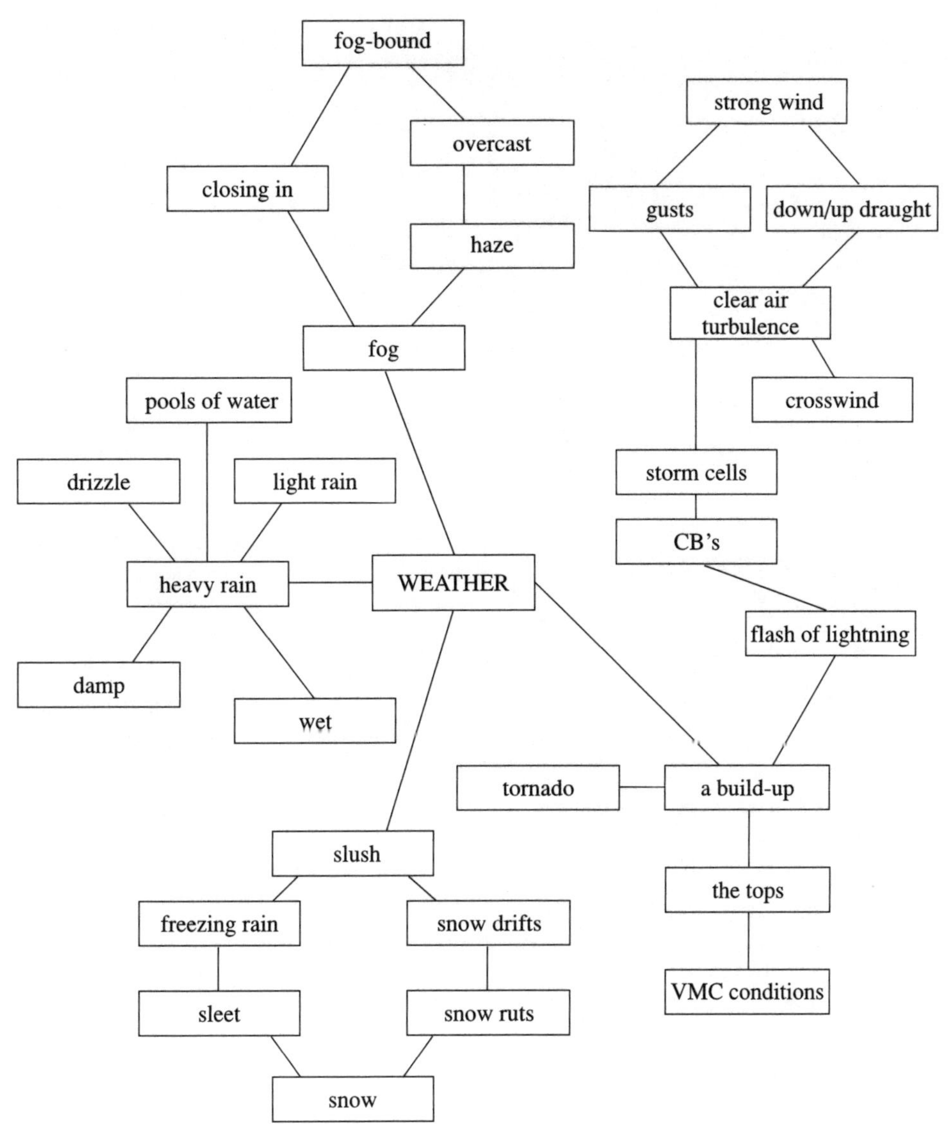

3.6.2 **Look, Listen and Write** (from page 145)

1 the cabin
2 the cockpit
3 a door
4 an aisle (or alley)
5 a row of seats
6 toilets
7 a galley
8 a jump seat
9 an oxygen mask
10 a life jacket (or life vest)
11 an escape slide (or chute)
12 a seat-belt

Part Four

Approach to parking

4.1 ARRIVAL (ATIS)

Key words and phrases

Check that you understand all the words and phrases in this list. Look up any new words in an aviation dictionary.

patches of fog	showers
vertical visibility	radar vectors
minima	instrument approach
QFE	unserviceable (US)
repairs	ILS (Instrument Landing System)
damp	turn-off
north/south/east/west	hectopascal
bird strike hazard	

Typical ATIS recording

Look at page 4 for a description of the items in these recordings.

Phraseology practice

Listen and Write Listen to the following ATIS recordings and make notes for each one in the table below.

1 Schiphol	
2 Rexbury	
3 Zurich	
4 Overby	
5 Baden	
6 Mauignac	
7 Heathrow	

8 Brest Guipavas	
9 Eggenfelden	
10 Rotterdam	
11 Tallin	
12 Khabarovsk	

Check Check your notes using the texts on page 154.

CHECK

4.1 **Listen and Write** (from page 152)

1 This is Schiphol Arrival information G, main landing runway 18R. Runway conditions runway 18R braking action good, braking action good, braking action medium to good, transition level 50, 230° 15 knots, variable between 200 and 260°, visibility 10 kms, scattered 1100 ft, few 1500 ft, cumulo nimbus, broken 4500 ft, temperature 10, dew point 9, QNH 994 hectopascal, temporary, visibility 6 kms, weather showers of rain, contact Approach and Arrival with callsign only, end of information Golf.

2 This is Rexbury arrival information Uniform, at 17.30 Zulu time. ILS approach landing runway 29, transition level 45, wind calm, visibility 220 metres, present weather: fog, vertical visibility 45 metres, check your minima, temperature 5, dew point 5, QNH 1020. Taxiway Yankee closed for repairs. This was information Uniform.

3 This is Zurich information India, landing runway 28, VOR DME approach, departure runway 32, met report Zurich 2050 wind 210° 6 knots, visibility 15 kms, cloud scattered 2500 ft, broken 3000 ft, temperature 3, dew point –2, QNH 1020 no sig, transition level 70 Urna arrival via Rilax, expect Rilax 1 Alpha arrival, Zurich information India.

4 This is Overby information India at 14.00 hours. ILS approach landing runway 33, take-off runway 33, transition level 35, wind 165° 21 knots, visibility 10 kms or more, present weather: rain showers, temperature 6, dew point 3, QNH 1006. This was information India.

5 Baden information Victor, meteorological report time 2150 expect ILS approach runway in use 21, transition level 60 wind 220° 05 knots, visibility 8 kms present weather light drizzle, cloud broken 1400 ft, temperature 03, dew point 02, QNH 1025 information Victor out.

6 This is Marignac Information Romeo recorded at 1930 UTC, runway in use 23, ILS approach, transition level 50, wind 320° 4 knots, visibility 10 kms, cloud broken 4000 ft, temperature +7, dew point +4, QNH 1028 QFE 1022, inform Merignac on first contact received Romeo information.

7 This is Heathrow arrival information K, 21.15 hours weather: wind 240° 07 knots, visibility 8 kms in haze, temperature +17, dew point +10, QNH 1018 millibars, 28R single runway operations, no turn-off available block 14. Ockam VOR US. Report aircraft type and information K received on first contact with Heathrow Approach.

8 Good afternoon, Brest Guipavas information Juliet recorded at 1200 UTC time. Approach locator ILS 25L, runway in use 25L. Planned departure route 4 Whisky, transition level 050. Caution bird strike around the airfield and special VFR conditions, wind 210° 13 knots, maximum 24 visibility 4500 metres present weather light drizzle and mist, clouds broken 1000 ft, temperature +17, dew point +15, QNH 1015 QFE 1003 inform Brest Guipavas on first contact that you have received Juliet information.

9 Guten tag, this is the latest weather report Eggenfelden at 18 hours 56 minutes Zulu, wind 250° 3 knots, visibility 8 kms, scattered 2700, overcast 4000 ft, temperature 0 Celsius, dew point –1 Celsius, QNH 1024 QFE 976 hectopascal.

10 This is Rotterdam information November, main landing runway 06, transition level 45, operational report: exit runway 24, holding 06 closed, runway approach lights runway 06 not available, 070° 3 knots, visibility less than 800 metres, RVR available on ATC frequencies, patches of fog, sky clear, temperature 11, dew point 11, QNH 1012 hectopascal, temporary, visibility 600 metres Acknowledge information November at first contact.

11 Tallin ATIS information Echo 2150, expect VOR, DME ILS approach, runway 26 in use, braking action good and runway dry, snow, transition level 50 wind 150° 03 knots, visibility 3700 metres.

12 Khabarovsk ATIS information Lima 0600 runway in use 23L parallel approach, NDB approach, VOR DME approach, visual approach, transition level 1500 metres runway out of operation, repair work in progress, outer runway 23R between taxiway 4 and taxiway 1 not available for repair, taxiway 2 taxiway 3 are out of operation, bird strike hazard in take-off and landing area.
Present weather wind 280° 4 metres per second, visibility above 10 kms cloud few cumulo nimbus 990 metres, temperature 33, dew point 13, QFE 990 hectopascal 742 mm, no sig, acknowledge information Lima, Khabarovsk.

4.2 APPROACH

4.2.1 Approach (routine)

Key words and phrases

Check that you understand all the words in the list below. Look up any new words in an aviation dictionary.

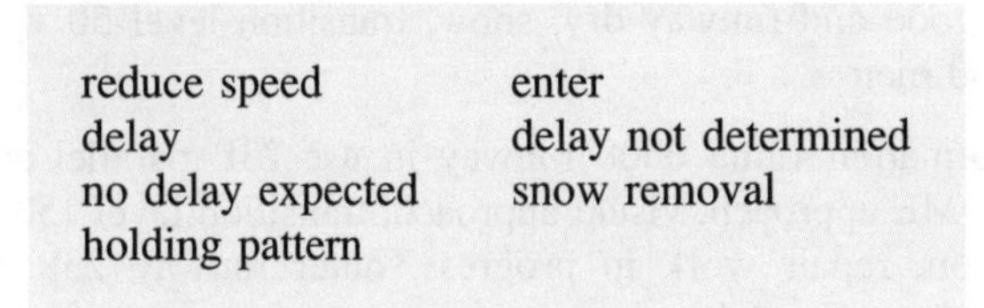

reduce speed
delay
no delay expected
holding pattern
enter
delay not determined
snow removal

Typical exchange

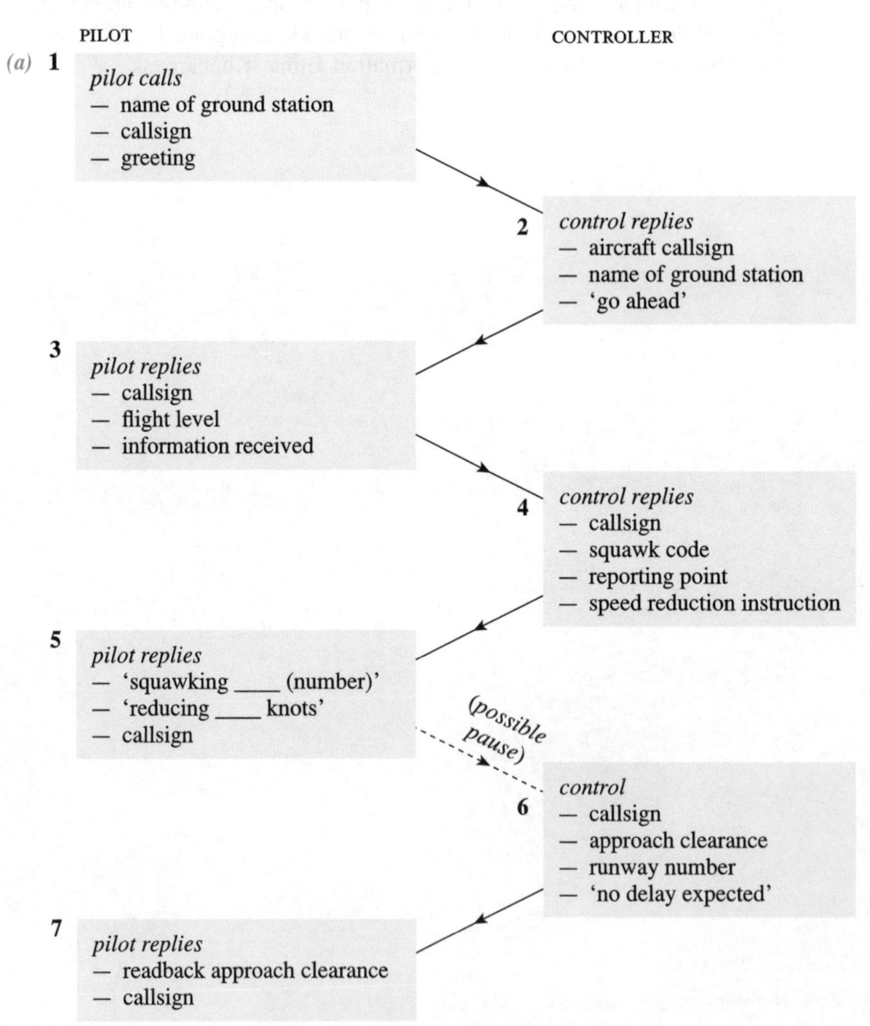

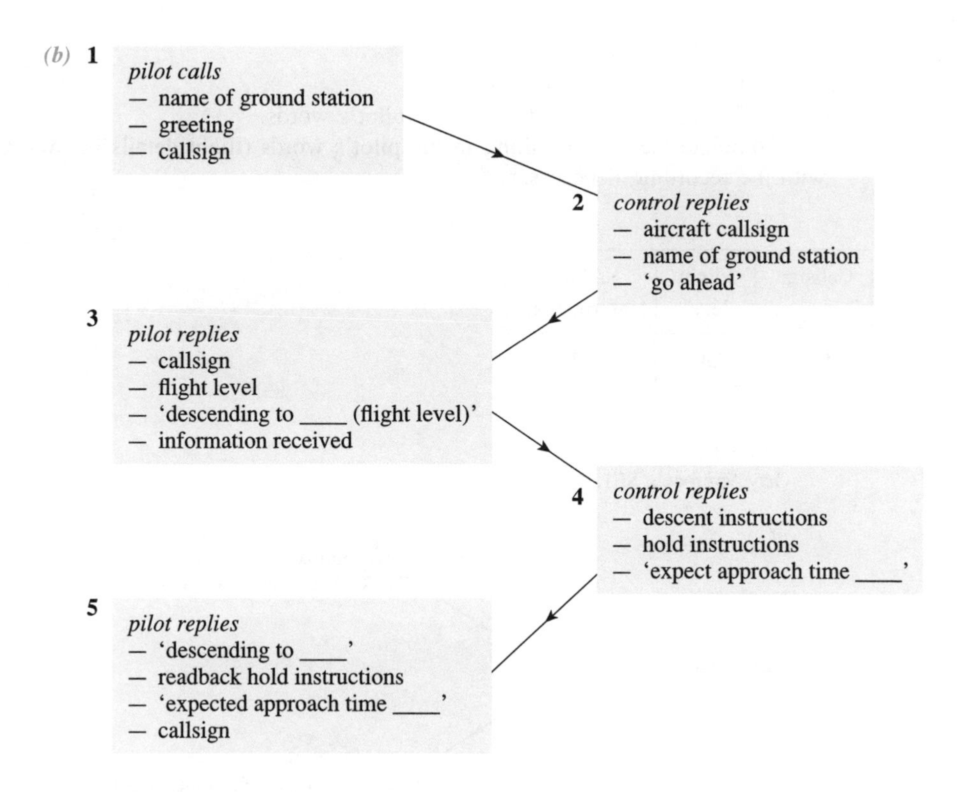

(b) 1
pilot calls
— name of ground station
— greeting
— callsign
2
control replies
— aircraft callsign
— name of ground station
— 'go ahead'
3
pilot replies
— callsign
— flight level
— 'descending to ____ (flight level)'
— information received
4
control replies
— descent instructions
— hold instructions
— 'expect approach time ____'
5
pilot replies
— 'descending to ____'
— readback hold instructions
— 'expected approach time ____'
— callsign

NOTES

— In (***a***) *pilot call* **1**, the greeting should be at the end. However, in practice it often comes between *name of ground station* and *callsign*, as in (***b***) **1**.
— In (***b***) *control reply* **4**, the callsign is not used, as this is part of a dialogue, and contact is clearly established (see notes on *Use of Callsigns* in 2.4.1, *Climb*).

Phraseology practice

Listen Listen to dialogue (***a***) on the CD.

Listen and Repeat Listen and repeat the pilot's words.

Write Complete the text by filling in the pilot's words (flight details below). Check with the recording if necessary.

Callsign	Flight level	ATIS information
SF153	50	M

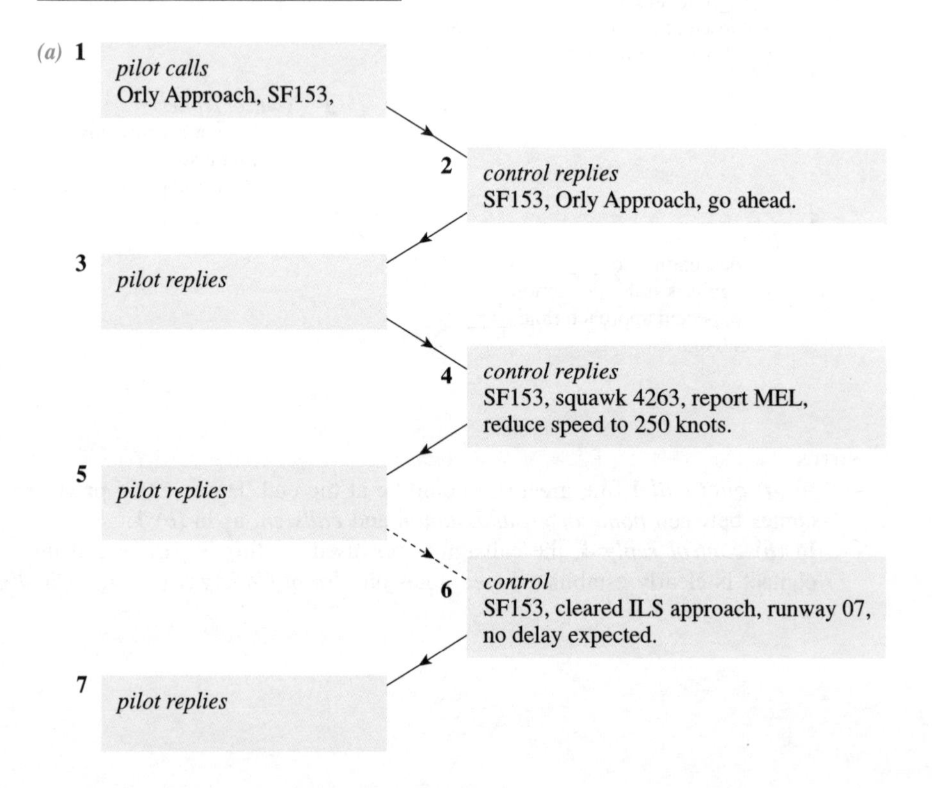

(*a*) 1
pilot calls
Orly Approach, SF153,
2
control replies
SF153, Orly Approach, go ahead.
3
pilot replies
4
control replies
SF153, squawk 4263, report MEL, reduce speed to 250 knots.
5
pilot replies
6
control
SF153, cleared ILS approach, runway 07, no delay expected.
7
pilot replies

Check Check your answers, page 162.

Listen Listen to dialogue (***b***) on the CD.
Listen and Repeat Listen again and repeat the pilot's words.
Write Complete the text by filling in the pilot's words (flight details below). Check with the recording if necessary.

Callsign	Flight level	ATIS information
AG235	150 ↘ 80	K

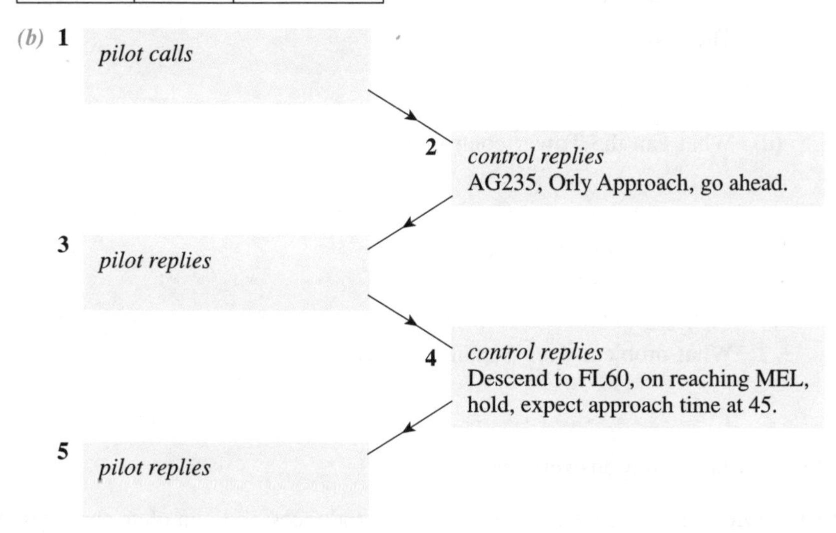

(*b*) 1
pilot calls
2
control replies
AG235, Orly Approach, go ahead.
3
pilot replies
4
control replies
Descend to FL60, on reaching MEL, hold, expect approach time at 45.
5
pilot replies

Check Check your answers, page 162.

Listen and Speak Listen to the CD. Using the flight details below, call Approach Control.

	Callsign	Flight level	ATIS information
1	SF153	↘ 50	M
2	AG235	150 ↘ 80	K
3	BI196	↘ 90	L
4	NJ342	130 ↘ 80	P
5	MO725	↘ 90	T

Check Check your answers, page 162.

4.2.2 Approach (non-routine)

Listen and Answer Listen to the dialogues and write down the answers to these questions. There are four questions for dialogue 1.

1(a) What is the problem?

. . . .

(b) What does the pilot do first?

. . . .

(c) Then what does he do?

. . . .

(d) What can the Tower controller see?

. . . .

2. Why did they overshoot?

. . . .

3. What problem does Sunair 572 have?

. . . .

Check Check your answers, page 163.

Listen and Write Listen to the following dialogues and complete the texts below.

1 PIL SF662, Orly Tower, our __________ __________ is __________.

CTL SF662, what are __________?

PIL Request proceed to __________ in order to __________ complete check.

CTL Roger, climb 2000 ft and turn left heading 350 to MEL VOR.

PIL __________ to 2000 ft, __________ left heading 350 to MEL.

(*pause*)

PIL SF662, __________ MEL 2000 ft, landing gear __________ but __________ not __________. We intend to __________ __________ near the Tower to have the __________ checked.

CTL Roger, make a low pass at 200 ft heading 200, __________ of Tower.

PIL At 200 ft, heading 200, North of Tower.

(*pause*)

CTL SF662 your landing gear __________ __________.

PIL SF662, __________ __________ and we intend to land.

2 PIL Sunair 594, ___________.

CTL Sunair 594, you're number 1 to land. ___________ ___________ at 600 ft 2 miles final, runway 07.

PIL Number 1 to land, Sunair 594.

(*pause*)

PIL Sunair 594, ___________.

CTL Sunair 594, ___________, when ___________ 1000 ft, turn right to Redhill VOR.

3 PIL Sunair 572, ___________ ___________ 10°. Request ___________ ___________ to runway 26 which is the ___________.

CTL Roger Sunair 572, ___________ ___________ over RIV VOR while we sort out the traffic, ___________ when ready.

PIL Thank you Winton, request ___________ for landing, Sunair 572.

Check Check your answers, page 164.

Your word list

Write down any words in the dialogues you do not understand, or are not sure about. Try to guess the meaning, in English or in your own language, and write it down. Then check with a dictionary.

CHECK

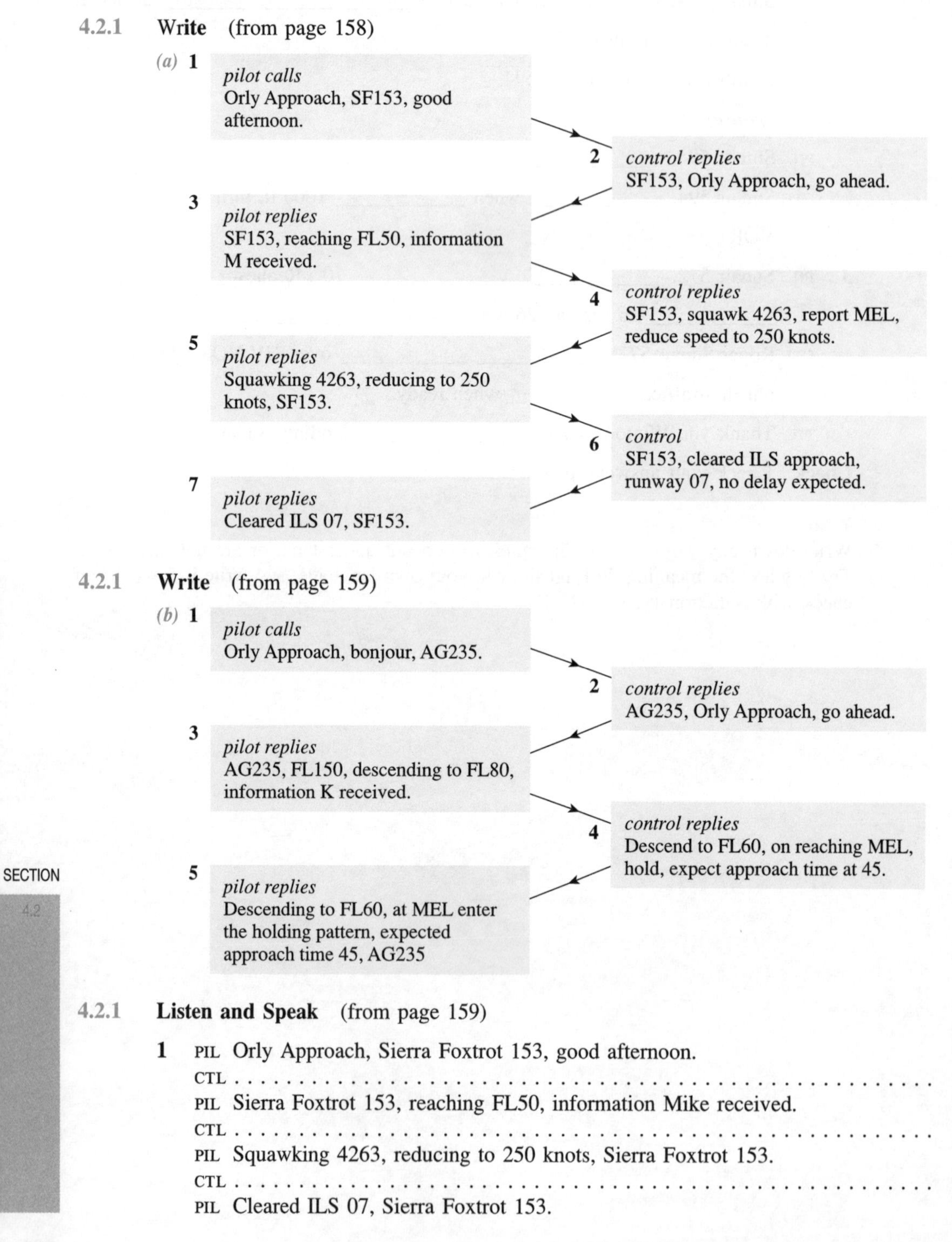

4.2.1 Write (from page 158)

(a)

1 *pilot calls*
Orly Approach, SF153, good afternoon.

2 *control replies*
SF153, Orly Approach, go ahead.

3 *pilot replies*
SF153, reaching FL50, information M received.

4 *control replies*
SF153, squawk 4263, report MEL, reduce speed to 250 knots.

5 *pilot replies*
Squawking 4263, reducing to 250 knots, SF153.

6 *control*
SF153, cleared ILS approach, runway 07, no delay expected.

7 *pilot replies*
Cleared ILS 07, SF153.

4.2.1 Write (from page 159)

(b)

1 *pilot calls*
Orly Approach, bonjour, AG235.

2 *control replies*
AG235, Orly Approach, go ahead.

3 *pilot replies*
AG235, FL150, descending to FL80, information K received.

4 *control replies*
Descend to FL60, on reaching MEL, hold, expect approach time at 45.

5 *pilot replies*
Descending to FL60, at MEL enter the holding pattern, expected approach time 45, AG235

4.2.1 Listen and Speak (from page 159)

1 PIL Orly Approach, Sierra Foxtrot 153, good afternoon.
CTL . . . .
PIL Sierra Foxtrot 153, reaching FL50, information Mike received.
CTL . . . .
PIL Squawking 4263, reducing to 250 knots, Sierra Foxtrot 153.
CTL . . . .
PIL Cleared ILS 07, Sierra Foxtrot 153.

2 PIL Orly Approach, bonjour, Alpha Golf 235.
CTL . . . .
PIL Alpha Golf 235, FL150, descending to FL80, information Kilo received.
CTL . . . .
PIL Descending to FL60, at Mike Echo Lima enter the holding pattern, expected approach time 45, Alpha Golf 235.

3 PIL Orly Approach, Bravo India 196, good morning.
CTL . . . .
PIL Bravo India 196, reaching flight level 90, information Lima received.
CTL . . . .
PIL Negative, reaching level 90, Bravo India 196.
CTL . . . .
PIL Squawking 3127, descending level 70, reducing 200 knots, cleared Mike Echo Lima, report reaching, Bravo India 196.
CTL . . . .
PIL Cleared ILS approach runway 26, Bravo India 196.

4 PIL Orly Approach, November Juliet 342, good afternoon.
CTL . . . .
PIL November Juliet 342, FL130, descending to level 80, information Papa received.
CTL . . . .
PIL Affirm, November Juliet 342.
CTL . . . .
PIL Descending to FL50, at Mike Echo Lima, enter the holding pattern, November Juliet 342.

5 PIL Orly Approach, Mike Oscar 725, good afternoon.
CTL . . . .
PIL Mike Oscar 725, reaching FL90, information Tango received.
CTL . . . .
PIL Squawking ident, descending to level 60, reducing to 210 knots, will report Mike Echo Lima on reaching, Mike Oscar 725.
CTL . . . .
PIL Cleared ILS 07, Mike Oscar 725.

4.2.2 Listen and Answer (from page 160)

1(a) What is the problem?
The left main landing gear is jammed.
(b) What does the pilot do first?
He carries out a complete check while in a holding pattern.
(c) Then what does he do?
He makes a low pass near the Tower.
(d) What can the Tower controller see?
He can see that the landing gear seems to be fully extended.

2. Why did they overshoot?
Because of wind shear on the approach.
3. What problem does Sunair 572 have?
They cannot extend the flaps more than 10°.

4.2.2 **Listen and Write** (from page 161)

1

PIL Sierra Foxtrot 662, Orly Tower, our left main landing gear is jammed.
CTL Sierra Foxtrot 662, what are your intentions?
PIL Request proceed to holding area in order to carry out complete check.
CTL Roger, climb 2000 ft and turn left heading 350 to Mike Echo Lima VOR.
PIL Climbing to 2000 ft, turning left heading 350 to Mike Echo Lima.
(*pause*)
PIL Sierra Foxtrot 662, over Mike Echo Lima 2000 ft, landing gear down but maybe not locked. We intend to make a low pass near the Tower to have the undercarriage checked.
CTL Roger, make a low pass at 200 ft heading 200, North of Tower.
PIL At 200 ft, heading 200, North of Tower.
(*pause*)
CTL SF662, your landing gear seems to be completely extended.
PIL SF662, request emergency services and we intend to land.

2

PIL Sunair 594, outer marker.
CTL Sunair 594, you're number 1 to land. Caution wind shear reported at 600 ft 2 miles final, runway 07.
PIL Number 1 to land, Sunair 594.
(*pause*)
PIL Sunair 594, going around.
CTL Sunair 594, standard procedure, when passing 1000 ft, turn right to Redhill VOR.

3

PIL Sunair 572, unable to extend flaps beyond 10°. Request high speed flat approach to runway 26 which is the longest available.
CTL Roger Sunair 572, proceed to holding pattern over RIV VOR while we sort out the traffic, call you back when ready.
PIL Thank you Winton, request emergency services for landing, Sunair 572.

4.3 FINAL APPROACH AND LANDING

4.3.1 Final approach and landing (routine)

Key words and phrases

Check that you understand the words and phrases below. Look up any new words in an aviation dictionary.

estimate	tower
straight-in approach	outer marker
established	

Typical exchange

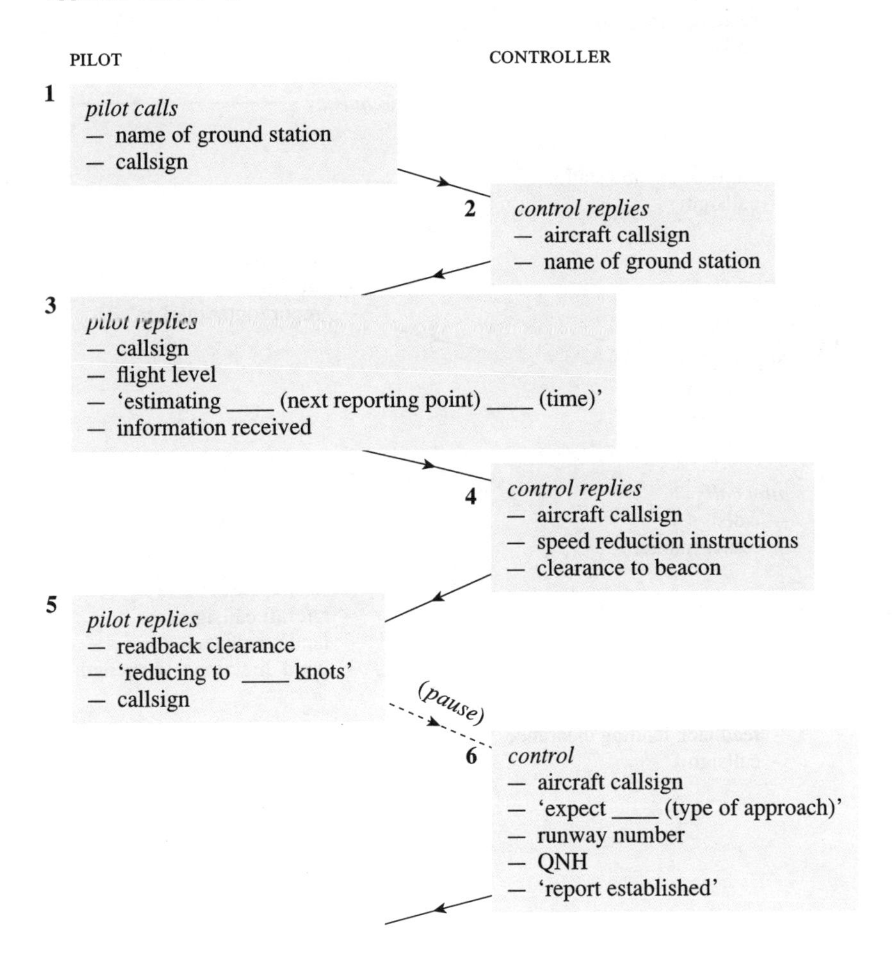

PILOT
CONTROLLER
1
pilot calls
— name of ground station
— callsign
2
control replies
— aircraft callsign
— name of ground station
3
pilot replies
— callsign
— flight level
— 'estimating ____ (next reporting point) ____ (time)'
— information received
4
control replies
— aircraft callsign
— speed reduction instructions
— clearance to beacon
5
pilot replies
— readback clearance
— 'reducing to ____ knots'
— callsign
(pause)
6
control
— aircraft callsign
— 'expect ____ (type of approach)'
— runway number
— QNH
— 'report established'

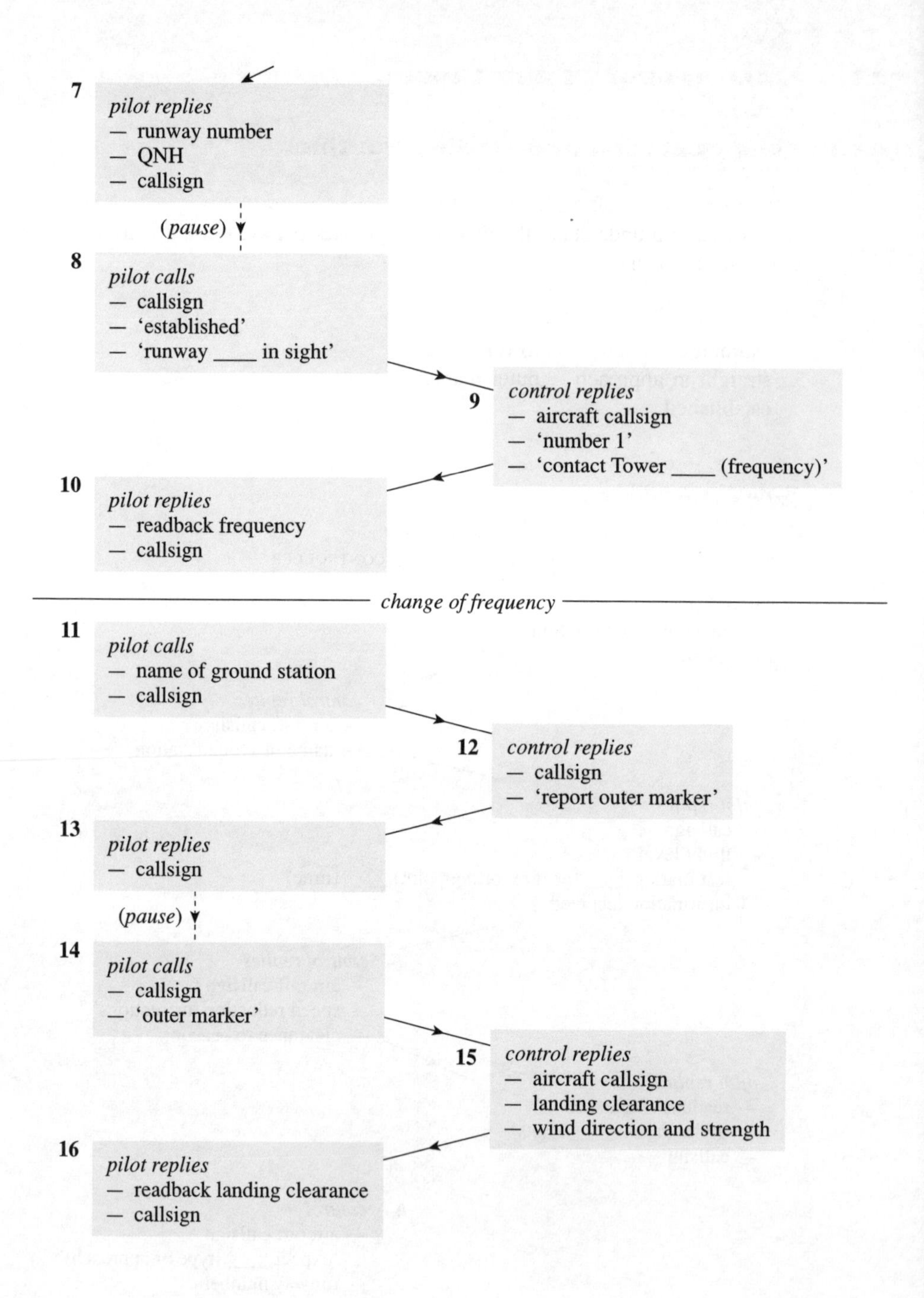
7
pilot replies
— runway number
— QNH
— callsign
(pause)
8
pilot calls
— callsign
— 'established'
— 'runway ____ in sight'
9
control replies
— aircraft callsign
— 'number 1'
— 'contact Tower ____ (frequency)'
10
pilot replies
— readback frequency
— callsign
change of frequency
11
pilot calls
— name of ground station
— callsign
12
control replies
— callsign
— 'report outer marker'
13
pilot replies
— callsign
(pause)
14
pilot calls
— callsign
— 'outer marker'
15
control replies
— aircraft callsign
— landing clearance
— wind direction and strength
16
pilot replies
— readback landing clearance
— callsign

Phraseology practice

Listen Listen to the dialogue.

Listen and Repeat Listen and repeat the pilot's words.

Write Complete the text of the dialogue below, using the flight details given.

Flight details:

callsign SF153, flight level 50, reporting point estimation RED 32, ATIS information M.

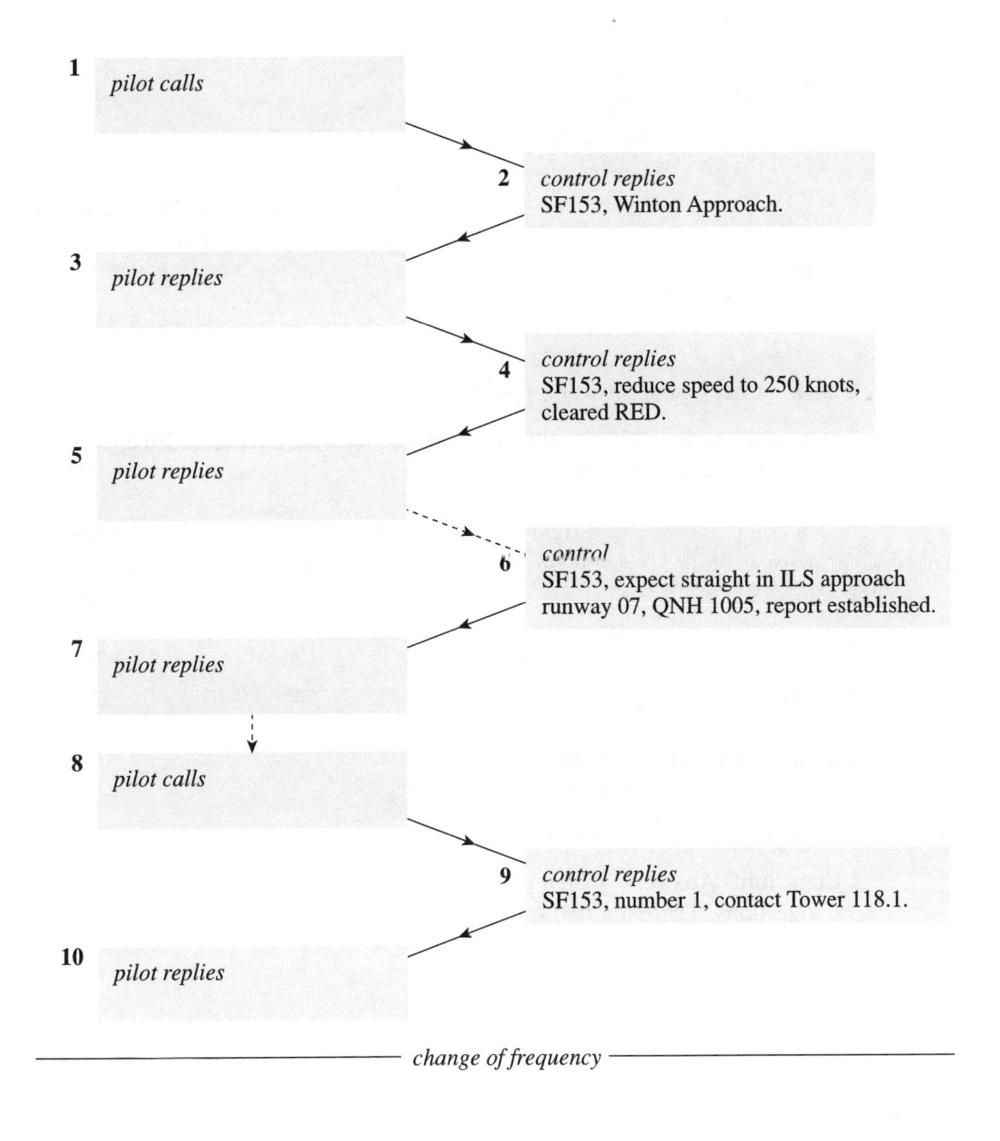

1 pilot calls
2 control replies
SF153, Winton Approach.
3 pilot replies
4 control replies
SF153, reduce speed to 250 knots, cleared RED.
5 pilot replies
6 control
SF153, expect straight in ILS approach runway 07, QNH 1005, report established.
7 pilot replies
8 pilot calls
9 control replies
SF153, number 1, contact Tower 118.1.
10 pilot replies
change of frequency

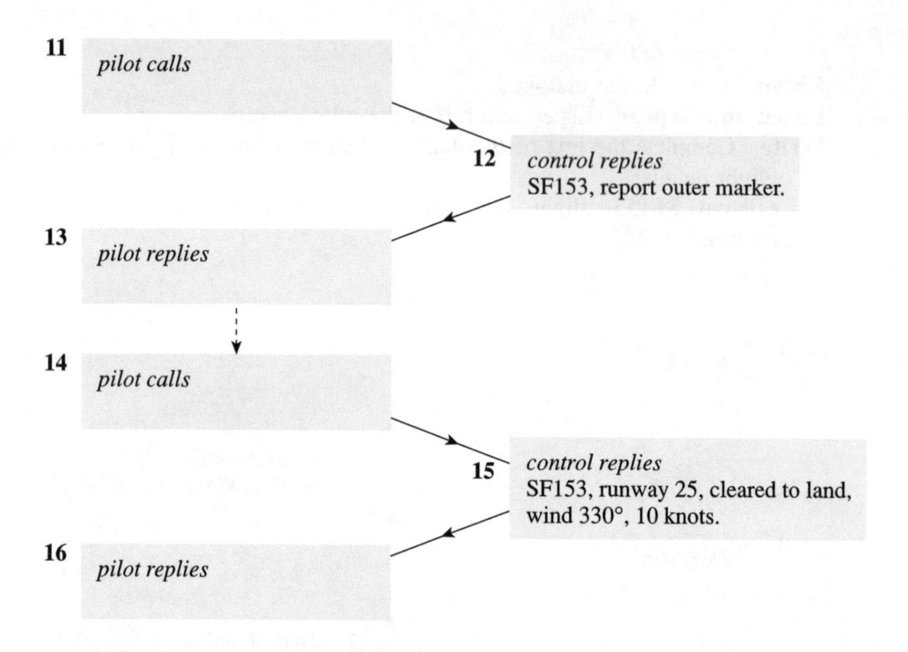
11
pilot calls
12
control replies
SF153, report outer marker.
13
pilot replies
14
pilot calls
15
control replies
SF153, runway 25, cleared to land, wind 330°, 10 knots.
16
pilot replies

Check Check your answers, page 171.

Listen and Speak Take the pilot's role in the following three recorded approach sequences. Use the flight details below.

	Callsign	Flight level	Estimated time at RED	ATIS
1	SF153	50	32	M
2	AG235	150 → 80	16	K
3	BI196	90	54	O

Check Check your answers, page 172.

4.3.2 Final approach and landing (non-routine)

Listen and Answer Listen to the dialogues and write down answers to these questions. There are two questions for each dialogue.

1(a) Why must Sunair go around?

. . . .

(b) What might cause problems on runway 12?

. . . .

2(a) Why can't Sunair 350 vacate the runway?

. . . .

(b) What do they ask the controller to do?

. . . .

3(a) Why must Sunair go around?

. . . .

(b) Why does the pilot decide to divert to Overby?

. . . .

Check Check your answers, page 173.

Listen and Write Listen to the dialogues again and complete the texts below.

1 PIL Winton Tower, Sunair 323, ____________ ____________, good morning.

CTL Sunair 323, good morning, you are ____________ ____________, report short final.

PIL Number 2 to land, Sunair 323.

(*pause*)

PIL Sunair 323, ____________.

CTL Sunair 323, the aircraft ____________ ____________ to ____________ the runway, go around.

PIL ____________, Sunair 323.

(*pause*)

PIL Approach, Sunair 323.

CTL Sunair 323, ____________ ____________, proceed to Redhill ____________ ____________, runway 25 is ________________ by a ________________ ____________.

PIL Roger, Sunair 323, ____________ to runway 12?

CTL Standby one, I'll call you back.

CTL Sunair 323, can you ________________ a ________________ of 18 knots ____________ to 25?

PIL Affirm, Sunair 323.

2 CTL Sunair 350, cleared to land, runway 25, wind 320° 12 knots.

PIL Cleared to land, runway 25, Sunair 350.

(*pause*)

PIL Winton Tower, Sunair 350, we ____________ ____________ and have at least 2 ____________ ____________. We are ____________ ____________, please advise ____________ and we request ____________ and buses to take the passengers ____________ ____________.

3 PIL Winton Tower, Sunair 697, ____________.

CTL Sunair 697, number 1 to land, ____________.

(*pause*)

CTL Sunair 697, go around, ____________, there's a ____________ ____________.

PIL ____________. Confirm the standard procedure, Sunair 697.

CTL Climb to 3000 ft ____________ ____________ and contact Approach on 121.3.

PIL Climbing to 3000 ft, and Approach on 121.3.

PIL Winton Approach, Sunair 697.

CTL Sunair 697, proceed to ____________ ____________ Redhill.

PIL ____________, we ____________ longer than five minutes, do you know ____________ ____________?

CTL Delay is ______ for the moment – there seems to be a problem with the ____________.

PIL Request ____________ to Overby, Sunair 697.

Check Check your answers, page 173.

Your word list

Write down any words in the dialogues you do not understand, or are not sure about. Try to guess the meaning, in English or in your own language, and write it down. Then check with a dictionary.

CHECK

4.3.1 **Write** (from page 167)

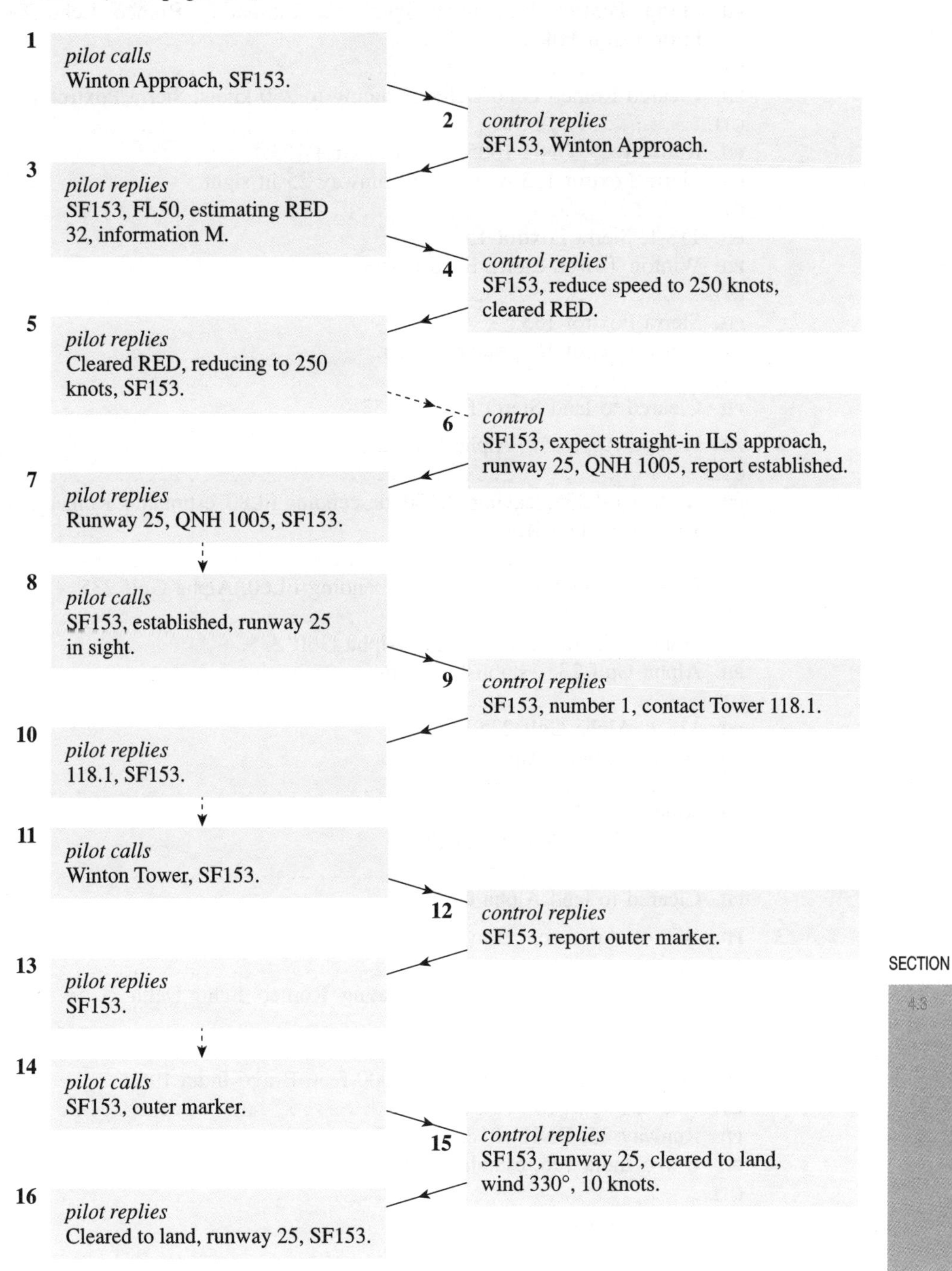

1
pilot calls
Winton Approach, SF153.
2
control replies
SF153, Winton Approach.
3
pilot replies
SF153, FL50, estimating RED 32, information M.
4
control replies
SF153, reduce speed to 250 knots, cleared RED.
5
pilot replies
Cleared RED, reducing to 250 knots, SF153.
6
control
SF153, expect straight-in ILS approach, runway 25, QNH 1005, report established.
7
pilot replies
Runway 25, QNH 1005, SF153.
8
pilot calls
SF153, established, runway 25 in sight.
9
control replies
SF153, number 1, contact Tower 118.1.
10
pilot replies
118.1, SF153.
11
pilot calls
Winton Tower, SF153.
12
control replies
SF153, report outer marker.
13
pilot replies
SF153.
14
pilot calls
SF153, outer marker.
15
control replies
SF153, runway 25, cleared to land, wind 330°, 10 knots.
16
pilot replies
Cleared to land, runway 25, SF153.

4.3.1 Listen and Speak (from page 168)

1 PIL Winton Approach, Sierra Foxtrot 153.

CTL . . . .

PIL Sierra Foxtrot 153, flight level 50, estimating Romeo Echo Delta 32, information Mike.

CTL . . . .

PIL Cleared Romeo Echo Delta, reducing to 250 knots, Sierra Foxtrot 153.

CTL . . . .

PIL Runway 25, QNH 1005, Sierra Foxtrot 153.

PIL Sierra Foxtrot 153 established, runway 25 in sight.

CTL . . . .

PIL 118.1, Sierra Foxtrot 153.

PIL Winton Tower, Sierra Foxtrot 153.

CTL . . . .

PIL Sierra Foxtrot 153.

PIL Sierra Foxtrot 153, outer marker.

CTL . . . .

PIL Cleared to land Sierra Foxtrot 153.

2 PIL Winton Approach, Alpha Golf 235.

CTL . . . .

PIL Alpha Golf 235, leaving FL150, descending FL80, estimating Romeo Echo Delta 16, information Kilo.

CTL . . . .

PIL Cleared Romeo Echo Delta, descending FL60, Alpha Golf 235.

CTL . . . .

PIL Squawking 4263, runway 25, Alpha Golf 235.

PIL Alpha Golf 235 established, runway 25 in sight.

CTL . . . .

PIL 118.1, Alpha Golf 235.

PIL Winton Tower, Alpha Golf 235.

CTL . . . .

PIL Alpha Golf 235.

PIL Alpha Golf 235, outer marker.

CTL . . . .

PIL Cleared to land Alpha Golf 235.

3 PIL Winton Approach, Bravo India 196.

CTL . . . .

PIL Bravo India 196, FL90, estimating Romeo Echo Delta at 54, information Oscar.

CTL . . . .

PIL Leaving FL90, descending to 4000 feet, Bravo India 196.

CTL . . . .

PIL Runway 25, QNH 1012, Bravo India 196.

PIL Bravo India 196, established ILS runway 07.

CTL . . . .

PIL 118.1, Bravo India 196.

PIL Winton Tower, Bravo India 196.

CTL . . . .

PIL Bravo India 196.
PIL Bravo India 196, outer marker.
CTL . . . .
PIL Cleared to land, Bravo India 196.

4.3.2 **Listen and Answer** (from page 168)

1(a) Why must Sunair go around?
The aircraft in front was unable to vacate the runway.
(b) What might cause problems on runway 12?
There is a strong crosswind.
2(a) Why can't Sunair 350 vacate the runway?
They aquaplaned and have at least 2 tyres blown out on main gear.
(b) What do they ask the controller to do?
Advise company maintenance and arrange for passenger steps and buses.
3(a) Why must Sunair go around?
The runway lights have failed.
(b) Why does the pilot decide to divert to Overby?
They are running short of fuel.

4.3.2 **Listen and Write** (from page 169)

1 PIL Winton Tower, Sunair 323, over outer marker, good morning.
CTL Sunair 323, good morning, you are number 2 for landing, report short final.
PIL Number 2 to land, Sunair 323.
(pause)
PIL Sunair 323, short final.
CTL Sunair 323, the aircraft in front of you is unable to vacate the runway, go around.
PIL Going around, Sunair 323.
(pause)
PIL Approach, Sunair 323.
CTL Sunair 323, climb to 4000 ft, proceed to Redhill holding pattern, runway 07 is blocked by a crashed aircraft.
PIL Roger, Sunair 323, may we proceed to runway 12?
CTL Standby one I'll call you back.
CTL Sunair 323, can you accept a crosswind of 18 knots gusting to 25?
PIL Affirm, Sunair 323.

2 CTL Sunair 350, cleared to land, runway 25, wind 320° 12 knots.
PIL Cleared to land, runway 25, Sunair 350.
(pause)
PIL Winton Tower, Sunair 350, we aquaplaned after touch-down and have at least 2 tyres blown out on right main gear. We are unable to vacate the runway, please advise company maintenance and we request passenger steps and buses to take the passengers to the terminal.

3 PIL Winton Tower, Sunair 697, long final.
CTL Sunair 697, number 1 to land, wind calm.
(pause)
CTL Sunair 697, go around, standard procedure, there's a runway lighting failure.
PIL Going around. Confirm the standard procedure, Sunair 697.
CTL Climb to 3000 ft on runway heading and contact Approach on 121.3.

PIL Climbing to 3000 ft, and Approach on 121.3.
PIL Winton Approach, Sunair 697.
CTL Sunair 697, proceed to holding area over Redhill.
PIL We're running low on fuel, we cannot hold longer than five minutes, do you know how long the delay will be?
CTL Delay is undetermined for the moment — there seems to be a problem with the generators.
PIL Request divert to Overby, Sunair 697.

4.4 AFTER LANDING

4.4.1 After landing (routine)

Key words and phrases

Check that you understand the following words and phrases. Look up any new words in an aviation dictionary.

vacated
inner/outer taxiway
turn-off

Typical exchange

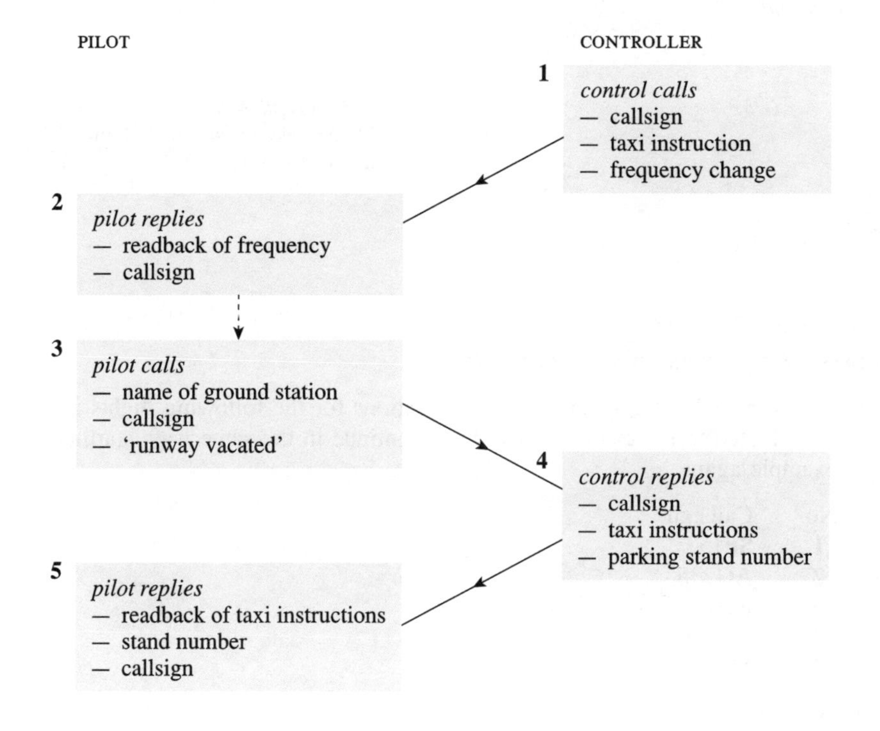

Phraseology practice

Listen Listen to the recorded dialogue.

Listen and Repeat Listen again and repeat the pilot's words.

Write Complete the text below by writing in the pilot's words. Check with the CD if necessary.

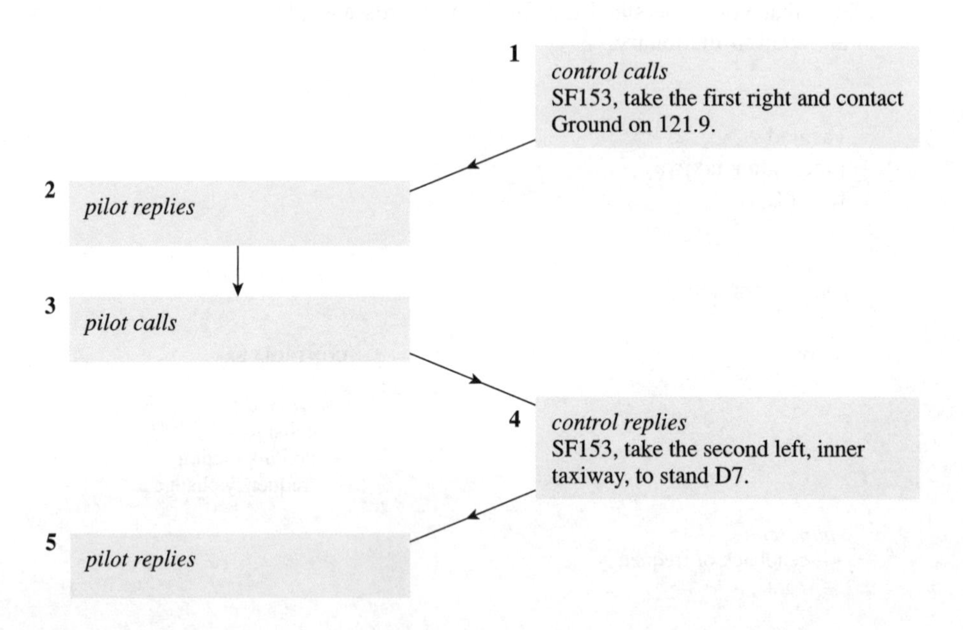

1
control calls
SF153, take the first right and contact Ground on 121.9.
2
pilot replies
3
pilot calls
4
control replies
SF153, take the second left, inner taxiway, to stand D7.
5
pilot replies

Check Check your answers, page 178.

Listen and Speak Reply to the taxi instructions for the following flights in a similar way. Listen to the example first. Then continue in the same way, starting with the example again.

No.	Callsign
1	SF153
2	AG235
3	BI196
4	NJ342
5	MO725

Check Check your answers, page 178.

4.4.2 After landing (non-routine)

Listen and Answer Listen to the dialogues and write down the answers to these questions.

1. Why does Sunair have to hold on the taxiway?

   . . . .

2. Why does Sunair need a tug?

   . . . .

Check Check your answers, page 179.

Listen and Write Listen to the dialogues again and complete the texts below.

1 CTL Sunair 229, take the ____________ ____________, then ____________ ____________.

PIL Sunair 229, ____________.

CTL Sunair 229, ____________, a 727 ____________ ____________ and is ____________ the taxiway. You'll have to wait ____________ ____________ beyond the next ____________.

PIL Roger, ____________ ____________, Sunair 229.

2 CTL Sunair 223, take the ____________ left and contact Ground on 121.7.

PIL 121.7, Sunair 223.

PIL Winton Ground, Sunair 223, good morning. We seem to have had ____________ ____________ on ____________. Request ____________ ____________.

CTL Roger, Sunair 223, can you ____________ ____________ 50 yards or so ____________ the next intersection?

PIL Affirm, I think we can ____________ that slowly.

CTL Thank you Sunair 223, we'll ____________ as soon as possible.

Check Check your answers, page 179.

Your word list

Write down any words in the dialogues you do not understand or are not sure about. Try to guess the meaning, in English or in your own language, and write it down. Then check with a dictionary.

CHECK

4.4.1 Write (from page 176)

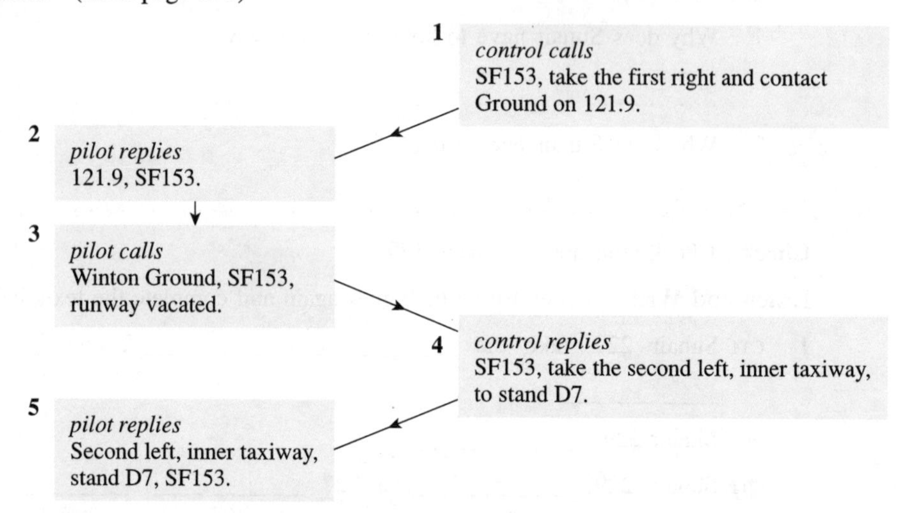

1
control calls
SF153, take the first right and contact Ground on 121.9.
2
pilot replies
121.9, SF153.
3
pilot calls
Winton Ground, SF153, runway vacated.
4
control replies
SF153, take the second left, inner taxiway, to stand D7.
5
pilot replies
Second left, inner taxiway, stand D7, SF153.

4.4.1 Listen and Speak (from page 176)

1 CTL . . . .
PIL 121.9, Sierra Foxtrot 153.
PIL Winton Ground, Sierra Foxtrot 153, runway vacated.
CTL . . . .
PIL Second left, inner taxiway, stand Delta 7, Sierra Foxtrot 153.

2 CTL . . . .
PIL 121.6, Alpha Golf 235.
PIL Winton Ground, Alpha Golf 235, runway vacated.
CTL . . . .
PIL Taxiway Bravo, stand Charlie 10, Alpha Golf 235.

3 CTL . . . .
PIL 121.8, Bravo India 196.
PIL Winton Ground, Bravo India 196, runway vacated.
CTL . . . .
PIL Turn right, outer taxiway, gate 39, Bravo India 196.

4 CTL . . . .
PIL 121.6, November Juliet 342.
PIL Winton Ground, November Juliet 342, runway vacated.
CTL . . . .
PIL Taxiway Bravo, stand 12, November Juliet 342.

5 CTL . . . .
PIL 121.6, Mike Oscar 725.
PIL Winton Ground, Mike Oscar 725, runway vacated.
CTL . . . .
PIL Straight ahead, first right, taxiway Bravo, stand 28, Mike Oscar 725.

4.4.2 **Listen and Answer** (from page 176)

1. Why does Sunair have to hold on the taxiway?
   A 727 has taken a wrong turning and is blocking the taxiway.
2. Why does Sunair need a tug?
   They have had a tyre blow out on the nose gear.

4.4.2 **Listen and Write** (from page 177)

1 CTL Sunair 229, take the first convenient turn-off, then turn right into taxiway Bravo.
PIL Sunair 229, runway vacated.
CTL Sunair 229, stop taxi, a 727 has taken a wrong turning and is blocking the taxiway. You'll have to wait until a tug pushes him back beyond the next intersection.
PIL Roger, holding, Sunair 229.

2 CTL Sunair 223, take the second left and contact Ground on 121.7.
PIL 121.7, Sunair 223.
PIL Winton Ground, Sunair 223, good morning. We seem to have had a nose gear tyre blow out on landing. Request a tug to tow us to the apron.
CTL Roger, Sunair 223, can you move forward under your own power, 50 yards or so until you're past the next intersection?
PIL Affirm, I think we can manage that, slowly.
CTL Thank you Sunair 223, we'll get a tug out to you as soon as possible.

4.5 REVIEW OF PART FOUR

4.5.1 Flight from Rexbury to Winton (approach and landing)

Listen and Read You are now in contact with Valley Control, cruising at FL270 and preparing for descent. You expect to change to Meadow Control soon. The next reporting point is RED (Redhill) VOR. For further details (Winton radio frequencies) turn to page 49.

Listen and Speak You are ready to begin your descent towards Winton. Listen to the recording, follow the instructions and reply to the controller. The recording begins with Winton ATIS.

Check Check your answers, page 182.

4.5.2 Flight from Dublin to Paris (descent and landing)

Listen and Read Flight plan details:

Callsign SF309. (Note that for historical reasons the callsign letters Sierra Foxtrot are sometimes pronounced as Safa.)

Listen and Speak Take the pilot's part. Follow the instructions and reply to the controller. SF309 is cruising at FL310 and preparing for descent. The recording begins with Paris Orly Arrival ATIS.

Check Check your answers, page 182.

Descent and Aborted Approach [illegible]

[illegible] Jubs [illegible] Winton information [illegible] Kenway [illegible] landing 25, for take-off 20, transition level [illegible], surface wind [illegible] visibility [illegible] metres, temperature [illegible] dew point [illegible]. On initial contact report information [illegible] received.

[illegible] Sultan 367, ready for descent.

[illegible]

[illegible] Descending FL [illegible] Meadow Control [illegible] affective.

[illegible] Meadow Control, Sultan 367, good afternoon.

[illegible] Descending FL 120, [illegible], Sultan 367.

[illegible] Winton Approach on 12[illegible], Sultan 367, goodbye.

[illegible] Winton Approach, Sultan 367, good afternoon.

[illegible] expecting [illegible] Runway 25, Sultan 367.

[illegible] Sultan 367, reaching FL 70, descending to [illegible].

[illegible] Winton Approach [illegible], Sultan 367, [illegible].

[illegible]

[illegible] Descending to [illegible] ft QNH [illegible] right [illegible] landing [illegible] Sultan 367.

[illegible] Descending to [illegible] ft [illegible] Sultan 367.

[illegible] Sultan 367 [illegible].

[illegible] Sultan 367 [illegible].

[illegible] Tower, Sultan 367, good afternoon.

[illegible] number [illegible] to land, Sultan 367.

[illegible] Sultan 367 [illegible].

[illegible]

[illegible] Sultan 367, [illegible].

CHECK

4.5.1 Listen and Speak (from page 180)

ATIS This is Winton information Lima recorded at 15.30 Zulu time. Runway for landing 25, for take-off 30, transition level 50, surface wind 280° 10 knots visibility 8000 metres, temperature 12, dew point 11, QNH 1020. On initial contact report information Lima received.

PIL Sunair 367, ready for descent.

CTL . . . .

PIL Descending FL190, Meadow Control 128.5, goodbye.

PIL Meadow Control, Sunair 367, good afternoon.

CTL . . . .

PIL Descending FL120, RED direct, Sunair 367.

CTL . . . .

PIL Winton Approach on 121.3, Sunair 367, goodbye.

PIL Winton Approach, Sunair 367, good afternoon.

CTL . . . .

PIL To intercept the Redhill VOR 070 radial and descending to FL60, expecting ILS approach runway 25, Sunair 367.

PIL Sunair 367, reaching FL70, descending to 60.

CTL . . . .

PIL Winton Radar on 121.1, Sunair 367, goodbye.

PIL Winton Radar, Sunair 367, good afternoon.

CTL . . . .

PIL Descending to 3000 ft, QNH 1020, turning right heading 160, Sunair 367.

CTL . . . .

PIL Descending to 2000 ft, turning right heading 230, Sunair 367.

PIL Sunair 367, established on the glide slope.

CTL . . . .

PIL Tower 118.1, Sunair 367, goodbye.

PIL Tower, Sunair 367, good afternoon.

CTL . . . .

PIL Number 2 to land, Sunair 367.

PIL Sunair 367, outer marker.

CTL . . . .

PIL Cleared to land, runway 25, Sunair 367.

PIL Sunair 367, runway vacated.

CTL . . . .

PIL 121.7, Sunair 367, goodbye.

PIL Ground, Sunair 367, good afternoon.

CTL . . . .

PIL Second left, inner taxiway, stand D7, Sunair 367.

4.5.2 Listen and Speak (from page 180)

ATIS landing runway 26, take-off runway 25, attention taxiway 2A closed, attention bird situation, surface wind 242° 13 knots, visibility 10 kms, temperature +10, dew point +8, QNH 1017 mb QFE 1006 mb, transition level 40, CDG is facing West, confirm information India received on initial contact.

PIL Paris, SF309, ready to descend.

CTL . . . .

PIL 124.05, SF309, goodbye.

PIL Paris, SF309, bonjour.

CTL . . . .

PIL Descending to FL240 initially, SF309.

CTL . . . .

PIL Descending to FL110, SF309.

CTL . . . .

PIL Descending to FL80, SF309.

CTL . . . .

PIL Turning left to Reymy, SF309.

PIL Reaching FL80, SF309.

CTL . . . .

PIL Orly Approach 120.85, SF309, goodbye.

PIL Orly Approach, SF309, good afternoon.

CTL . . . .

PIL Squawking 4244, SF309.

PIL SF309, reaching Reymy.

CTL . . . .

PIL TSU, radial 075, runway 26, SF309.

CTL . . . .

PIL 300, SF309.

CTL . . . .

CTL . . . .

PIL Reducing to 250 knots, descending to 4000 ft, QNH1017, SF309.

PIL SF309, reaching 4000 ft.

CTL . . . .

PIL Descending to 3000 ft, SF309.

CTL . . . .

PIL Heading 170, SF309.

CTL . . . .

PIL Turning right heading 230, cleared ILS 26, SF309.

CTL . . . .

PIL 180 knots till OYE, change 118.7, SF309, goodbye.

PIL Orly, SF309, bonjour.

CTL . . . .

PIL Roger.

CTL . . . .

PIL Negative, 180 knots, SF309.

PIL SF309, over outer marker.

CTL ....

PIL Cleared to land, SF309.

CTL ....

PIL First right, Ground 121.7, SF309.

PIL Ground, SF309, runway vacated.

CTL ....

PIL Delta 8, SF309.

4.6 SUPPLEMENTARY VOCABULARY

Aviation jobs

Read and Write Here is a table with the names of *jobs* in aviation, followed by a list of *definitions* of the jobs. Match the jobs with the definitions, and write the definitions in the table.

Jobs	Definitions
co-ordinator	
ticket sales clerk	
controller	
station manager	
flight engineer	
purser	
captain	
reservations clerk	
customs officer	
shuttle bus driver	
marshaller	
flight attendant	
baggage handler	

DEFINITIONS

a person who works in the cabin
the third crew member in the cockpit
this person helps the pilot to park the plane
the person in the left-hand seat in the cockpit
the boss of the ground staff
the person in charge of the bus from the plane to the terminal
someone who loads and unloads the luggage
this person may work in the Tower
the person who can inspect passengers' luggage
the person who sells tickets
the person who works mainly on computer and the telephone
the first person to come on board when a flight arrives
the chief of the cabin crew

Check Check your answers, page 186.

CHECK

4.6 Read and Write (from page 185)

Jobs	Definitions
co-ordinator	the first person to come on board when a flight arrives
ticket sales clerk	the person who sells tickets
controller	this person may work in the Tower
station manager	the boss of the ground staff
flight engineer	the third crew member in the cockpit
purser	the chief of the cabin crew
captain	the person in the left-hand seat in the cockpit
reservations clerk	the person who works mainly on computer and the telephone
customs officer	the person who can inspect passengers' luggage
shuttle bus driver	the person in charge of the bus from the plane to the terminal
marshaller	this person helps the pilot to park the plane
flight attendant	a person who works in the cabin
baggage handler	someone who loads and unloads the luggage

Part Five

Final review

5.1 REXBURY TO WINTON (COMPLETE FLIGHT)

Scenario

Read

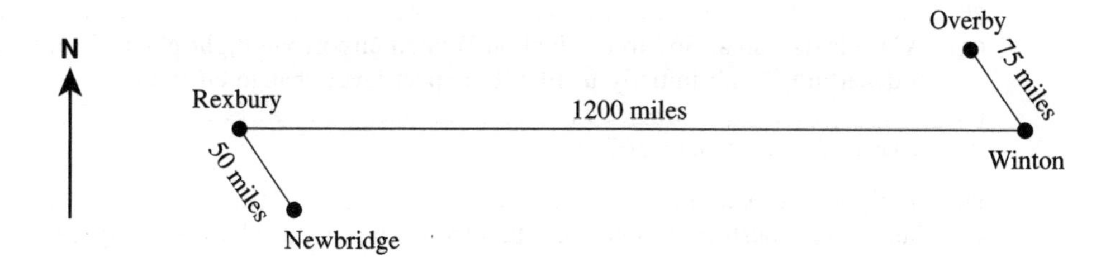

Winton is 1200 nautical miles East of Rexbury. The alternate for Winton is Overby, 75 nautical miles North West of Winton. Newbridge Airport is 50 miles South East of Rexbury.

Rexbury Airport
Runway: 29
Taxiways: Yankee, Delta
SID's: November 2, Romeo I, Golf 5
Tower frequency: 118.300
Approach frequency: 120.200
Rexbury Area Control: 128.900

Winton Airport
Runways: 07, 12, 25, 30
Taxiways: Inner/Outer
Tower frequency: 118.100
Winton Radar frequency: 121.100
Approach frequency: 121.300
Ground frequency: 121.700
VOR—RED (Redhill)

En route
New County Upper Control: 135.900
Valley Control: 128.500
Meadow Control: 126.300

Reporting points
RIV (River)
BCK (Blackrock)
LAK (Lake)
RED (Redhill)

Listen and Read You are flying from Rexbury to Winton. Your callsign is Sunair 367, your stand is 19. The time is 13.40. The recording begins with ATIS information, and then asks you to make initial contact with Rexbury Ground.

Listen and Speak Follow the instructions on the CD, and reply to the controller. If necessary, you can read the controller's part included below. But then try to reply *without* reading the controller's part.

Check Check your answers, page 193.

Audioscript of recorded simulation (controller's part only). The dotted lines (. . .) show where the pilot (you) should speak.

ATIS (*twice*): This is Rexbury departure information Foxtrot at 13.30 Zulu time. Take-off and landing runway 29, wind 260° 12 knots, CAVOK, temperature 14, dew point 11, QNH 1023, no sig. This was information Foxtrot.

PIL (*call Rexbury Ground*). . . . .

CTL Good afternoon, Sunair 367, go ahead.

PIL (*ask for start-up*) . . . .
CTL Say again stand number, Sunair 367.
PIL . . . .
CTL Sunair 367, start-up approved.
PIL . . . .

CTL Sunair 367, here is your ATC clearance.
PIL . . . .
CTL ATC clears Sunair 367 to destination Winton airport via flight planned route, Golf 5 departure, climb initially to FL110, expect level change en route.
PIL . . . .
CTL That is correct, Sunair 367.

PIL (*call for push-back*) . . . .
CTL Sunair 367, push-back approved, taxi to holding point 29 via taxiway Delta.
PIL . . . .

CTL Sunair 367, contact Tower now on 118.3.
PIL . . . .

PIL (*call reaching holding point*) . . . .
CTL Sunair 367, report the 727 on final in sight.
PIL . . . .
CTL Behind the landing 727, line up behind.
PIL . . . .
PIL (*call ready for departure*) . . . .
CTL Sunair 367, runway 29, cleared for take-off, wind 255° 13 knots.
PIL . . . .

CTL Sunair 367, airborne 04, climb on present heading to FL110, contact Rexbury Control on 128.8.
PIL . . . .

PIL . . . .
CTL Sunair 367, Rexbury Control, good afternoon. Turn right now heading 050 and continue climb to FL220.
PIL . . . .

CTL Sunair 367, proceed now to Romeo India Victor VOR and recleared to FL270, cruising level.
PIL . . . .
PIL (*ask if you can have FL330*) . . . .
CTL Standby Sunair, I'll call you back.

CTL Sunair 367, can you accept FL370?
PIL (*you can't*) . . . .
CTL Sunair 367, climb to FL270, report when reaching.
PIL . . . .

PIL (*call at FL270*) . . . .
CTL Roger, Sunair 367, change now to New County Upper Control, frequency 135.9, goodbye.
PIL . . . .

PIL (*call New County Upper Control*) . . . .
CTL Good afternoon, Sunair 367, continue to Blackrock, report when reaching.

PIL . . . .

(*you now tune in to Winton Volmet*)

VOLMET This is Winton Volmet. This is Winton Volmet.

Winton airport at 14.30. 280° 10 knots, 8000 metres, temperature 12, dew point 11, QNH 1020, no sig.

Overby at 14.30. 240° 12 knots, 10 kms or more, temperature 8, dew point 6, QNH 1020, no sig.

Newbridge at 14.30. 250° 4 knots, 3000 metres, mist, temperature 6, dew point 4, QNH 1016, no sig.

CTL Sunair 367, unknown traffic 10 o'clock, 8 miles, moving from left to right.
PIL (*you see the traffic, reply*). . . . .
CTL Roger.

CTL Sunair 367, contact Valley Control now on 128.5, goodbye.
PIL . . . .
PIL (*call Valley Control*) . . . .
CTL Sunair 367, good afternoon, continue to Blackrock, report reaching.
PIL . . . .

PIL (*call over Blackrock*) . . . .
CTL Roger, Sunair 367, proceed to Lima Alpha Kilo direct.
PIL . . . .

PIL (*you want to turn 30° right to avoid build-up*). . . . .
CTL Roger, Sunair 367, what is your present heading?
PIL (*025°, reply*). . . . .
CTL Sunair 367, turn right heading 050° for 15 miles, report back on track.

PIL (*you have passed the build-up*) . . . .
CTL Roger, Sunair 367, resume own navigation to Lake.
PIL . . . .

PIL (*call over LAK*). . . . .
CTL Sunair 367, proceed to Romeo Echo Delta, call me back when ready for descent.
PIL . . . .

(*you now tune in to Winton ATIS*)
ATIS (*twice*) This is Winton information Lima recorded at 15.30 Zulu time. Runway for landing 25 for take-off 30, transition level 50, surface wind 280° 10 knots, visibility 8000 metres, temperature 12, dew point 11, QNH 1020. On initial contact report information Lima received.

PIL (*ask for descent*) . . . .
CTL Sunair 367, descend to FL190 and contact Meadow Control on 128.5, goodbye.
PIL . . . .

PIL (*call Meadow Control*) . . . .

CTL Good afternoon, Sunair 367, radar contact, descend to FL120 Romeo Echo Delta VOR direct.

PIL . . . .

CTL Sunair 367, you are approaching Romeo Echo Delta, contact Winton Approach now on 121.3, goodbye.

PIL . . . .

PIL *(call Winton Approach)* . . . .

CTL Good afternoon, Sunair 367, radar identified, passing Romeo Echo Delta VOR. Intercept radial 070 Romeo Echo Delta VOR and descend to flight level 60, expect radar vectoring to ILS runway 25, report crossing 70.

PIL . . . .

PIL *(call reaching 70)* . . . .

CTL Sunair 367, contact Winton Radar on 121.1, goodbye.

PIL . . . .

PIL *(call Winton Radar)* . . . .

CTL Good afternoon, 367, radar contact, descend to 3000 ft, QNH 1020. Take heading 160.

PIL . . . .

CTL Sunair 367, continue descent to 2000 ft, turn right heading 230, cleared for ILS approach runway 25, report established.

PIL . . . .

PIL *(call established)* . . . .

CTL Sunair 367, contact Tower on 118.1, goodbye.

PIL . . . .

PIL *(call Tower)* . . . .

CTL Good afternoon, Sunair 367, number 2 to land, number 1 at touch down, report over outer marker.

PIL . . . .

PIL *(call at outer marker)* . . . .

CTL Sunair 367, clear to land runway 25, wind 260° 08 knots.

PIL . . . .

PIL *(call runway vacated)* . . . .

CTL Roger, Sunair 367, contact Ground on 121.7.

PIL . . . .

PIL *(call Ground)* . . . .

CTL Sunair 367, good afternoon, take the second left onto the inner taxiway, stand Delta 7.

PIL . . . .

CHECK

5.1 **Listen and Read** (from page 189)

ATIS This is Rexbury departure information Foxtrot at 13.30 Zulu time. Take-off and landing runway 29, wind 260° 12 knots, CAVOK, temperature 14, dew point 11, QNH 1023, no sig. This was information Foxtrot.

PIL Rexbury Ground, Sunair 367, good afternoon.

CTL ....

PIL Sunair 367, stand 19, information Foxtrot received, request start-up.

CTL ....

PIL Stand 19, Sunair 367.

CTL ....

PIL Starting up, Sunair 367.

CTL ....

PIL Ready to copy.

CTL ....

PIL Sunair 367 is cleared to Winton via flight planned route, Golf 5 departure, climb to FL110 initially, level change en route.

CTL ....

PIL Sunair 367, request push-back

CTL ....

PIL Holding point 29, taxiway D, Sunair 367.

CTL ....

PIL Tower on 118.3, goodbye.

PIL Rexbury Tower, Sunair 367, good afternoon, reaching holding point 29.

CTL ....

PIL Sunair 367, 727 in sight.

CTL ....

PIL Behind the landing 727 line up, Sunair 367.

PIL Ready for departure, runway 29, Sunair 367.

CTL ....

PIL Cleared for take-off, runway 29, Sunair 367.

CTL ....

PIL Climbing to FL110, Rexbury Control on 128.8, Sunair 367, goodbye.

PIL Rexbury Control, Sunair 367, good afternoon.

CTL ....

PIL Right turn, heading 050, climbing to FL220, Sunair 367.

CTL ....

PIL Climbing to FL270, direct to Romeo India Victor VOR, Sunair 367.

PIL Sunair 367, is FL330 available?

CTL ....

CTL ....

PIL Negative, Sunair 367.

CTL ....

PIL Climbing to FL270, Sunair 367.

PIL Sunair 367, reaching FL270.

CTL ....

PIL 135.9, Sunair 367, goodbye.

PIL New County Upper Control, Sunair 367, good afternoon.

CTL ....

PIL Continue to Blackrock, report reaching, Sunair 367.

VOLMET This is Winton Volmet. This is Winton Volmet.

Winton airport at 14.30, 280° 12 knots, 8000 metres, temperature 12, dew point 11, QNH 1020, no sig.

Overby at 14.30, 240° 12 knots, 10 kms or more, temperature 8, dew point 6, QNH 1020, no sig.

Newbridge at 14.30, 250° 4 knots, 3000 metres, mist, temperature 6, dew point 4, QNH 1016, no sig.

CTL ....

PIL Roger, traffic in sight, Sunair 367.

CTL ....

CTL ....

PIL 128.5, Sunair 367, goodbye.

PIL Valley Control, Sunair 367, good afternoon. Estimating BCK at 48.

CTL ....

PIL Roger, continue to Blackrock.

PIL Sunair 367, over Blackrock this time, estimating LAK at 15.

CTL ....

PIL Roger.

PIL Sunair 367, request turn right 30° to avoid build-up.

CTL ....

PIL 025°, Sunair 367.

CTL ....

PIL Turning right, heading 050, Sunair 367.

PIL Sunair 367, we have passed the build-up, are now back on track.

CTL ....

PIL Proceeding to Lake, Sunair 367.

PIL Over LAK this time, Sunair 367.

CTL ....

PIL To RED, Sunair 367.

ATIS This is Winton information Lima recorded at 15.30 Zulu time. Runway for landing 25 for take-off 30, transition level 50, surface wind 280° 10 knots, visibility 8000 metres, temperature 12, dew point 11, QNH 1020. On initial contact report information Lima received.

PIL Sunair 367, ready for descent.

CTL ....

PIL Descending FL190, Meadow Control 128.5, goodbye.

PIL Meadow Control, Sunair 367, good afternoon.

CTL ....

PIL Descending FL120, RED direct, Sunair 367.

CTL ....

PIL Winton Approach on 121.3, Sunair 367, goodbye.

PIL Winton Approach, Sunair 367, good afternoon.

CTL ....

PIL To intercept the Redhill VOR 070 radial and descending to FL60, expecting ILS approach runway 25, Sunair 367.

PIL Sunair 367, reaching FL70, descending to 60.

CTL ....

PIL Winton Radar on 121.1, Sunair 367, goodbye.

PIL Winton Radar, Sunair 367, good afternoon.

CTL ....

PIL Descending to 3000 ft, QNH 1020, turning right heading 160, Sunair 367.

CTL ....

PIL Descending to 2000 ft, turning right heading 230, Sunair 367.

PIL Sunair 367, established on the glide slope.

CTL ....

PIL Tower 118.1, Sunair 367, goodbye.

PIL Tower, Sunair 367, good afternoon.

CTL ....

PIL Number 2 to land, Sunair 367.

PIL Sunair 367, outer marker.

CTL ....

PIL Cleared to land, runway 25, Sunair 367.

PIL Sunair 367, runway vacated.

CTL ....

PIL 121.7, Sunair 367, goodbye.

PIL Ground, Sunair 367, good afternoon.

CTL ....

PIL Second left, inner taxiway, stand D7, Sunair 367.

5.2 DUBLIN TO PARIS (COMPLETE FLIGHT)

Read Before you start this simulation, study the following details carefully.

Dublin airport: runways 11, 17, 23
Tower frequency 118.6

Route to Paris and reporting points:
Liffy
Wallasey (WAL)
Telba
Midhurst (MID)
Sitet
Etrat
Reymy
Toussus
Orly (OYE)

Frequencies en route

Dublin Control	128.0	France Control	132.0
London Control	128.05	Paris Control	124.05
London Control	133.7	Orly Approach	120.85
London Control	127.7	Orly Tower	118.7

(NOTE: The recording is based on pre-2005 frequencies.)

Orly airport: runway 26,
Ground frequency 121.7

Listen and Read You are flying from Dublin to Paris. Your callsign is SF309. Note that the callsign letters Sierra Foxtrot are often abbreviated to Sierra Fox, and are sometimes pronounced as Safa. The recording begins by asking you to make initial contact with Dublin Ground.

Listen and Speak Follow the instructions on the CD, and reply to the controller. If necessary, you can read the controller's part below. But then try to reply *without* reading the controller's part.

Check Check your answers, page 200.

Audioscript of Dublin–Paris simulation (controller's part only). The dotted lines (. . .) show where the pilot (you) should speak.

PIL (*call Ground*) . . . .
CTL SF309, Ground, good morning.
PIL (*ready to start-up in 20 minutes*) . . . .
CTL Yes, that is OK, no restrictions into Orly.
PIL (*ask for departure runway*) . . . .
CTL Runway 17, surface wind 110° 20 knots.
PIL . . . .
CTL 309, Ground, your ATC clearance.
PIL . . . .
CTL SF309, cleared Dublin to Paris, Orly via Liffy Blue 1, flight planned route, FL230, to request level change.
PIL . . . .

CTL ... request level change is correct, cleared enter backtrack runway 11, contact Dublin Tower frequency 118.6, good morning.

PIL ....

PIL *(call Tower)* ....

CTL Roger, 309, backtrack 11, expedite the taxi please and cleared to line up and hold runway 17.

PIL ....

CTL That's it 309.

PIL *(call ready to depart)* ....

CTL Roger, 309 is clear to take-off runway 17. It's a left turn-out direct for Liffy, wind is 100° 20 knots.

PIL ....

CTL That is correct.

CTL 309 airborne, time 23, contact Dublin Control 128.0.

PIL ....

PIL *(call Dublin)* ....

CTL SF309, direct Liffy climb FL230.

PIL ....

CTL SF309, report FL.

PIL *(level 100)* ....

CTL SF309, continue climb to 230, call London 128.05.

PIL ....

PIL *(call London)* ....

CTL SF309, squawk 5260, maintain 230 on reaching.

PIL ....

CTL SF309, climb to FL290.

PIL ....

CTL SF309, climb to FL330.

PIL ....

CTL SF309, what is your heading?

PIL *(100)* ....

CTL SF309, roger, turn right heading 125.

PIL ....

PIL *(call FL330)* ....

CTL SF309, resume own navigation to Honiley.

PIL ....

CTL SF309, correction the last message. You can set course direct to Midhurst.

PIL ....

CTL SF309, contact London 133.7, good day.

PIL ....

PIL *(call London)* ....

CTL SF309, good day, maintain FL330, present position direct Midhurst.

PIL . . . .
CTL SF309, contact London now 127.7.
PIL . . . .

PIL *(call London)* . . . .
CTL SF309, good afternoon, maintain FL330.
PIL . . . .

CTL SF309.
PIL . . . .
CTL SF309, descend to FL310.
PIL . . . .

CTL SF309, continue now with Paris 132.0.
PIL . . . .

PIL *(call Paris)*. . . . .
CTL SF309, bonjour, maintain FL310 standard routing, Reymy clearance limit, runway 26 at Orly, squawk 0444.
PIL . . . .
(be ready to copy Orly ATIS)

ATIS . . . landing runway 26, take-off runway 25, attention taxiway 2A closed, attention bird situation, surface wind 242° 13 knots, visibility 10 kms, temperature +10, dew point +8, QNH 1017 mb, QFE 1006 mb, transition level 40, Charles de Gaulle is facing West.* Confirm information I received on initial contact.

PIL *(call and ask for descent)* . . . .
CTL SF309, cleared FL 250, contact Paris 124.05, goodbye.
PIL . . . .

PIL *(call Paris)* . . . .
CTL SF309, good evening, clearance FL240 initially, I'll call you back.
PIL . . . .

CTL SF309, recleared down FL110.
PIL . . . .

CTL SF309, recleared down FL80 now.
PIL . . . .

CTL SF309, you turn left to Reymy now.
PIL . . . .

PIL *(call reaching FL80)*
CTL SF309, roger, call Orly Approach now 120.85, goodbye sir.
PIL . . . .

---

* Charles de Gaulle is facing West means that aircraft are taking off from Charles de Gaulle towards the West. There are two large international airports in the Paris region, Paris Orly and Paris Charles de Gaulle and the direction in which a/c take off at one airport affects which SID's (Standard Instrument Departure) may be used at the other.

PIL (*call Orly*)
CTL Good afternoon, 309, your squawk on 4244.
PIL . . . .

PIL (*call reaching Reymy*)
CTL SF309, radar contact, cross to TSU now radar vectoring runway 26 after Toussus radial 075.
PIL . . . .

CTL SF309, what's your speed?
PIL (*300*) . . . .
CTL Roger.

CTL SF309, reduce 250 knots and after descend 4000 ft, QNH 1017.
PIL . . . .

PIL (*call reaching 4000 ft*) . . . .
CTL Roger, descend 3000 ft.

CTL SF309, heading 170.
PIL . . . .

CTL SF309, turn right heading 230 cleared ILS 26.
PIL . . . .

CTL SF309, maintain 180 knots minimum till OYE, call Airport 118.7, bye.
PIL . . . .

PIL (*call Orly*) . . . .
CTL SF309, bonjour, report passing outer marker runway 26.
PIL . . . .

CTL SF309, 160 knots?
PIL (*your speed is 180 knots, reply*) . . . .
CTL OK.

PIL (*call over outer marker*) . . . .
CTL SF309, clear to land, wind 240° 12 knots.
PIL . . . .

CTL SF309, first right and call Ground 121.7.
PIL . . . .

PIL (*call Ground, runway vacated*) . . . .
CTL SF309, bonjour, taxi for D8.
PIL . . . .

CHECK

5.2 **Listen and Speak** from page 196

PIL Dublin Ground, SF309.

CTL ....

PIL We'll be ready to start-up in 20 minutes.

CTL ....

PIL SF309, what is the departure runway?

CTL ....

PIL 17, 110° 20 knots.

CTL ....

PIL Ready to copy, SF309.

CTL ....

PIL SF309 is cleared to Paris, Orly via Liffy Blue 1, flight planned route, FL230, to request level change en route.

CTL ....

PIL Backtrack runway 11, Tower 118.6, SF309.

PIL Tower, SF309, good afternoon.

CTL ....

PIL Backtrack 11, expediting, approved to line up and wait runway 17.

CTL ....

PIL SF309, ready to depart.

CTL ....

PIL Cleared to take-off runway 17, left turn-out direct Liffy, 100° 20 knots.

CTL ....

CTL ....

PIL Dublin 128.0, SF309, goodbye.

PIL Dublin, SF309, good afternoon.

CTL ....

PIL Direct Liffy, climbing FL230, SF309.

CTL ....

PIL FL100, SF309.

CTL ....

PIL Climbing to FL230, London 128.05, SF309.

PIL London, SF309, good afternoon.

CTL ....

PIL Maintain 230 on reaching, squawking 5260.

CTL ....

PIL Climbing to FL290, SF309.

CTL ....

PIL Climbing to FL330, SF309.

CTL ....

PIL Heading 100, SF309.

CTL ....

PIL Turning right, heading 125.

PIL SF309, reaching FL330.

CTL ....

PIL Own navigation to Honiley, SF309.

CTL ....

PIL Direct to Midhurst, SF309.

CTL ....

PIL London 133.7, SF309, good day.

PIL London, SF309, good afternoon.

CTL ....

PIL Maintaining FL330, direct Midhurst, SF309.

CTL ....

PIL London 127.7, SF309.

PIL London, SF309, good afternoon.

CTL ....

PIL Maintaining FL330, SF309.

CTL ....

PIL Go ahead, SF309.

CTL ....

PIL Descending to FL310.

CTL ....

PIL Paris 132.0.

PIL Paris, SF309, Paris, good afternoon.

CTL ....

PIL Maintaining FL310, cleared to Reymy, squawking 0444.

ATIS ....

PIL Paris, SF309, ready to descend.

CTL ....

PIL 124.05, SF309, goodbye.

PIL Paris, SF309, bonjour.

CTL ....

PIL Descending to FL240 initially, SF309.

CTL ....

PIL Descending to FL110, SF309.

CTL ....

PIL Descending to FL80, SF309.

CTL ....

PIL Turning left to Reymy, SF309.

PIL Reaching FL80, SF309.

CTL ....

PIL Orly Approach 120.85, SF309, goodbye.

PIL Orly Approach, SF309, good afternoon.

CTL ....
PIL Squawking 4244, SF309.

PIL SF309, reaching Reymy.
CTL ....
PIL TSU, radial 075, runway 26, SF309.
CTL ....
PIL 300, SF309.
CTL ....

CTL ....
PIL Reducing to 250 knots, descending to 4000 ft, QNH1017, SF309.

PIL SF309, reaching 4000 ft.
CTL ....
PIL Descending to 3000 ft, SF309.

CTL ....
PIL Heading 170, SF309.

CTL ....
PIL Turning right heading 230, cleared ILS 26, SF309.
CTL ....
PIL 180 knots till OYE, change 118.7, SF309, goodbye.

PIL Orly, SF309, bonjour.
CTL ....
PIL Roger.

CTL ....
PIL 160 knots, SF309.

PIL SF309, over outer marker.
CTL ....
PIL Cleared to land, SF309.

CTL ....
PIL First right, Ground 121.7, SF309.

PIL Ground, SF309, runway vacated.
CTL ....
PIL Delta 8, SF309.

Audioscript for controller's part and for non-dialogue tasks

The controller's words will not normally be read by the student. However, it may occasionally be useful for students to see the controller's words, for example in pairwork practice. There may also be occasions when the teacher wishes to read out the controller's words to students.

To avoid duplication, reference is made to the CHECK Sections, in cases where the controller's words can be found there.

1.1.1 *(page 4)*
Listen
Listen and Repeat
Write
See CHECK section (*page 7*)

1.1.1 *(page 4)*
Listen and Speak

1 PIL *(ask for departure information)* . . . .
CTL SF398, runway in use 29, wind 350° 23 knots gusting 30, temperature 12, dew point 10, runway is wet, braking action good, QNH1023.
PIL . . . .

2 PIL *(ask for departure information)* . . . .
CTL Kilo Mike 563, 60° 18 knots, temperature –2, dew point –6, QNH 1008, take-off runway 08.
PIL . . . .

3 PIL *(ask for departure information)* . . . .
CTL Sierra Victor 295, QNH 1014, temperature 23, dew point 21, surface wind 180° 9 knots, take-off runway 23.
PIL . . . .

4 PIL *(ask for departure information)* . . . .
CTL Charlie Uniform 759, latest take-off data — wind calm, temperature 18, dew point 16, runway in use 33R, QNH 1015, taxiway India closed.
PIL . . . .

5 PIL *(ask for departure information)* . . . .
CTL Juliet Delta, runway in use 19 Left, 260° 10 knots gusting to 25, QNH 1005, temperature 8, dew point 5.
PIL . . . .

6 PIL *(ask for departure information)* . . . .
CTL Echo November 926, runway in use 21, wind 320° 5 knots, temperature +2, dew point minus 1, QNH 1019.
PIL . . . .

1.1.2 *(page 5)*
Write (Exercises 1 and 2)
See CHECK Section (*pages 7–9*)

1.2 *(page 11)*
Listen
Listen and Repeat
Write
See CHECK Section (*page 12*)

1.2 *(page 11)*
Listen and Speak

1 CTL SF196, here is your clearance.
PIL . . . .
CTL Rexbury ATC clears SF196 to Winton via flight planned route, N2 departure, left turnout after departure, climb to and maintain FL250, request level change en route, contact 120.2 when airborne, and squawk 2514.
PIL . . . .

2 CTL Sunair 926, here is your clearance.
PIL . . . .
CTL Frankfurt ATC clears Sunair 926 to Paris Charles de Gaulle, via Upper Red 10, Standard Instrument Departure 31, climb to and maintain FL290, contact Approach on 120.1 when airborne.
PIL . . . .

3 CTL Sunair 831, here is your clearance.
PIL . . . .
CTL Rexbury ATC clears Sunair 831 to Winton via flight planned route, Romeo 1 departure, left turn-out after departure, FL210 initially, request level change en route, contact Approach on frequency 120.2 when airborne.
PIL . . . .

4 CTL Sunair 435, clearance.
PIL . . . .
CTL Winton ATC clears Sunair 435 to Rexbury, Oscar 3 departure, climb on runway heading to FL160, squawk 1537, contact 121.3 when airborne.
PIL . . . .

5 CTL Sunair 921, here is your clearance.
PIL . . . .
CTL Winton ATC clears Sunair 921 to Rexbury, Whisky 1 departure, flight planned route, FL180 initially, request level change en route, squawk 1525, frequency 121.3 when airborne.
PIL . . . .

1.3.1 *(page 15)*
Listen
Write

1 PIL Winton Ground, SF153, good morning.

CTL Go ahead, Sierra Fox 153.
PIL Sierra Fox 153, stand Bravo 5, information Juliet, request start-up for Athens.
CTL Sierra Fox 153, start-up approved.
PIL Starting up, Sierra Fox 153.

2 PIL Winton Ground, FBG, good morning.
CTL Go ahead, Fox Bravo Golf.
PIL Fox Bravo Golf, stand Charlie 8, information Kilo, request start-up for New York.
CTL Fox Bravo Golf, standby for start.
PIL Standing by, Fox Bravo Golf.

3 PIL Winton Ground, AG235, good morning.
CTL Go ahead, Alpha Golf.
PIL Alpha Golf 235, gate 21, information Mike, request start-up for Frankfurt.
CTL Alpha Golf 235, start-up approved.
PIL Starting up, Alpha Golf 235.

4 PIL Winton Ground, THI, good morning.
CTL Go ahead, Tango Hotel India.
PIL Tango Hotel India, stand Alpha 9, information Charlie, request start-up for Rome Fiumiccino.
CTL Tango Hotel India, standby for start.
PIL Standing by, Tango Hotel India.

5 PIL Winton Ground, NUM, good morning.
CTL Go ahead, November Uniform Mike.
PIL November Uniform Mike, gate Delta 7, information India, request start-up for Cairo.
CTL November Uniform Mike, start-up approved.
PIL Starting up, November Uniform Mike.

6 PIL Winton Ground, WJD, good morning.
CTL Whisky Juliet Delta, stand 13, information Lima, request start-up for London, Heathrow.
CTL Whisky Juliet Delta, standby for start.
PIL Standing by, Whisky Juliet Delta.

1.3.1 (*page 15*)
Listen and Repeat
Write
See CHECK Section, (*page 20*)

1.3.1 (*page 16*)
Listen and Speak

1 PIL (*call Winton Ground*) . . . .
CTL Go ahead, Sierra Foxtrot 153.
PIL . . . .
CTL Sierra Fox 153, start-up approved.
PIL . . . .

2 PIL (*call Winton Ground*) . . . .
CTL Go ahead, Foxtrot Bravo Golf.
PIL . . . .
CTL Fox Bravo Golf, standby for start.
PIL . . . .
CTL Fox Bravo Golf, start-up approved.
PIL . . . .

3 PIL (*call Winton Ground*) . . . .
CTL Go ahead, Alpha Golf.
PIL . . . .
CTL Say again, gate number.
PIL . . . .
CTL Alpha Golf 235, start-up approved.
PIL . . . .

4 PIL (*call Winton Ground*) . . . .
CTL Say again, callsign.
PIL . . . .
CTL Go ahead, Tango Hotel India.
PIL . . . .
CTL Tango Hotel India, start-up approved.
PIL . . . .

5 PIL (*call Winton Ground*) . . . .
CTL Go ahead, November Uniform Mike.
PIL . . . .
CTL Say again, stand number.
PIL . . . .
CTL November Uniform Mike, stand by for start.
PIL . . . .
CTL November Uniform Mike, start-up approved.

6 PIL (*call Winton Ground*) . . . .
CTL Say again, callsign.
PIL . . . .
CTL Go ahead, Whisky Juliet Delta.
PIL . . . .
CTL Whisky Juliet Delta, start-up approved.
PIL . . . .

1.3.1 (*page 17*)
Listen
Listen and Repeat
Write
See CHECK Section (*page 21*)

1.3.1 (*page 18*)
Listen and Speak

1 PIL (*ask for start-up*) . . . .
CTL Sierra Foxtrot 153, start-up at 35.
PIL . . . .

2 PIL (*ask for start-up*) . . . .
CTL Fox Bravo Golf, expect departure at 45, start-up at your discretion.
PIL . . . .

3 PIL (*ask for start-up*) . . . .
CTL Alpha Golf, slot time 55, start-up at your discretion.
PIL . . . .

4 PIL (*ask for start-up*) . . . .

CTL Taxi Hotel India, expect departure at 05, start-up at your discretion.
PIL . . . .

5 PIL (*ask for start-up*) . . . .
CTL Standby, November Uniform Mike, I'll call you back.
CTL November Uniform Mike, what is your gate number?
PIL . . . .
CTL November Uniform Mike, start-up approved.
PIL . . . .

6 PIL (*ask for start-up*) . . . .
CTL Say again, callsign.
PIL . . . .
CTL Whisky Juliet Delta, slot time 10, start-up at your discretion.
PIL . . . .

7 PIL (*ask for start up*) . . . .
CTL Echo Sierra Quebec, start-up at 50.
PIL . . . .

8 PIL (*ask for start-up*) . . . .
CTL Kilo Victor X-Ray, start-up approved.
PIL . . . .

9 PIL (*ask for start-up*) . . . .
CTL Yankee Foxtrot Lima, slot time 15, start-up at your discretion.
PIL . . . .

10 PIL (*ask for start-up*) . . . .
CTL Oscar Papa Romeo, say again stand number.
PIL . . . .
CTL Oscar Papa Romeo, expect departure at 25, start-up at your discretion.
PIL . . . .

1.3.2 (*page 18*)
Listen and Answer
Listen and Write
See CHECK Section (*page 23*)

1.4.1 (*page 24*)
Listen
Listen and Repeat
Write
See CHECK Section (*page 27*)

1.4.1 (*page 25*)
Listen and Speak

1 PIL (*ask for push-back*) . . . .
CTL SF153, roger, push-back approved.
PIL . . . .

2 PIL (*ask for push-back*) . . . .
CTL FBG, hold position, I'll call you back.
PIL . . . .
CTL FBG, push-back approved.
PIL . . . .

3 PIL (*ask for push-back*) . . . .
CTL AG235, expect 1 minute delay, due 747 passing behind you.
PIL . . . .

4 PIL (*ask for push-back*) . . . .
CTL THI, push-back approved.
PIL . . . .

5 PIL (*ask for push-back*) . . . .
CTL NUM, hold position.
PIL . . . .
CTL NUM, expect 1 minute delay due DC9 passing behind to park.
PIL . . . .

6 PIL (*ask for push-back*) . . . .
CTL WJD hold position.
PIL . . . .
CTL WJD, say again stand number.
PIL . . . .
CTL WJD, expect a couple of minutes delay, due to DC10 passing behind to park.
PIL . . . .

1.4.2 (*page 25*)
Listen and Answer
Listen and Write
See CHECK Section (*page 28*)

1.5.1 (*page 29*)
Look, Listen and Write

1. Take the second turning on the left.
2. Go straight ahead at the intersection.
3. Give way to the aircraft arriving on your left.
4. Take the first turning on the right.
5. Give way to the aircraft on your right.
6. There's an aircraft overtaking you on your right.
7. Take the first left turn-off.
8. Take the third turning on the left.
9. Follow the aircraft in front of you.

1.5.1 (*page 32*)
Look and Speak
See CHECK Section (*page 37*)

1.5.2 (*page 34*)
Listen
Listen and Repeat
Write
See CHECK section (*page 38*)

1.5.2 (*page 35*)
Listen and Speak

1 PIL (*ask for taxi*) . . . .
CTL SF133, taxi via taxiway C to holding point 29L.
PIL . . . .
CTL SF133, give way to the 747 passing left to right.
PIL . . . .

2 PIL (*ask for taxi*) . . . .
CTL SF133, taxi via taxiway C to holding point 29L.
PIL . . . .
PIL (*call near holding point, ask to cross runway*) . . . .
CTL SF133, negative, hold short runway 29L.
PIL . . . .
CTL SF133, cross runway 29L, report vacated.
PIL . . . .
PIL (*call runway vacated*) . . . .

3 PIL (*ask for taxi*) . . . .
CTL SF133, taxi to holding pont 09. Give way to the company aircraft passing behind.
PIL . . . .
CTL SF133, follow the 767 to taxiway D.
PIL . . . .

4 PIL (*ask for taxi*) . . . .
CTL SF133, taxi via taxiway E to holding point runway 18.
PIL . . . .
CTL SF133, hold at the next intersection and give way to the aircraft coming from your left.
PIL . . . .
PIL (*call near holding point, ask to cross runway*) . . . .
CTL SF133, cross runway 18, report vacated.
PIL . . . .
PIL (*call runway vacated*) . . . .

5 PIL (*ask for taxi*) . . . .
CTL SF133, after the Airbus passing right to left, taxiway I to holding point runway 31.
PIL . . . .
CTL SF133, expedite taxi.
PIL . . . .
PIL (*call near holding point, ask to cross runway*) . . . .
CTL SF133, negative, hold short of runway 31.
PIL . . . .
CTL SF133, cross runway 31, report vacated.
PIL . . . .
PIL (*call runway vacated*) . . . .

6 PIL (*ask for taxi*) . . . .
CTL SF133, taxiway D to holding point runway 14.
PIL . . . .
CTL SF133, hold at the next intersection, give way to the aircraft coming from your right.
PIL . . . .

1.6.1 (*page 42*)
Listen (dialogues ***a***, ***b***, ***c***)
Listen and Repeat (dialogues ***a***, ***b***, ***c***)
Listen and Write (dialogues ***a***, ***b***, ***c***)
See CHECK Section (*page 45*)

1.6.1 (*page 43*)
Listen and Speak

1 PIL . . . .
CTL Sierra Fox 153, line up and wait.
PIL . . . .

2 PIL . . . .
CTL Fox Bravo Golf, report the Airbus on final in sight.
PIL . . . .
CTL Fox Bravo Golf, behind the landing Airbus on final line up behind.
PIL . . . .

3 PIL . . . .
CTL Alpha Golf 235, hold short of the runway, you're number 2 for departure after the Airbus.
PIL . . . .
CTL Alpha Golf 235, line up and wait.
PIL . . . .

4 PIL . . . .
CTL Echo Sierra Quebec, report the 767 on final, 5 miles, in sight.
PIL . . . .
CTL Echo Sierra Quebec, behind the landing 767 on final line up behind.
PIL . . . .

5 PIL . . . .
CTL Kilo Victor X-ray, hold short of the runway, you're number 2 for departure after the Air France.
PIL . . . .
CTL Kilo Victor X-ray, line up and wait.
PIL . . . .

6 PIL . . . .
CTL Yankee Foxtrot Lima, line up and wait.
PIL . . . .

7 PIL . . . .
CTL Oscar Papa Romeo, hold position, you're number 2 for departure.
PIL . . . .
CTL Oscar Papa Romeo, line up and wait.

8 PIL . . . .
CTL Zulu Echo 692, negative departure, I'll call you back.

CTL Zulu Echo 692, line up and wait.
PIL . . . .

1.6.2 (*page 44*)
Listen and Answer
Listen and Write
See CHECK Section (*page 46*)

1.7.2 (*page 49*)
Listen and Speak

ATIS (*twice*) This is Rexbury departure information Fox at 13.30 Zulu time. Take-off and landing runway 29, wind 260° 12 knots, CAVOK, temperature 14, dew point 11, QNH 1023, no sig. This was information Fox.

PIL (*call Rexbury Ground*) . . . .
CTL Good afternoon, Sunair 367, go ahead.
PIL (*ask for start-up*) . . . .
CTL Say again stand number, Sunair 367.
PIL . . . .
CTL Sunair 367, start-up approved.
PIL . . . .
CTL Sunair 367, here is your ATC clearance.
PIL . . . .
CTL ATC clears Sunair 367 to destination Winton airport via flight planned route, Golf 5 departure, climb initially to FL110, expect level change en route.
PIL . . . .
CTL That is correct, Sunair 367.
PIL (*call for push-back*) . . . .
CTL Sunair 367, push-back approved, taxi to holding point 29 via taxiway Delta.
PIL . . . .
CTL Sunair 367, contact Tower now on 118.3.
PIL . . . .
PIL (*call reaching holding point*) . . . .
CTL Sunair 367, report the 727 on final in sight.
PIL . . . .
CTL Behind the landing 727, line up behind.

1.7.3 (*page 49*)
Listen and Speak

PIL (*call Ground*) . . . .
CTL SF309, Ground, good morning.
PIL (*ready to start-up in 20 minutes*) . . . .
CTL Yes, that is OK, no restrictions into Orly.
PIL (*ask for departure runway*) . . . .
CTL Runway 17, surface wind 110° 20 knots.
PIL . . . .
CTL 309, Ground, your ATC clearance.
PIL . . . .
CTL SF309, cleared Dublin to Paris, Orly via Liffy Blue 1, flight planned route, FL230, to request level change.
PIL . . . .
CTL Request level change is correct, cleared enter backtrack runway 11, contact Dublin Tower frequency 118.6, good morning.
PIL . . . .
PIL (*call Tower*) . . . .
CTL Roger, 309, backtrack 11, expedite the taxi please and cleared to line up and hold on runway 17.
PIL . . . .
CTL That's it, 309.

2.1 (*page 63*)
Listen and Read

1 MAYDAY MAYDAY MAYDAY, Winton Tower, Sunair 379, engine no. 1 on fire, intend to land at Overby, present position 50 miles North of Winton, FL200, heading 290.
2 PAN PAN, PAN PAN, PAN PAN, Winton Tower, Sunair 639, 35 miles North West of Winton, FL170, passenger seriously ill, suspected heart attack, request priority landing.

2.1 (*page 63*)
Listen and Speak
See CHECK Section (*page 65*)

2.2.1 (*page 66*)
Listen
Listen and Repeat
Write
See CHECK Section (*page 71*)

2.2.1 (*page 67*)
Listen and Speak

1 PIL (*ready for departure, tell control*) . . . . . .
CTL SF153, runway 29L, cleared for take-off, wind 290° 12 knots.
PIL . . . .

2 PIL (*ready for departure, tell control*) . . . . . .
CTL FBG, runway 18, cleared for immediate take-off, wind 200° 8 knots.
PIL . . . .

3 PIL (*ready for departure, tell control*) . . . . . .
CTL AG235, runway 31, negative departure, I'll call you back.
CTL AG235, runway 31, cleared now for take-off, wind calm.
PIL . . . .

4 PIL (*ready for departure, tell control*) . . . . . .
CTL ESQ, runway 07, cleared for take-off, wind 005° 19 knots.
PIL . . . .

2.2.1 (*page 68*)
Listen
Listen and Repeat
Write
See CHECK Section (*page 71*)

2.2.1 (*page 68*)
Listen and Speak

1 PIL (*ready for departure, tell control*) . . . . . .
CTL SF153, runway 29L, cleared for take-off, wind 290° 12 knots, report airborne.
PIL . . . .
CTL SF153, runway 29L, take-off immediately or vacate runway 29L.
PIL . . . .

2 PIL (*ready for departure, tell control*) . . . . . .
CTL FBG, runway 18 cleared for take-off, wind 200° 8 knots.
PIL . . . .
CTL FBG, hold position, cancel take-off, I say again, cancel take-off.
PIL . . . .

3 PIL (*ready for departure, tell control*) . . . . . .
CTL AG235, runway 31, cleared for take-off, wind calm.
PIL . . . .
CTL AG235, stop immediately, AG235, stop immediately.
PIL . . . .

4 PIL (*ready for departure, tell control*) . . . . . .
CTL Juliet Delta India, runway 07 cleared for take-off, wind 120° 16 knots.
PIL . . . .
CTL Juliet Delta India, stop immediately, Juliet Delta India, stop immediately.
PIL . . . .

5 PIL (*ready for departure, tell control*) . . . . . .
CTL Mike Papa Hotel, runway 07 cleared for take-off, wind 150° 11 knots.
PIL . . . .
CTL Mike Papa Hotel, runway 07, take-off immediately or vacate runway.
PIL . . . .

6 PIL (*ready for departure, tell control*) . . . . . .
CTL Romeo Sierra Tango, runway 26 cleared for take-off, wind 340° 5 knots.
PIL . . . .
CTL Romeo Sierra Tango, runway 26, hold position, cancel take-off, I say again, cancel take-off.
PIL . . . .

7 PIL (*ready for departure, tell control*)
CTL Delta November Oscar, runway 12 cleared for take-off, wind 090° 7 knots.
PIL . . . .
CTL Delta November Oscar, stop immediately, Delta November Oscar, stop immediately.
PIL . . . .

8 PIL (*ready for departure, call control*) . . . . .
CTL Uniform Charlie Quebec, runway 25, cleared for take-off, wind 170° 13 knots.
PIL . . . .
CTL Hold position, Uniform Charlie Quebec, cancel take-off, I say again, cancel take-off, vehicle obstructing runway.
PIL . . . .

2.2.2 (*page 69*)
Listen and Answer
Listen and Write
See CHECK Section (*page 73*)

2.3.1 (*page 75*)
Listen and Write

1. Climb straight ahead.
2. Turn right, heading 190.
3. Climb so as to cross Delta at FL190.
4. Turn left, heading 190.
5. Climb to FL190.
6. Climb on present heading.
7. Climb on track to Delta.
8. Continue present heading until FL150.
9. Expedite climb to FL190.

2.3.1 (*page 76*)
Listen and Speak

1 CTL Turn left heading 190.
PIL . . . .

2 CTL Climb to FL220.
PIL . . . .

3 CTL Climb straight ahead.
PIL . . . .

4 CTL Turn left, heading 260.
PIL . . . .

5 CTL Climb on track to Papa.
PIL . . . .

6 CTL Climb on present heading to FL270.
PIL . . . .

7 CTL Turn right heading 310.
PIL . . . .

8 CTL Climb so as to cross Zulu at FL150.
PIL . . . .

9 CTL Continue present heading until FL190.
PIL . . . .

10 CTL Climb on track to Zulu.
PIL . . . .

11 CTL Expedite climb to FL170.
PIL . . . .

2.3.1 (*page 76*)
Listen
Listen and Repeat
Write
See CHECK Section (*page 79*)

2.3.1 (*page 77*)
Listen and Speak

1 CTL SF153, airborne 33, turn right heading 130, continue climb to FL150.
PIL . . . .
CTL Contact 125.8, goodbye.
PIL . . . .

2 CTL AG235, airborne 29, climb on present heading to FL110.
PIL . . . .
CTL Contact now 129.6, goodbye.
PIL . . . .

3 CTL YFL, airborne 58, turn left heading 230, expedite climb to FL70.
PIL . . . .
CTL Contact Approach on 129.7.
PIL . . . .

4 CTL OPR, airborne 42, climb so as to cross November at FL90.
PIL . . . .
CTL Contact 128.6, goodbye.
PIL . . . .

5 CTL DNO, turn right heading 190, continue climb to FL130.
PIL . . . .
CTL Contact 132.9, goodbye.
PIL . . . .

6 CTL ZE692, airborne 42, climb on present heading to FL130.
PIL . . . .
CTL Contact now 134.2.
PIL . . . .

2.3.2 (*page 77*)
Listen and Answer
Listen and Write
See CHECK Section (*page 80*)

2.4.1 (*page 83*)
Listen
Listen and Repeat
Write
See CHECK Section (*page 86*)

2.4.1 (*page 84*)
Listen and Speak

1 CTL SF153, contact Delta Control on 128.7, goodbye.
PIL . . . .
PIL (*call Delta Control*) . . . .
CTL Delta Control, good morning SF153.
PIL . . . .
CTL Climb to flight level 210, report reaching, maintain present heading.
PIL . . . .
PIL (*call reaching 210*) . . . .
CTL Roger, SF153, climb to level 310.
PIL . . . .
CTL Change now 129.4, goodbye.
PIL . . . .

2 CTL AG235, change to Foxtrot Control now on 132.4.
PIL . . . .
PIL (*call Fox Control*) . . . .
CTL Foxtrot Control, good morning AG235.
PIL . . . .
CTL Climb to FL210, report passing 180, maintain present heading.
PIL . . . .
PIL (*call passing FL180*) . . . .
CTL Roger, AG235, turn right heading 330 and climb to level 280.
PIL . . . .
CTL Contact India Control on 131.7, goodbye.
PIL . . . .

3 CTL YFL, contact Mike Control on 126.5.
PIL . . . .
PIL (*call Mike Control*) . . . .
CTL Mike Control, good morning YFL.
PIL . . . .
CTL Climb to FL250, expedite until passing level 150.
PIL . . . .
CTL YFL, turn right, correction, turn left heading 180.
PIL . . . .
CTL Contact Papa Control on 128.9.
PIL . . . .

4 CTL OPR, change now to November Control on 127.3.
PIL . . . .
PIL (*call November Control*) . . . .
CTL November Control, good morning OPR.
PIL . . . .

CTL Turn right heading 230 and climb to FL240, report reaching.
PIL . . . .
PIL (*call reaching FL240*) . . . .
CTL Roger, OPR, climb to level 290.
PIL . . . .
CTL Change now to Alpha Control on 129.5.

5 CTL DNO, contact Whisky Control on 133.2.
PIL . . . .
PIL (*call Whisky Control*) . . . .
CTL DNO Whisky Control, good morning.
PIL . . . .
CTL Climb to FL250, report passing 150.
PIL . . . .
PIL (*call passing FL150*) . . . .
CTL Roger, DNO, turn left heading 160, climb to FL270.
PIL . . . .
CTL Contact now Zulu Control on 129.5.
PIL . . . .

6 CTL ZE692, change to Foxtrot Control on 126.9.
PIL . . . .
PIL (*call Foxtrot Control*) . . . .
CTL Foxtrot Control, good morning ZE.
PIL . . . .
CTL Turn right heading 130, climb to FL210, expedite until passing 150.
PIL . . . .
CTL ZE692, report reaching level 210.
PIL . . . .
PIL (*call reaching level 210*) . . . .
CTL Roger, ZE, contact Delta Control on 128.2.
PIL . . . .

2.4.2 (*page 85*)
Listen and Answer
Listen and Write
See CHECK Section (*page 88*)

2.5.1 (*page 90*)
Listen
Listen and Repeat
Write
See CHECK Section (*page 92*)

2.5.1 (*page 90*)
Listen and Speak

1 PIL (*contact Echo control*) . . . .
CTL Go ahead 153.
PIL . . . .
CTL Maintain present heading, climb flight level 210, report when reaching.
PIL . . . .
PIL (*you are now reaching level 210, call control*) . . . .
CTL Roger, Sierra Fox 153, climb to level 270.
PIL . . . .
CTL Negative, not at the moment, can you accept level 390?
PIL . . . .
CTL Change now to 129.4.
PIL . . . .
CTL Goodbye Sierra Fox 153.

2 PIL (*contact control*) . . . .
CTL Go ahead Alpha Golf 235.
PIL . . . .
CTL Turn right heading 290, I'll call you back for further climb.
PIL . . . .
CTL Alpha Golf 235, climb now to flight level 280.
PIL . . . .
CTL Negative, can you accept level 410?
PIL . . . .
CTL Change now to 131.7.
PIL . . . .
CTL Goodbye.

3 PIL (*contact control*) . . . .
CTL Go ahead Yankee Foxtrot Lima.
PIL . . . .
CTL Maintain your heading, and climb to level 190, report reaching.
PIL . . . .
PIL (*you've reached level 190, call control*) . . .
CTL Roger, Yankee Foxtrot Lima, climb to level 330.
PIL . . . .
CTL Call 126.8.
PIL . . . .
CTL Goodbye.

4 PIL (*contact control*) . . . .
CTL Go ahead Oscar Papa Romeo.
PIL . . . .
CTL Turn left heading 160, I'll call you back.
PIL . . . .
CTL Oscar Papa Romeo, climb to level 250.
PIL . . . .
CTL 290 is unavailable due to heavy traffic. Can you accept 390?
PIL . . . .
CTL Climb then to level 250, report reaching.
PIL . . . .
PIL (*you're reaching 250, call control*) . . . . .
CTL Roger Oscar Papa Romeo, contact 132.9.

5 PIL (*contact control*) . . . .
CTL Go ahead Delta November Oscar.
PIL . . . .
CTL Maintain present heading, climb FL170, report when reaching.

PIL . . . .
PIL (*you're reaching level 170, call control*)
CTL Roger, Delta November Oscar, climb now to level 210.
PIL . . . .
CTL Change now to 129.3.
PIL . . . .
CTL Goodbye.

6 PIL (*contact control*) . . . .
CTL Go ahead Zulu Echo 692.
PIL . . . .
CTL Turn left heading 010, climb level 170, report passing 150.
PIL . . . .
PIL (*you are now passing level 150, call control*)
CTL Roger Zulu Echo, climb 290.
PIL . . . .
CTL 330 is unavailable, can you accept 410?
PIL . . . .
CTL Change now to 133.2.
PIL . . . .
CTL Goodbye.

2.5.2 (*page 91*)
Listen and Answer
Listen and Write
See CHECK Section (*page 94*)

2.6.1 (*page 96*)
Listen and Speak

PIL (*call ready for departure*)
CTL Sunair 367, runway 29, cleared for take-off, wind 255° 13 knots.
PIL . . . .
CTL Sunair 367, airborne 04, climb on present heading to FL110, contact Rexbury Control on 128.8.
PIL . . . .
PIL . . . .
CTL Sunair 367, Rexbury Control, good afternoon. Turn right now heading 050 and continue climb to FL220.
PIL . . . .
CTL Sunair 367, proceed now to Romeo India Victor VOR and recleared to FL270, cruising level.
PIL . . . .
PIL (*ask if you can have FL330*) . . . .
CTL Standby Sunair, I'll call you back.
CTL Sunair 367, can you accept FL370?
PIL (*you can't*) . . . .
CTL Sunair 367, climb to FL270, report when reaching.
PIL . . . .
PIL (*call at flight level 270*) . . . .
CTL Roger, Sunair 367, change now to New County Upper Control, frequency 135.9, goodbye.
PIL . . . .

2.6.2 (*page 96*)
Listen and Speak

PIL (*call ready to depart*) . . . .
CTL Roger, SF309 is clear to take-off runway 17, it's a left turn-out direct for Liffy, wind is 100° 20 knots.
PIL . . . .
CTL That is correct.
CTL 309, airborne time 23, contact Dublin Control 128.0.
PIL . . . .
PIL (*call Dublin*) . . . .
CTL SF309, direct Liffy climb FL230.
PIL . . . .
CTL SF309, report FL.
PIL (*level 100*) . . . .
CTL SF309, continue climb to 230, call London 128.05.
PIL . . . .
PIL (*call London*) . . . .
CTL SF309, squawk 5260, maintain 230 on reaching.
PIL . . . .
CTL SF309, climb to FL290.
PIL . . . .
CTL SF309, climb to FL330.
PIL . . . .

2.7.2 (*page 102*)
Look, Listen and Repeat
Look, Listen and Speak
See CHECK Section (*page 105*)

2.7.3 (*page 104*)
Listen and Write
See CHECK Section (*page 107*)

3.1 (*page 112*)
Listen and Write
See CHECK Section (*page 114*)

3.2.1 (*page 116*)
Listen and Write

1. Omit position reports this frequency.
2. Next report at Alpha.
3. Resume position reporting.
4. Report intercepting the 120 radial of the Alpha VOR.
5. Report 5 miles from Alpha DME.

6. Report passing the Alpha VOR 342 radial.
7. Report passing Alpha.
8. Omit position reports until Alpha.
9. Report intercepting the 210 radial of the Alpha VOR.
10. Report 15 miles from Alpha DME.

3.2.1 (*page 117*)
Listen
Listen and Repeat
Write
See CHECK Section (*page 120*)

3.2.1 (*page 118*)
Listen and Speak

1 CTL Go ahead SF153.
PIL . . . .
CTL Roger, SF, next report at Zulu.

2 CTL Go ahead Alpha Golf 235.
PIL . . . .
CTL Roger, Alpha Golf, omit position reports this frequency.
PIL . . . .

3 CTL Go ahead Bravo India 196.
PIL . . . .
CTL Roger, Bravo India, next report at Tango.
PIL . . . .

4 CTL Go ahead November Juliet 342.
PIL . . . .
CTL Roger, November Juliet, report intercepting 340 radial Fox VOR.
PIL . . . .

5 CTL Go ahead Mike Oscar 725.
PIL . . . .
CTL Roger, Mike Oscar, report 10 miles from Sierra DME.
PIL . . . .

3.2.2 (*page 118*)
Listen and Answer
Listen and Write
See CHECK Section (*page 121*)

3.3.1 (*page 122*)
Listen and Write

1. Unknown traffic 10 o'clock, 5 miles crossing left to right.
2. Unknown same direction traffic overtaking you on the left.
3. Unknown fast moving traffic closing 7 miles.
4. Unknown traffic, 3 o'clock crossing right to left.
5. Unknown traffic, 10 o'clock, climbing.
6. Unknown traffic, parallel, overtaking you on the right.
7. Unknown traffic, 3 o'clock, 8 miles descending.

3.3.1 (*page 124*)
Listen
Listen and Repeat
Listen and Write
See CHECK Section (*page 127*)

3.3.1 (*page 124*)
Listen and Speak

1 CTL Sierra Foxtrot 153, unknown traffic 10 o'clock, 5 miles, crossing left to right.
PIL . . . .
CTL Turn left heading 050.
PIL . . . .
CTL Sierra Foxtrot, clear of traffic, resume own navigation direct Charlie, magnetic track 070, distance 27 miles.
PIL . . . .

2 CTL Sierra Foxtrot 153, unknown traffic, same direction overtaking you on the left.
PIL . . . .
CTL Turn right heading 170.
PIL . . . .
CTL Sierra Foxtrot, clear of traffic, resume own navigation direct to Delta, magnetic track 149.
PIL . . . .

3 CTL Sierra Foxtrot 153, unknown traffic, 2 o'clock, closing 10 miles.
PIL . . . .
CTL Turn right heading 250.
PIL . . . .
CTL Sierra Foxtrot, clear of traffic, resume own navigation direct Echo, magnetic track 227, distance 33 miles.
PIL . . . .

3.3.1 (*page 124*)
Listen
Listen and Repeat
Write

CTL Sierra Foxtrot 153, traffic at your 2 o'clock position, 6 miles, moving right to left.
PIL Traffic in sight.

3.3.1 (*page 125*)
Listen, Speak and Write

1 CTL Sierra Foxtrot 153, unknown traffic at your 9 o'clock position, 6 miles moving left to right.
PIL . . . .

2 CTL Sierra Foxtrot 153, unknown traffic closing 10 miles.
PIL . . . .

3 CTL Sierra Foxtrot 153, unknown fast moving traffic, 4 o'clock, climbing.
PIL . . . .

4 CTL Sierra Foxtrot 153, unknown traffic, opposite direction 11 o'clock, 9 miles.
PIL . . . .

5 CTL Sierra Foxtrot 153, unknown same direction traffic, overtaking you on the left.
PIL . . . .

6 CTL Sierra Foxtrot 153, unknown traffic 10 o'clock, 5 miles, moving right to left.
PIL . . . .

3.3.2 *(page 125)*
Listen and Answer
Listen and Write
See CHECK Section (*page 128*)

3.4.1 *(pages 132–133)*
Listen (dialogues ***a*** and ***b***)
Listen and Repeat (dialogues ***a*** and ***b***)
Write (dialogues ***a*** and ***b***)
See CHECK Section (*pages 135–136*)

3.4.1 *(page 133)*
Listen and Speak

1 CTL SF153, squawk ident.
PIL . . . .
CTL SF153, radar contact, descend to FL220.
PIL . . . .
CTL SF153, continue descent to FL110, report passing 150.
PIL . . . .
PIL *(you are reaching 150, call control)*
CTL SF153, confirm leaving level 150.
PIL . . . .

2 CTL AG235, squawk 2744.
PIL . . . .
CTL AG235, descend now to FL210.
PIL . . . .
CTL AG235, recleared to FL150, increase rate of descent so as to cross Tango at level 150, report passing FL180.
PIL . . . .
PIL *(you are reaching 180, call control)*
CTL Confirm leaving level 190, AG235.
PIL . . . .

3 CTL BI196, squawk ident.
PIL . . . .
CTL BI196, radar contact, descend to FL190.
PIL . . . .
CTL BI196, continue descent to FL190, report passing 160.
PIL . . . .
PIL *(you are reaching 160, call control)* . . . .
CTL Confirm leaving level 160, BI196.
PIL . . . .

4 CTL NJ342, squawk 4526.
PIL . . . .
CTL NJ342, descend now to FL130.
PIL . . . .
CTL NJ342, recleared to FL80, increase your rate of descent to cross Sierra at level 80, report passing FL110.
PIL . . . .
PIL *(you are reaching 110, call control)* . . . .
CTL Confirm leaving FL130, NJ.
PIL . . . .

5 CTL MO725, squawk ident.
PIL . . . .
CTL MO725, radar contact, descend to FL170.
PIL . . . .
CTL MO725, recleared to FL90, increase rate of descent to cross Delta at level 90, report passing FL140.
PIL . . . .
PIL *(you are reaching 140, call control)* . . . .
CTL Confirm leaving FL140, MO.
PIL . . . .

3.4.2 *(page 134)*
Listen and Answer
Listen and Write
See CHECK Section (*page 137*)

3.5.1 *(page 138)*
Listen and Speak

PIL *(call New County Upper Control)* . . . .
CTL Good afternoon Sunair 367, continue to Blackrock, report when reaching.
PIL . . . .
(you now tune in to Winton Volmet)
VOLMET This is Winton Volmet. This is Winton Volmet.

Winton airport at 14.30. 280° 10 knots, 8000 metres, temperature 12, dew point 11, QNH 1020, no sig.

Overby at 14.30. 240° 12 knots, 10 kms or more, temperature 8, dew point 6, QNH 1020, no sig.

Newbridge at 14.30. 250° 4 knots, 3000 metres, mist, temperature 6, dew point 4, QNH 1016, no sig.

CTL Sunair 367, unknown traffic 10 o'clock, 8 miles moving from left to right.

PIL (*you see the traffic*) . . . .
CTL Roger.
CTL Sunair 367, contact Valley Control now on 128.5, goodbye.
PIL . . . .
PIL (*call Valley Control*) . . . .
CTL Sunair 367, good afternoon, continue to Blackrock, report reaching.
PIL . . . .
PIL (*call over Blackrock*) . . . .
CTL Roger, Sunair 367, proceed to Lima Alpha Kilo direct.
PIL . . . .
PIL (*you want to turn 30° right to avoid build-up*)
CTL Roger, Sunair 367, what is your present heading?
PIL (*025*) . . . .
CTL Sunair 367, turn right heading 050° for 15 miles, report back on track.
PIL (*you have passed the build-up, call control*)
PIL . . . .
CTL Roger, Sunair 367, resume own navigation to Lake.
PIL . . . .
PIL (*call over LAK*) . . . .
CTL Sunair 367, proceed to Romeo Echo Delta, call me back when ready for descent.

3.5.2 (*page 138*)
Listen and Speak

CTL SF309, what is your heading?
PIL (*100*) . . . .
CTL 309, roger, turn right heading 125.
PIL . . . .
PIL (*call FL330*) . . . .
CTL F309, resume own navigation to Honiley.
PIL . . . .
CTL SF309, correction the last message, you can set course direct to Midhurst.
PIL . . . .
CTL SF309, contact London 133.7, good day.
PIL . . . .
PIL (*call London*) . . . .
CTL SF309, good day, maintain FL330, present position, direct Midhurst.
PIL . . . .
CTL SF309, contact London now 127.7.
PIL . . . .
PIL (*call London*) . . . .
CTL 309, good afternoon, maintain FL330.
PIL . . . .
CTL SF309.
PIL . . . .
CTL 309, descend to FL310.
PIL . . . .
CTL SF309, continue now with Paris 132.0.
PIL . . . .
PIL (*Call Paris*) . . . .
CTL SF309, bonjour, maintain FL310 standard routing, Reymy clearance limit, runway 26 at Orly, squawk 0444.
PIL . . . .

3.6.1 (*page 142*)
Listen and Write

sandstorm; wet; CAVOK; calm; drizzle; broken; headwind; overcast; VMC conditions; damp, tornado; flooded; mist; heavy rain; crosswind; drift; (thick/dense) fog; gusts; CB's; icy patches; light rain; strong wind; fog patches; water spout; (in and out of) the tops; turbulence; haze; standing water; ceiling; sleet; snow; dispersing; hail; cirrus; lightning; pools of water; closing in; clear air turbulence; fog-bound; a flash of lightning; snow ruts; hailstones; severe/moderate turbulence; slush; a bank of clouds; freezing rain; windshear; a build-up; snow drifts; to be struck by lightning; icing; down/up-draught; storm cells; black ice; a rainbow.

Listen and Check
See CHECK Section (*page 146*)

3.6.2 (*page 144*)
Look, Listen and Repeat
Look, Listen and Write
Look, Listen and Speak
See CHECK Section (*page 147*)

4.1 (*page 151*)
Listen and Write
See CHECK Section (*page 154*)

4.2.1 (*pages 158–159*)
Listen (dialogues ***a*** and ***b***)
Listen and Repeat (dialogues ***a*** and ***b***)
Write (dialogues ***a*** and ***b***)
See CHECK Section (*page 162*)

4.2.1 (*page 159*)
Listen and Speak

1 PIL (*call Approach*)
CTL Sierra Foxtrot 153, Orly Approach, go ahead.
PIL . . . .
CTL Sierra Foxtrot 153, squawk 4263, report Mike Echo Lima, reduce speed 250 knots.
PIL . . . .

CTL Sierra Foxtrot 153, cleared ILS approach, runway 07, no delay expected.
PIL . . . .

2 PIL (*call Approach*) . . . .
CTL Alpha Golf 235, Orly Approach, go ahead.
PIL . . . .
CTL Descend to FL60, on reaching Mike Echo Lima hold, expected Approach time is 45.
PIL . . . .

3 PIL (*call Approach*) . . . .
CTL Bravo India, Orly Approach, go ahead.
PIL . . . .
CTL Confirm reaching level 80, Bravo India.
PIL . . . .
CTL Bravo India 196, squawk 3127, descend to flight level 70, cleared to Mike Echo Lima, report reaching, reduce speed 200 knots.
PIL . . . .
CTL Bravo India 196, cleared ILS approach runway 26, no delay expected.
PIL . . . .

4 PIL (*call approach*) . . . .
CTL November Juliet 342, Orly Approach, go ahead.
PIL . . . .
CTL November Juliet, confirm leaving level 130.
PIL . . . .
CTL Descend to flight level 50, hold at Mike Echo Lima, delay not determined, snow removal in progress.
PIL . . . .

5 PIL (*call Approach*) . . . .
CTL Mike Oscar 725, Orly Approach, go ahead.
PIL . . . .
CTL Mike Oscar 725, squawk ident, descend to flight level 60, report Mike Echo Lima on reaching, reduce speed 210 knots.
PIL . . . .
CTL Mike Oscar 725, cleared ILS approach runway 07, no delay expected.
PIL . . . .

4.2.2 (*page 160*)
Listen and Answer
Write
See CHECK Section (*pages 163–164*)

4.3.1 (*page 167*)
Listen
Listen and Repeat
Listen and Write
See CHECK Section (*page 171*)

4.3.1 (*page 168*)
Listen and Speak

1 PIL (*Sierra Foxtrot 153, call Winton Approach*)
CTL Sierra Foxtrot 153, Winton Approach.
PIL . . . .
CTL Sierra Foxtrot 153, reduce speed to 250 knots, cleared Romeo Echo Delta.
PIL . . . .
CTL Sierra Foxtrot 153, expect straight in ILS approach runway 25, QNH 1005, report established.
PIL . . . .
PIL (*call established*) . . . .
CTL Sierra Foxtrot 153, number 1, contact Tower 118.1.
PIL . . . .
PIL (*call Tower*) . . . .
CTL Sierra Foxtrot 153, report outer marker.
PIL . . . .
PIL (*call outer marker*) . . . .
CTL Sierra Foxtrot 153, runway 25, cleared to land, wind 330° 10 knots.
PIL . . . .

2 PIL (*Alpha Golf 235, call Winton Approach*)
. . . .
CTL Alpha Golf 235, Winton Approach.
PIL . . . .
CTL Alpha Golf 235, descend flight level 60, cleared Romeo Echo Delta.
PIL . . . .
CTL Alpha Golf 235, squawk 4263, expect straight in ILS approach runway 25, report established.
PIL . . . .
PIL (*call established*) . . . .
CTL Alpha Golf 235, number 1 for landing, contact Tower 118.1.
PIL . . . .
PIL (*call Tower*) . . . .
CTL Alpha Golf 235, report outer marker.
PIL . . . .
PIL (*call outer marker*) . . . .
CTL Alpha Golf 235, cleared to land, runway 25, wind 60 degrees, 13 knots.
PIL . . . .

3 PIL (*Bravo India 196, call Winton Approach*)
. . . .
CTL Bravo India 196, Winton Approach, go ahead.
PIL . . . .
CTL Bravo India 196, descend flight level, correction, descend to altitude 4000 ft.
PIL . . . .
CTL Bravo India 196, expect straight in approach runway 25, QNH 1012, report established.
PIL . . . .
PIL (*call established*) . . . .

CTL Bravo India 196, you're number 1 to land, contact Tower 118. 1.

PIL . . . .

PIL (*call Tower*) . . . .

CTL Bravo India 196, report outer marker.

PIL . . . .

PIL (*call outer marker*) . . . .

CTL Bravo India 196, cleared to land, runway 25, wind 185°, 20 knots gusting up to 30.

PIL . . . .

4.3.2 (*pages 168–169*)
Listen and Answer
Listen and Write
See CHECK Section (*page 173*)

4.4.1 (*page 176*)
Listen
Listen and Repeat
Write
See CHECK Section (*page 178*)

4.4.1 (*page 176*)
Listen and Speak

1 CTL Sierra Foxtrot 153, take the first right and contact Ground on 121.9.

PIL . . . .

PIL (*call runway vacated*) . . . .

CTL Sierra Foxtrot 153, take the second left, inner taxiway, to stand Delta 7.

PIL . . . .

2 CTL Alpha Golf 235, take the first left and contact Ground 121.6.

PIL . . . .

PIL (*call runway vacated*) . . . .

CTL Alpha Golf 235, straight ahead to the second intersection, taxiway Bravo, stand Charlie 10.

PIL . . . .

3 CTL Bravo India 196, second left turn-off and contact Ground 121.8.

PIL . . . .

PIL (*call runway vacated*) . . . .

CTL Bravo India 196, turn right at the intersection, outer taxiway to gate 39.

PIL . . . .

4 CTL November Juliet 342, take the first left and contact Ground 121.6.

PIL . . . .

PIL (*call runway vacated*) . . . .

CTL November Juliet 342, straight ahead, taxiway Bravo, to stand 12.

PIL . . . .

5 CTL Mike Oscar 725, first left turn-off and contact Ground on 121.6.

PIL . . . .

PIL (*call runway vacated*) . . . .

CTL Mike Oscar 725, straight ahead at the intersection, then first right and taxiway Bravo to stand 28.

PIL . . . .

4.4.2 (*page 176–177*)
Listen and Answer
Listen and Write
See CHECK Section (*page 179*)

4.5.1 (*page 180*)
Listen and Speak

ATIS (*twice*) This is Winton information Lima recorded at 15.30 Zulu time. Runway for landing 25, for take-off 30, transition level 50, surface wind 280° 10 knots, visibility 800 metres, temperature 12, dew point 11, QNH 1020. On initial contact report information Lima received.

PIL (*ask for descent*)

CTL Sunair 367, descend to flight level 190 and contact Meadow Control on 128.5, goodbye.

PIL . . . .

PIL (*call Meadow Control*) . . . .

CTL Good afternoon, Sunair 367, radar contact, descend to flight level 120, Romeo Echo Delta VOR direct.

PIL . . . .

CTL Sunair 367, you are approaching Romeo Echo Delta, contact now Winton Approach on 121.3, goodbye.

PIL . . . .

PIL (*call Winton Approach*) . . . .

CTL Good afternoon, Sunair 367, radar identified, passing Romeo Echo Delta VOR, intercept radial 070 Romeo Echo Delta VOR and descend to flight level 60, expect radar vectoring to ILS runway 25, report crossing 70.

PIL . . . .

PIL (*call reaching 70*) . . . .

CTL Sunair 367, contact Winton Radar on 121.1, goodbye.

PIL . . . .

PIL (*call Winton Radar*) . . . .

CTL Good afternoon, 367, radar contact, descend to 3000 ft, QNH 1020. Take heading 160.

PIL . . . .

CTL Sunair 367, continue descent to 2000 ft, turn right heading 230, cleared for ILS approach runway 25, report established.

PIL . . . .

PIL (*call established*) . . . .

CTL Sunair 367, contact Tower on 118.1, goodbye.

PIL . . . .
PIL (*call Tower*) . . . .
CTL Good afternoon, Sunair 367, number 2 to land, number 1 touching down, report over outer marker.
PIL . . . .
PIL (*call at outer marker*) . . . .
CTL Sunair 367, clear to land runway 25, wind 260° 08 knots.
PIL . . . .
PIL (*call runway vacated*) . . . .
CTL Roger, Sunair 367, contact Ground on 121.7.
PIL . . . .
PIL (*call Ground*) . . . .
CTL Sunair 367, good afternoon, take the second left onto the inner taxiway, stand Delta 7.
PIL . . . .

4.5.2 (*page 180*)
Listen and Speak

(*be ready to copy Orly ATIS*)
ATIS . . . landing runway 26, take-off runway 25, attention taxiway 2A closed, attention bird situation, surface wind 242° 13 knots, visibility 10 kms, temperature +10°, dew point +8°, QNH 1017 mb, QFE 1006 mb, transition level 40, Charles de Gaulle is facing West. Confirm information India received on initial contact.

PIL (*call and ask for descent*) . . . .
CTL SF309, cleared FL250 contact Paris 124.05, goodbye.
PIL . . . .

PIL (*call Paris*) . . . .
CTL SF309, good evening, clearance FL240 initially, I'll call you back.
PIL . . . .

CTL SF309, recleared down FL110.
PIL . . . .

CTL SF309, recleared down FL80 now.
PIL . . . .

CTL SF309, you turn left to Reymy now.
PIL . . . .

PIL (*call reaching FL80*) . . . .
CTL SF309, roger, call Orly Approach now 120.85, goodbye sir.
PIL . . . .

PIL (*call Orly*) . . . .
CTL Good afternoon 309, your squawk on 4244.
PIL . . . .

PIL (*call reaching Reymy*) . . . .
CTL 309, radar contact, cross to TSU now, radar vectoring, runway 26, after Toussus radial 075.
PIL . . . .

CTL SF309, what's your speed?
PIL (*300*) . . . .
CTL Roger.
CTL SF309, reduce 250 knots and after descend 4000 ft, QNH 1017.
PIL . . . .

PIL (*call reaching 4000 ft*) . . . .
CTL Roger, descend 3000 ft.

CTL 309, heading 170.
PIL . . . .

CTL SF309, turn right heading 230, cleared ILS 26.
PIL . . . .

CTL SF309, maintain 180 knots minimum till OYE, call Airport 118.7, bye.
PIL . . . .

PIL (*call Orly*) . . . .
CTL SF309, bonjour, report passing outer marker, runway 26.
PIL . . . .

CTL SF309, 160 knots?
PIL (*your speed is 180 knots, reply*)
CTL OK.

PIL (*call over outer marker*) . . . .
CTL SF309, clear to land, wind 240° 12 knots.
PIL . . . .

CTL SF309, first right and call ground 121.7.
PIL . . . .

PIL (*call Ground, runway vacated*) . . . .
CTL 309, bonjour, taxi for Delta 8.
PIL . . . .

5.1 (*page 189*)
Listen and Speak
For controller's part, see pages 189–192

5.2 (*page 196*)
Listen and Speak
For controller's part, see pages 196–199

APPENDIX
TCAS Traffic-Alert and Collision Avoidance system

Read

TCAS (part of the ACAS system: Airborne Collision Avoidance System) is a traffic-alerting and collision avoiding system designed to help safety in the air. TCAS is a system used for detecting and tracking transponder equipped aircraft coming too near your own aircraft. (These are called 'intruders'.)
For TCAS to work between 2 aircraft the 'intruding' aircraft must have a working SSR (Secondary Surveillance Radar) transponder. TCAS analyses the replies from the transponder to get the range and bearing of the other aircraft. If the other aircraft is reporting altitude (mode C), the relative altitude is also known.
If the system sees that a possible collision danger exists, it gives visual and audio directions to the crew for **vertical** avoidance manoeuvres. If both aircraft carry TCAS, the 2 systems will communicate with each other and give both crews warnings what to do. If one crew is told to climb, the other will be instructed to descend.

If another aircraft is detected inside certain limits, TCAS will first give the crew a Traffic Advisory (TA). A voice announcement is heard in the cockpit, advising 'TRAFFIC, TRAFFIC'.
If an intruder comes too close, TCAS will give what is a called a Resolution Advisory (RA) and then the crew must act. A synthesised voice announces a vertical manoeuvre command: 'CLIMB. CLIMB' or 'DESCEND, DESCEND'. The crew must act immediately. They must notify ATC as soon as possible.

ICAO TCAS RT phraseology :
Clearance ± : altitude or level)

SITUATION	PHRASEOLOGIES
After a flight crew starts to deviate from any ATC clearance or instruction to comply with an ACAS resolution advisory (RA)	PIL TCAS RA CTL ROGER
After the response to an ACAS RA is completed and a return to the ATC clearance or instruction is initiated	PIL CLEAR OF CONFLICT, RETURNING TO (assigned clearance ±) CTL ROGER (or alternative instructions)
After the response to an ACAS resolution advisory is completed and the assigned ATC clearance or instruction has been resumed	PIL CLEAR OF CONFLICT (assigned clearance ±) RESUMED CTL ROGER (or alternative instructions)
After and ATC clearance or instruction contradictory to the ACAS RA is received, the flight crew will follow the RA and inform ATC directly (pilot and controller interchange)	PIL Unable, TCAS RA. CTL ROGER

TCAS Phraseology practice

Read

Examples:

ACAS	TRAFFIC TRAFFIC
ACAS	DESCEND DESCEND
PIL	(call sign) TCAS RA (*Pronunciation 'teekas ar ay'*)
CTL	(call sign) roger
ACAS	CLEAR OF CONFLICT
PIL	(call sign) clear of conflict, returning to FL150 (assigned clearance)
CTL	(call sign) roger (or alternative instructions, e.g. a heading)
PIL	(call sign) clear of conflict, FL150 resumed.
CTL	(call sign) roger

If unable to comply with a clearance as a result of a TCAS alert

CTL	(call sign) climb to FL150
PIL	Unable TCAS resolution RA
CTL	roger

Read and write

Write the pilot's words

1. You are flying at FL150, callsign Sunair 123

ACAS	TRAFFIC TRAFFIC
(a little later)	
ACAS	CLIMB CLIMB
PIL	______________________________
CTL	Sunair 123 roger.
(after some time)	
ACAS	CLEAR OF CONFLICT
PIL	______________________________
CTL	Sunair 123 roger
PIL	______________________________
CTL	Sunair 123, roger

2. You are flying at FL150, callsign Sunair 123

ACAS	TRAFFIC TRAFFIC
ACAS	CLIMB CLIMB
CTL	Sunair 123, descend to FL130
PIL	______________________________
CTL	Sunair 123 roger
PIL	______________________________
CTL	Sunair 123 roger.

3. You are flying at FL150, callsign Sunair 123

ACAS	TRAFFIC TRAFFIC
(a little later)	
ACAS	DESCEND DESCEND

PIL	______________________________
CTL	Sunair 123 roger.
(after some time)	
ACAS	CLEAR OF CONFLICT
PIL	______________________________
CTL	Sunair 123 roger
PIL	______________________________
CTL	Sunair 123, roger

4. You are flying at flight level 150, callsign Sunair 123

ACAS	TRAFFIC TRAFFIC
ACAS	DESCEND DESCEND
CTL	Sunair 123, climb to FL 170
PIL	______________________________
CTL	Sunair 123 roger

Check

1.

ACAS	TRAFFIC, TRAFFIC
ACAS	CLIMB, CLIMB
PIL	Sunair 123 TCAS RA
CTL	Sunair 123 roger.
(after some time)	
ACAS	CLEAR OF CONFLICT
PIL	Sunair 123 TCAS RA, clear of conflict, returning to FL150
CTL	Sunair 123 roger.
PIL	Sunair 123, clear of conflict, FL150 resumed
ATC	Sunair 123 roger.

2. You are flying at FL150, callsign Sunair 123

ACAS	TRAFFIC TRAFFIC
ACAS	CLIMB CLIMB
CTL	Sunair 123, descend to FL130
PIL	Sunair 123 unable TCAS RA
CTL	Sunair 123 roger

3. You are flying at FL150, callsign Sunair 123

ACAS	TRAFFIC TRAFFIC
(a little later)	
ACAS	DESCEND DESCEND
PIL	Sunair 123 TCAS RA.
CTL	Sunair 123 roger.
(after some time)	
ACAS	CLEAR OF CONFLICT
PIL	Sunair 123, clear of conflict, returning to FL150
CTL	Sunair 123 roger
PIL	Sunair 123, clear of conflict, FL150 resumed.
CTL	Sunair 123, roger

4. You are flying at FL150, callsign Sunair 123

ACAS	TRAFFIC TRAFFIC
ACAS	DESCEND DESCEND
CTL	Sunair 123, climb to FL170
PIL	Sunair 123 unable TCAS RA
CTL	Sunair 123 roger